A Kid in the Great Depression
By
Lou Tyrrell

LHDJ Content, Inc.
300 East 34th Street,
Ste. 27D.
New York, N.Y. 10016

This book is dedicated to my sister Gen.

And her son, Barry.

Genevieve Fialk, who took care of me through

the hard times and let me share her bedroom.

Gen, now 91years young lives a happy life

at Daughter's of Israel Nursing Home,

West Orange, New Jersey under the watchful

eye of my favorite nephew Barry Fialk.

God bless them both.

4

I was born, so said Mr. Dickens in his "David Copperfield." The problem was I was born too late. Twenty-seven minutes too late to arrive on New Years day. It was day two of 1925. I don't remember a thing. 1926 is also pretty hazy but things began to clear by Christmas of 1927. I had a Christmas stocking hanging on the mantle over the fireplace. My big sister, Gen, gave me a little chocolate Santa Claus sticking out of my stocking. I stood in front of the fire sucking on it. My hand was chocolate, my chin was chocolate and my bright white shirt was growing brown spots all down the front.

My Dad laughed, picked me up and carried me to the big Christmas tree that filled the corner of the room. "Let's see what Santa Claus has brought you, Bruz." He said sliding a huge green and red package out on the carpet. "This is yours. Come on, open it." My mother and sister crowded around as I tore the pretty paper open. I saw silver handlebars. "OOOH," I said.

"Hurry up, Bruz, I can't wait." My father urged. I kept tearing. A shiny red tricycle appeared, sparkling amongst the pile of shredded wrapping paper. "Bikey, Bikey!" I screamed, jumping on the black seat, pedaling off into the dining room. My mother, father and big sister smiling down on me, proud of what their little Bruzzilah could do.

I have a big brother named Jay. He isn't there in my memory picture. He's nearly fourteen years older than me. He's almost a man. He was probably playing baseball in the park. He played ball anytime he could get a game. My mother named me Louis, after her father. Jay hated the name. "Let's call him 'Brother,'" he said, "Anything's better than Louis. Hey, kid, let me hear you say Brother."

I looked up at my brother Jay who was half a head taller than my father. "Bruzzy." I said. And from that moment on I was Bruzzy. Kindergarten, I was Bruzzy, Grammar School I was Bruzzy, Bruzzy in Junior High,

Not until my second year in high school, when we moved to New York, did I become Lou.

I rode my Christmas present up and down the sidewalk outside our house on Pacific Avenue in Glendale. California, in 1927, was wide-open spaces. A wonderland populated by few people with very good weather. The rains came in February; the humidity was usually very low. In 1927 there were fewer people in the whole state than now live in Los Angeles County. There was no place better for a little boy to grow up.

My mom held my hand on the front porch as we waved goodbye to my dad who was off to work. He waved back from the open cabin in his old Ford truck. "Why don't you ride Bikey while I straighten up, Bruz. The garage door is open." I nodded and ran up the driveway.

I pulled the bike through the open door of the garage, sat on the seat, held my legs straight out and coasted down the driveway. I took a deep breath when the inside wheel lifted off the ground as I turned onto the sidewalk. I zoomed over the bump where a big tree root had cracked the walk, sailed past Tarpley's Newspaper and Candy Store, looped around at the corner and flew into the return trip. I could do this for hours, my little legs pushing the pedals round and round as the multi colored houses sailed by. Ladies watched me from their porches, the mailman dodged past laughing while Mr. Tarpley stood on the stairs in front of his store waving each time I passed by.

I was speeding right along when Mr. Tarpley yelled, "Hey, Bruz pull over for minute." I put my shoes on the sidewalk and slid to a stop right in front of the store. It wasn't a real store. There weren't any stores on Pacific Avenue. It was the basement of his house. They had dug away the ground, put a window and door in the basement wall and the store was born. "Don't you need a rest, Bruz, you've been at that for more than an hour. I could offer you a cold drink or maybe some candy."

"Candy, candy, prease." I said jumping off the trike, doing the steps sideways so my little legs reached, following Mr.Tarpley into his store.

6

He took down a big glass container filled with balls of candy. Red balls. Green balls. Yellow, purple, all the colors of the rainbow. "They're brand new, Bruz, they call them Jawbreakers, you can't chew them, you have to suck them, interested?" I shook my head yes. "Can I have a yellow one?" He held out the candy, "Take what you like. Don't chew. Suck."

"Uh huh." I took a yellow one and put it in my mouth. It didn't fit. It was too big. I opened my mouth as far as I could, wiggled it around and slid it in between my teeth. My mouth was full, fuller than I had ever felt. I couldn't spit it out! Terrified, I ran for my mother leaving bikey alone in front of the store. I ran up the street trying to yell Mommy but nothing came out.

My mother was sitting on the front porch crocheting, the long bedspread covering her lap. She saw me coming and put her work aside. I ran across the lawn and she came down the stairs. I pointed to my mouth and garbled something she didn't understand. She grabbed me by my shoulders and sat me on the top step. "Relax, Bruzzilah, there's nothing wrong with you, just relax, suck on your candy." She spoke so softly and so confidently I could feel the terror melting away. She rubbed my neck, "just relax, sweetheart, suck your candy." "No like candy." I muttered.

"I gave him a jawbreaker, it's too big for his mouth, Sorry, Mrs. Tyrrell. Here's his bike," Tarpley called from the edge of the lawn.

"Fine, Mr. Tarpley, he'll be just fine in a moment. Are you sucking, Boobalah?" I nodded. I could feel the candy getting smaller. My Mom wasn't scared at all so I just kept sucking. Suddenly I spit it out and it bounced onto the lawn. "I don't like lemon, Mommy, it was a pretty yellow ball, but it was lemon, Mommy, and I couldn't pit it out."

"Well it's out now, right there on the lawn. Next time you look at candy take a purple one. That's grape and you love grape." You go down and beg Mr. Tarpleys pardon, you scared him; after he was nice enough to give you candy.

Then, come home and we'll have a nice lunch." She bent over, kissed me, mussed my hair, climbed the stairs and started to push her work into a bag. I walked to Tarpley's thinking I had a wonderful mother; there wasn't another mother like her in the whole world.

2

My father was born in a small town called Monroe in Pennsylvania on April Ninth, 1880. He graduated from high school when he was eighteen. His family were show people who traveled with light opera companies. For some unknown reason he joined the circus as a maintenance man. They called them roustabouts. They schlepped the ropes, drove stakes into the ground, dug holes for poles, dragged canvas and put up the tents. My dad was special, very handy with tools and kept all the circus equipment running.

Blood being thicker than water, he couldn't ignore his show biz background, learned the art of slack wire walking and did his act at every show, after putting up the tent and fixing the door on the tiger's cage, of course. He was 22 when the circus landed in Jersey City for a two week run. He remembered his Uncle Dave lived there. He got a bus to Journal Square where Dave lived in a fancy apartment house. He walked up three flights and knocked on the door. It opened. "What the hell are you doing in the circus? That's the bottom rung of show business, Kid, even vaudeville is better, Your father can't stand the Tyrrell name in such a low class business, now come on in, sit down and Belle will make some coffee." He stepped back, smiling as his nephew shuffled into the room. Before the visit was over twenty-two year old Bill Tyrrell joined his Uncle Dave's roofing business. He gave two weeks notice to the circus and bid a fond farewell to his slack wire career.

"Take me with you, Bill, I'm sick of this job. Maybe if I hang around here in the roofing business I can get back in my dad's good graces." The guys were sitting around a fire chewing the rag after the last show. Tommy Manville had run away from home and joined the circus. He and Bill had been friends for nearly a year. "What the hell, if I can learn the business why can't you. Let me work it out with my uncle." In less than a month Manville and Tyrrell lived in a one-bedroom walkup and went to work each day with the Dave Tyrrell Roofers. Within five years Bill and Tommy were experts, each with his own crew, while poor Uncle Dave was bed ridden with some strange rare illness.

"You want to do the Linden job or the one in Ridgefield Park?" Bill asked Tommy sitting at the kitchen table in their fancy three-bedroom apartment, one floor down from Uncle Dave. "Let's toss for it, Bill, Ridgefield Park is closer to home."

"Call!" My father said, as he flipped a quarter into the air, slapping his hand over it as it hit the table."

"Heads!" Tommy called. Bill lifted his hand, "Tails, you lose!"

"I always lose." Tommy complained.

"Ridgefield Park is a nice town," my father thought as his men unloaded a ladder and laid it against the front corner of the roof. It was a big house, he thought, wealthy people must live here. It was painted dark blue with white shutters at the windows; it had a wide lawn with squares of slate making a path to the big front porch. Two white rocking chairs moved in the warm breeze as the screen door flew open and a golden Springer Spaniel came bounding down the steps, sniffing around Bill's shoes.

"Wait, Beauty, wait for me!' a voice called out as the door swung open revealing a lovely young lady in a gold sweater and skirt, her red hair piled on top of her head. She was wearing white tennis shoes. Bill was struck by lightning. "Hey Bill!" His crew chanted, "The ladder is ready, the job is waiting!" "Son-of-a-bitch," Bill thought as he dragged himself away to go to work. The lovely young thing hooked a leash to Beauty's collar and strolled off up the road.

Bill climbed the ladder, joined his men to figure out the problems of the job. He checked the angles of the roof, the chimneys at each end then returned to the ground just as the lovely thing returned. "Good morning, Miss," My father stuttered, "Could you tell your father the roofers are here?" "Sure, he's in the kitchen. It's in the back of the house. He wouldn't know you were here." She took her dog and went in. Bill Tyrrell's mouth watered as he watched her walk away.

An instant later she led a tall red haired man down the front steps. They approached Bill and he stuck out his hand.

"Lockman. Louis Lockman. You the boss?"

"Yes sir, Bill Tyrrell's the name." He shook the customer's hand. "We'd like to start right away, if that's okay with you."

"You see any problems?"

"No, sir. Simple, straight forward." Bill smiled. The lovely young thing stared at him.

"Well, any problems, just tell Dottie here, she'll find me. Oh excuse me, Mr. Tyrrell this is my daughter, Dorothy Lockman."

Bill and Dorothy were married two years later.

"Hey Bruz, I've got to go check on a job up in the hills, you want to come along?" I was watching the chickens scratching for their breakfast but there was no way I'd miss the chance to ride in the truck with my father. "Sure Dad!" I yelled running over to grab his big hand. The old Ford didn't have a self-starter. It had a crank. You stuck it in the hole at the base of the radiator and spun it to start the engine. My Dad put me in charge of the choke. This was not an easy job. It demanded good eye-hand coordination. My dad spun the crank, the engine coughed, "Now!" He yelled. "Choke it!" I pulled the lever on the steering column and the engine coughed; caught and rumbled into life. "Good work, Son. You can choke for me anytime," he laughed, shoving the crank into its place under the seat, climbing up behind the wheel. I sat straight up, proud of my father's compliment. He drove out of the driveway turned right and headed for the hills.

We drove up pretty streets, past Hoover High where my brother was a junior and into the rich neighborhood of Glendale. Beautiful homes, one right after the other, no poor people here. Times were good and houses were popping up everywhere. People loved California. They would come for a visit and never go home. The more people the better the future of the roofing business.

It was a long low ranch style house that angled up into a second floor and went deep into the property. A big house built for big shots. The exterior was complete, they were working on the interior and dad was going to put on a red tile roof. Hundred pound barrels of tar were lined up behind a machine that melted the tar and kept it at the proper temperature for application. Stack after stack of red Spanish tile hid behind a wall of tarpaper rolls guarding the easily breakable tiles. "Stand over there by the tiles, Bruz, I've got to go up on the roof and see how we're doing." My dad lifted me down to the ground and we walked up the rise. I stopped by the tiles and he walked over to a keg of tar. He grabbed each end of the keg, swung it up on his shoulder and walked over to the front porch. He put the keg on the ground, stepped up on the barrel, took hold of the roof with his right hand and pulled himself up. He put his left hand on the roof and pushed himself erect. I was mesmerized. My dad was a giant. He didn't need a ladder, just a keg of tar.

A big man came to the kegs of tar. He picked up an axe, rolled a keg free, set his feet and cut the keg in half, cut the halves in quarters and kicked the wood splinters into the fire. He put four pieces of tar on a metal shelf that dropped the tar into a big pot that bubbled big black bubbles making a blub, blub noise. I saw my dad walking down the roof of the front porch, he kneeled down, grabbed the edge, hung himself off the roof and dropped to the ground. "My dad can fly," I thought, "My dad can do anything." A tinkling bell filled the neighborhood. The Good Humor man was coming along. "Hey, Bruz, come on, let's get some ice cream!" I ran over and grabbed his big hand looking at him in awe.

We sat in the truck. One of his roofers was handling the crank and my father stole my choke job. We took a bite of our Good Humors while the engine turned over. We were half way home when my father threw his ice cream stick out on the street, I still had a couple of bites to go. I savored the last bites, licked off the little chocolate on the stick and noticed some writing. "What's this say?" I held the stick out. He looked away from the road. "Free Good Humor." He said looking back at the road, "You get a free Good Humor, I didn't even look at my stick." He stopped the truck. He turned it around and we drove back and found his stick.

12

He got out, picked up the stick and got back in. He looked at his stick. "Nope, No luck. Bruzzy, you're the lucky one in this family."

3

My dad had just got home from work, he came in the front door and my mom ran out of the kitchen to kiss him. "You're home early, darling. Is there something wrong?" She brushed some tar off his shoulder and put it in her apron pocket.

"Nothing, same shit. We ran out of tile and it would take longer to get it from Burbank than we had left of the workday, so we came home. No big deal. But I can sure use my big chair." My dad had his own chair. Big. Overstuffed. It had a big square ottoman for his legs. We weren't told not to sit in it, but none of us had the nerve to sit in our father's chair. It was his. We all respected that. He walked over to his chair, lowered his tired body into it, swinging his legs up on the ottoman, he leaned back, breathed deeply and said to no one, "There's no place like home."

I was sitting across the room playing with alphabet blocks trying to spell the words my big sister was teaching me. At the moment I was working on CAT, which we didn't have. The back door crashed open and Jay came bounding out of the kitchen. "Hi, everyone, I hit a home run! It rolled all the way up to the gym, I really caught the son-of a-bitch…"

"Watch the language, son, your little brother's in the room." Jay was being quietly reprimanded.

"You curse in front of him all the time, what's the difference?" "Oh, Oh," I thought, "Big mistake arguing with my father." They always seemed on the verge of a fight. I was sure Dad had the advantage.

"All right, Jay, I don't want any back talk. I've had a hard day. I'd like to be playing ball too. You'll find out very soon what responsibility means, now take your bat and glove to your room. Supper will be ready soon."

"Yes sir." Jay answered, "Sorry I talked back. Sorry, Bruz, I shouldn't curse in front of you." Suddenly Mom appeared in the room, "Oh, Jay, Darling, did you have a nice game?"

"I hit a home run."

"Isn't that wonderful. You're a terrific player. Now go get yourself ready for supper the ham is almost ready." She watched him go up the stairs. "Bill, you should get that tar off your hands before supper, why don't you use the sink in the laundry, there's some turpentine in there." She leaned down and kissed his thin graying hair.

"Yes, my love." My father put both his hands on the arms of his chair and pushed himself up, he grabbed his wife, hugged her, kissing the top of her red head. "I love you." He said and walked from the room. There was no doubt my father was in love with his wife and his wife returned the favor. Their bedroom was off limits and if it was really necessary to disturb them in their room, the rule was to knock and wait for permission to come in. That was the one unbreakable rule of the Tyrrell household.

I was learning a lot about personalities sitting there playing with my blocks. There was some problem between my brother and my father that I didn't understand but I knew I would find the answer someday. Right now I was busy memorizing D-O-G, I knew Gen would be testing me very soon. I had to be prepared. I heard her voice and looked up. She was standing in the archway between the living and dining rooms. "Bruz, dinner is almost ready, don't you think you ought to wash your hands and face before sitting at the dining room table? You'd make Momma very proud if she didn't have to tell you." I put the blocks in the box, the box in the coat closet, went upstairs to wash my hands and face. Why was everyone in this house smarter than me? It just wasn't fair.

Dad sat at the head of the table, my mother at the foot, opposite the kitchen door; Jay was on her left and Gen sat next to dad. I had the whole side of the table to myself. I sat on a fat pillow so I could reach my plate. I had my own little silver service, a little spoon, a little fork and a little knife. I was an important person to have his own silver. My sister filled the water glasses with iced tea while my mother put a big baked ham in the middle of the table.

She brought in a tray of sweet potatoes and Gen delivered a bowl of beets. My father stood up and took a long knife and a big fork and carved slice after slice off the ham.

"Jay, please pass me your mother's plate." Jay put the plate next to my father. My father put meat, potatoes and beets, artistically arranged on the plate, a sprig of parsley in the center and asked Jay to pass it to Mom.

"May I have your plate, Jay, please?" My father asked.

"I don't want any beets, please, dad. I hate pickled beets." Handing his plate to his father.

"They're your mother's pickled beets. They're delicious. She worked a whole week canning those beets last year. Just for us."

"Bill! He doesn't want any beets. Just give him ham and potatoes. Gen go slice up a tomato for your brother." My dad didn't say a thing, Genevieve got up quietly and went into the kitchen. Jay sat looking at the tablecloth until his father handed him his plate with a sprig of parsley in the center. My father fixed my sister's plate, then put a piece of ham, a small sweet potato and some beets on my plate, reached over and cut up my food and dropped a spring of parsley in the center. He made his own plate. Gen brought Jay's tomatoes, my father tasted his ham and dinner was underway. I tasted the beets. They were very good. What was Jay's problem?

Dinner was delicious. We were enjoying my mothers marvelous cooking. "I got a job." Jay said spearing a slice of tomato. "When I graduate, I can go to work for J. J. Newberry, I start in the stock room, but they start everybody there, I could work myself up to be president. How about that?"

"That's wonderful, Son. Where would you work?" My father asked haltingly.

"L.A., but I can walk up to Brand Boulevard and catch the trolley, it's no big deal."

"Well, perhaps you should hear your father's and my news and see how it might affect your plans. We've bought a new house, just over on Lake Street. It will be ready in two months, so you should check out how you get to L.A. from there."

"I was hoping you would come in with me when you graduated, Son, I have a very good business and it could be yours someday. I wish you'd think about that." My dad was practically begging.

"I don't want to be a roofer, Dad. I hate tar all over me and the dirt and dust. I want to dress in a suit, with a tie and polished shoes. I don't want to be a laborer; I want to work in a store. Serve people. A nice clean store." Jay looked straight at his father as he made his speech, I had a feeling he had practiced it many times.

"Well, you think about it. Find out how you get to L.A. from Lake Street, maybe you'll see some advantage to getting your hands dirty." He forked a piece of sweet potato into his mouth and sipped some iced tea.

"Jay-wah, baby, you do with your life what you want to do, we each get our chance and this is yours. You want to be a stock clerk in L.A.? Be a stock clerk and I'll love you just as much. Your father and I will help you in any way we can. We just want to see you happy. Now, anyone for hot apple pie and vanilla ice cream?"

4

The sun streamed in the wide window above the sink where my mother was preparing my favorite breakfast. Sugar toast! Toasted rye bread spread with butter and covered with sugar put under the flame in the broiler until the sugar was melted, speckled brown and crispy. I loved it with a big glass of cold milk, right out of the icebox. "Bruzzy, you and I have a lot of work to do. We have to be out of this house by the fifteenth of December, a little more than two months. You will be in charge of counting the animals, so we can figure out what we'll do with the ones we can't eat." I giggled. I thought my mom was funny. "While you're working on that I'll gather everything we can throw out and put it in the garage. When I'm finished we'll call the junkman and he will take it all away. That will save your father moving it to Lake Street. Would you like to do that? I waggled my head up and down. My mouth full of sugar toast made talking impossible.

I ran out to the chicken coop. I saw all the chickens, stretching their legs, spreading their wings, getting ready for a busy day scratching up their food. My dad threw a few handfuls of corn into the coop before he went to work and I was responsible for filling the mash feeders every afternoon. Mom thought I was too little for such a big responsibility, but so far I have never missed a day. The ducks stayed off by themselves. There were only three waddling around the coop, the others had gone into mom's blue roasting pan. I remember the day I climbed up into my father's big old truck and we drove through the hills past Eagle Rock and into Pasadena. My father knew a farmer there who supplied fertilized duck eggs. He bargained the price and finally settled for two-dozen eggs.

I followed my dad into the garage where his incubator was set up on an old table in a back corner. He had me count as he placed the eggs around the lamp. "Well, Bruz. Now we wait. Pretty soon those eggs will crack open and we'll have a bunch of baby ducks to look after. If you're good, I'll let you take care of them. Would you like that?"

I got so excited I couldn't answer so I just shook my head. He laughed, mussed my blonde curls, scooped me into his arms and carried me into the house. I forgot all about the ducks. I was very busy keeping bikey happy, going for milk at Tarpley's, helping my mother shop at the Grand Central Market and best of all riding with my father to the gas station on Sundays to fill up his old Ford truck.

Then one morning my bedroom door swung open, "Hey Bruz! You asleep? Come on, rise and shine, there's something you have to see in the garage." I jumped out of bed, put on my pants and shirt and ran barefoot down the stairs and outside where my dad stood by the garage door. I ran to the door. There, before my eyes was a bevy of little yellow ducks falling all over themselves. They were hissing and bumping around on a big blue double mattress on the floor of the garage. "How many, how many daddy?" I implored. "Count them, you can count." "One, two...I can't they don't stay still. I don't care how many I love them all." My dad showed me a bag of special food and the three little bowls to put on the mattress. "You have to fill those bowls three times a day and you must keep water in the water bowl. Then in a few weeks they'll be big enough to go in the coop where you can watch them grow." He didn't tell me they would be our Easter dinner.

I did as I was told. I took care of those little ducks, watched them grow day by day. Make their messes on the blue mattress. Finally we put sixteen ducks into the coop. And now as we were preparing to move I could count only three ducks. I didn't bother my head about it.

I reported to my mother on my animal counting task. We had three ducks, five Rhode Island Red hens, two White leghorn hens and six Plymouth Rocks. My father had taught me well.

My mother swung the garage doors open. One door laid against the fence the other pushed into the back yard. The garage was crowded with junk. The big blue duck mattress was rolled up and tied leaning against the sidewall. There was an old icebox, the top door hanging open, a rusted lawn mower, a broken bamboo rake, piles of newspapers, magazines, some old books, many pairs of shoes, all sizes and a torn beach chair.

My mother shook her head as the tinkle of the junkman's bell sounded in the neighborhood. "Junk Man! Junk Man!" Mr. Orzatti crooned, in his almost baritone voice. My mother waved her hand from the drive and Mr. Orzatti pulled his old buggy over to the curb. Climbed down from his perch and strolled up the driveway.

"You need the Junkman Missus?" in his broken English.

"Take a look at the stuff in the garage, please." My mother asked. I watched them standing in the middle of the doorway discussing items, making estimates, working hard on a deal. Finally they settled and Mr. Orzatti laid two dollars and two quarters in my mother's hand. He walked down the driveway, got up on his wagon driving his scrawny white horse to push it up the drive. He piled all the junk, the icebox, the papers, all the shoes on top of the junk already on board. Then he laid the mattress on the top, climbed back on the wagon, tapped his horse and was gone. Peace returned to Pacific Avenue.

Not twenty minutes later mom opened the front door to a very upset junkman. "Lady, your mattress kept falling off my wagon so I unrolled it and it's filthy. Such dirty people used that mattress. How could anyone sleep on such a mattress? I just don't understand how people can live in such filth. I bought that stuff in good faith. That mattress is worthless. You owe me fifty cents." Mom paid quietly. She never mentioned my father's ducks.

5

It was a big tan stucco house, two bay windows with brown shutters on the ground floor. It had a wide front porch and a glistening Spanish tile roof. We were standing in the double driveway looking at our new home. It was huge. It looked like a mansion to me. I looked up the drive and saw the two-car garage far behind the house and then a very deep back yard. My mother spoke to my sister and me. "Your dad is putting his business in the back yard, there's room for all his trucks and all the materials he keeps in Burbank, so he will be home a lot more than he has been."

The house fronted on a wide green lawn with hedges down each property line. The walk was off the drive and curved up to the front steps. Three steps up to the porch where we met an imposing front door. Much bigger to little me than the door at Pacific Avenue, I hoped we could afford a screen door so I wouldn't have to face opening that giant gate. My mother pushed a key into the lock and the big door swung open without a problem. I felt much better.

"Oh Mom! This is beautiful!" My sister Gen exclaimed. "Look at the big foyer and the staircase and the ceiling so high." My mom just smiled. "It's a lovely house, children," she said. "You'll both love your rooms. We'll be very happy here." I followed the ladies into the huge space. They chattered in the foyer, chuckled in the dining room, laughed in the kitchen, complained in the laundry room, swooned in the living room and we hadn't climbed the stairs yet. Upstairs was even better. The master bedroom had a bathroom right in through a door in the bedroom. You didn't need to walk out in the hall. Which was good because there wasn't any upstairs hall, just a balcony that ran around the whole downstairs space.

Gen's bedroom was very big, twice the size of Pacific Avenue and Jay had a great corner room with windows looking out into the backyard. "Where do I get to sleep, Mom, there's no rooms left, don't I get a room!" I pouted.

She smiled and took me by the hand. We walked out of Jay's room onto the balcony, I saw a glass door at the head of the stairway. "Open that door, it's a special room for our baby." My mom pointed the way. I ran over and pulled the door open and was in a glassed in room that went halfway across the back of the house…it really was a porch but they had made it into a bedroom just for me. I was one happy little brother.

It was dinnertime on Pacific Avenue. My dad dished out my mother's fabulous lamb stew and passed the bowls around. "We're moving to Lake Street, this Saturday and Sunday." My father said to the table. "My men and our three trucks will move us and we'll sleep in Lake Street on Sunday night. I know you have ball games, Jay, and that's all right, my guys are used to working together so you might just get in the way. Make sure you have all your stuff packed by Saturday except your Sunday clothes cause everything except beds and furniture will be moved on Saturday. Now let's enjoy your mother's stew."

I heard the sound of trucks pulling up in front of the house. I ran out on the front porch and saw two Ford trucks exactly like my dad's and six men in tar-spotted clothing climb out on the sidewalk. Things began to happen. Boxes piled up on the back of one truck and furniture started appearing on the other. I had to keep out of the way or I would be piled on the truck with the rest of the junk. Bikey traveled on the seat of dad's chair and by noon both trucks were piled as high as they could be piled. My mother gave the men lunch and they headed off to Lake Street, about a twenty-minute drive. Mom drove our Essex out of the driveway and waved as she headed for the new house. Genevieve and I were left home alone. We spent the afternoon eating up all the fruit that was left in the icebox, sweeping up the empty rooms and waiting for our folks to come back. By suppertime Mom and Dad returned and fed us franks, baked beans and some of Mom's canned peaches. Sunday morning, before the Examiner was dropped on our porch the trucks and men had returned. Pacific Avenue was fast emptying out. Jay helped. Carrying beds and pots and pans he became friends with all dad's men, even rode on the back of a truck on the trip to the new house. Pacific Avenue was history; the Tyrrells now lived on Lake Street.

Everyone was working. Chairs moving around, carpets pulled here and there. Mom checking exactly where the dining room table should be. She was very happy. She had a new gas stove and a refrigerator. No more ice man. We had progressed. I ran for my room to escape the madness in the house. My room was peaceful, quiet. I could look over the backyard, watch a lovely brown horse graze in the fields beyond our fence. I could see a playground across the street. See kids playing in the schoolyard. My new room was great. I fell on my little bed and fell fast asleep.

My dad made his specialty for breakfast. We all sat in our new kitchen as he piled his Western omelet on our plates. The family was dead tired but it was Monday morning and here we were in a mansion and I was anxious to explore. I ran out into the back yard and discovered a new sandbox my dad had built, a big square with a seat that ran all around and piled full of white sand. Heaven. A few feet away from my sandbox was my dad's new office. A little house about ten feet square. He would run his roofing business from there while I built sand castles in the sunshine.

The back yard was huge. The first third filled with kegs of tar, rolls of tarpaper and stack after stack of bright red Spanish tile. Then a sea of grass with beautiful flower beds on each side, fenced in by a 4 foot fence. It was ten times the size of our little triangular yard on Pacific Avenue. I would spend many happy days playing there.

I could hear yelling from the playground across the street where the School summer camp was in session. I walked to the fence to watch the kids. I wanted to join them. I skipped down the drive, ran around the corner sat on the curb and watched a game of kick ball in noisy progress. A tall man came out of the gate and walked to his car. "You look unhappy sitting there, young man, you want to play with the kids?" He called across the street.

"I can't cross the street by myself." He walked across the street. "Come, I'll take you to the playground." He grabbed my hand. He took me right into the play ground and left me standing watching the game. A boy kicked the ball and it came right to me. I caught it and threw it back. Another ball came to me. I caught it and threw it back.

A lady called out, "You want to play with us?" "Sure!" I yelled. The kids laughed. I was in the game. I was having a lot of fun when a loud bell rang out and the lady grabbed the ball. "Lunchtime, Kids," She called, they all ran off into the building leaving me and the ball all alone."

"Come, Bruzzy, let's have lunch!" My mother was standing at the gate waiting for me. I ran to her. "Mommy, Mommy, I played kick ball with the kids and I kicked one right over everybody's heads. It was a home run, I want to play some more. Can I play some more?"

"Come home, have some lunch and I'll bring you back. You can play if they ask you." She took my hand as we crossed the street.

"The man who crossed you knocked on the door. He told me you were in the playground. When I heard the lunch bell I came over to pick you up. You must have someone help you across the street, honey, or else you should find me and I'll cross you. Just until you're a little older, Okay?" Did anybody have a better mother? From that day on I practically lived in the schoolyard.

6

Every morning when I opened my eyes I would stand by the window and watch the brown horse chewing his breakfast. I wanted to know that horse. He looked like a friend but he was in that lot and I was behind a wire fence. I'd have my breakfast and go to the playground and forget about my friend the horse. But the next morning I would see him and want to pet his shiny neck.

One day, after many days of watching the horse, I went out into the back and walked to the fence. All the trucks, the roofers and my father had gone off to work and I was alone in the huge back yard. I looked through the wire. The horse was very close it seemed. I stuck my Ked into the wire, grabbed the fence to climb. Too big, the fence was too big I had to start higher. I looked around the yard and saw a milk carton leaning against my father's office. I investigated. I dragged the wooden box to the fence. I stood it on end against the wire. I got my knee up on top of the box and pulled against the fence till I stood. I could reach the bar at the top of the fence, my shoe went into the wire and I pulled up again. I was climbing. Suddenly I was lying on the wobbly top bar. I got my foot over into the wire and got down to the ground. I sat down catching my breath; I was struck with the fact that I could climb a fence. Imagine that. Now I could go meet my friend, the horse. I trotted across the big pasture and stood near the horse. He whinnied and stamped his foot. "I'm your friend, horsey." I called and came a little closer. He threw his head in the air and stamped again. "I want to be your friend, don't be scared, I'm your friend. Don't you want a friend? You're out here all by yourself all day. I could be your friend." I was standing right next to him. I could see his sides heave as he breathed in and out. I put my hand on his smooth warm neck and his skin wiggled under my palm. "You see? I'm not going to hurt you. I'm your friend. I'm going to call you Brownie. You like that name Brownie?" I kept rubbing his neck and he grumbled deep in his throat.

He was tied to a long thin rope so he had lots of walking room. I could see the grass marked by his hooves where he traveled at the end of his tether. There was a big brown box with a step built right where he could walk. If I could get him to go there I could climb up on the box and get on his back. I decided to try. I took hold of the halter he was wearing and gave a little pull. That great big horse came right along. I walked him to the box, he stopped right along side of it. Boy, I thought I was pretty smart to get the horse to stand right where I wanted him to stand. I climbed the step and stood on the box. I petted the big animal on his back and he made noises in his throat. He stood absolutely still. I took hold of his mane and put my leg over his back and fell into a sitting position. The horse took a couple of steps to the side. I said, "Nice, Brownie, walk Brownie, take me for a little ride, Brownie." What else could I say I had never seen a cowboy movie so I didn't know what you said to get a horse moving? Brownie turned his head, looked at me and began walking at the end of his rope around a big circle. I was in seventh heaven. I was riding a horse. Brownie was my horse and I was riding him. He walked past the box three times and then he stopped right at the box. He turned, looked at me and shook his head. "End of the line." I thought so I slid off his back on to the big brown box. Brownie stamped his foot a couple of times and went back to eating his grass. I patted his neck and whispered in his ear. "I'll see you tomorrow."

I walked back to the fence where the box was propped. On the wrong side! I looked up at the top of the fence. I was in trouble. The box was inside and I was outside. If I wanted over I had to climb. I stuck my foot in the wire and pulled myself up, stuck my other foot in wire and pulled up again and suddenly I was at the top, I threw my leg over and got my foot into the wire. I climbed down, past the box, right to the ground. I could climb a fence. I could ride a horse. I was a big boy!

I dreamed of the big brown horse that waited for me in the pasture behind our house. I jumped up in the morning and there he was eating his grass. I'll bet he's waiting for me. I ran down for breakfast. My dad was sitting at the table with my mother. They were talking.

"Your father is working in his office today, Bruz, so if you play in the sandbox don't make a lot of noise." She patted my hand. "I'm making some sugar toast for you than you can go out and play."

"Can I go across the street to the schoolyard, Mom. Maybe there's a ball game."

"Eat your breakfast and I'll cross you. I'll come get you at lunchtime. Are you having lunch with us, dear? I have some chicken, I could make some sandwiches."

"I'd love to, Darling. I have some billing to do and I need to order tile. Call me when you want to eat." He got up, leaned over and kissed my mothers head, messed my hair and went out the back door." No horseback riding today, I thought.

The sound of the trucks pulling out of the yard woke me the next morning. I looked out. The trucks were loaded with tar and roofing paper and tiles, looked like the start of a new job. I looked at the fence. I looked at Brownie. I was going riding.

Brownie saw me coming and walked over to the box. I was amazed. I walked over, "Hello Brownie, how's my good friend this morning?" He grumbled in his throat and tossed his head. I petted his neck. He pushed me with his head towards the big box. He wanted me on his back. He liked me on his back. I got settled on his back and he walked past the box twice and started to trot. I bounced up and down but held tightly on his mane. He passed the box and walked again, stopping to let me off. He had given me his ride. I stayed a few minutes petting him and talking to him then headed for the fence, he walked with me as far as his rope allowed. He whinnied and went back to eating grass. I did the fence. My Mom took me to the schoolyard.

Every morning for the rest of the week I rode Brownie till he put me off. Climbed the fence and spent the rest of the time at the schoolyard. It was a great life. I watched Jay-wah play ball in the schoolyard on Saturday. Sunday my dad packed us off to the beach. I slept in the car with my head in Gen's lap on the way home, a perk for being the baby of the family.

My dad woke me Monday morning and sat down on my bed. I sat up and wondered if I was in trouble. "Mr. Carle, who lives behind us, told me you've been riding his horse. Is that true?"

"Yes sir, Brownie, he's my friend. He likes me to ride on him. Do I have to stop?"

"The horse you call Brownie belongs to Mr. Carle's daughter. She has gone to live with her grandmother back east and the horse is very lonely for her. Carle figured out you were riding him because the horse was suddenly happier even though his master was still off in New England. He would like you to keep being friendly with the horse while he's still around. He said you could pick some free apricots as a reward."

I was so happy I couldn't answer. I just laughed out loud. "Oh boy, that's great. I'll ride him every day. I'll be his best friend."

"Well, son, you do what you want but Mr. Carle thinks three or four times a week would be good, so if I were you, I would do what he wants. You could walk down School Street and around the front of his house come up the drive to get to the horse. That way you wouldn't have to cross any streets or climb any fences. What do you think?"

"Oh, I'll climb the fence. It's easy and Brownie can see me coming and feel as happy as me. I won't hurt your fence, Daddy. I'll take care." My father laughed, stood up and messed my hair. Patted my head and left my room. I ran over to the window to look at my friend Brownie in the pasture behind our house. Over the weeks Brownie walked, trotted, cantered and finally galloped around the big circle. I was very comfortable hanging on to his mane, keeping my knees tight against his sides. I was in another world. Then one Sunday morning I looked out my window and Brownie was gone. And Mr. Carle was gone. New people were picking apricots in his orchard. New people. People who didn't know me, didn't talk with my dad and didn't live in the house. They just picked the apricots. I didn't ride again for several years, but that's another story.

7

Summer was over. School was about to start. Genevieve into the fifth grade. Jay, a senior in Hoover High would graduate in January. I wormed my way into being a guest student in Kindergarten. I was best at recess. Sandbox was my second best subject. But the teacher, who ran the summer camp, loved me. She liked having me around. I could sharpen pencils, clean the blackboard and sit quietly while she read stories. It was hard work but I loved school.

My mother became very involved in school politics. She ran bake sales, put together raffles she conned out of local businesspeople, held luncheons for special teachers, helped the principal with various jobs and Tyrrell became an important name at Franklin School.

Sandra Blaine lived in the house next door to us on Lake Street. She was in first grade. My dad and her father would chat across the hedge when dad was trimming it or mowing the lawn. Sandra's dad was a lawyer who saw my father as potential business. Mr. Blaine, a very tall man had long grey hair. He looked mean to me.

I sat in the sandbox at recess filling a bucket with wet sand making a row of sand cakes when Sandra sat down on the sand box. "You have such a beautiful sandbox in your own backyard. Much nicer than this why do you play in this one?"

I thought that was a dumb question. How could a first grader be so dumb? "I'm here. My sand box is across the street." I answered.

"I know that. Do you think I'm stupid? Why don't I come over after school and we could play in your sandbox?" She said, being very friendly.

"Sure. Come over at four. I don't have to go in till five-thirty." She shook her head, smiled and ran away just as the bell ended recess. Sandra was head and shoulders taller than me. She was very pretty with long red-blonde curls framing a cupid face.

She came over every day after school and we played in the sand box or played catch with a beach ball. One day she brought some jacks and taught me how to pick them up while the ball was still in the air. She drew a Hop Scotch plan on the back walk and we hopped and hopped on many afternoons. Sandra was fun.

My dad was leaning on the door of his office watching me pile sand up and push it over. "Where's your young lady friend today, Bruz?" He called out.

"She's coming in a little while, she had to shop with her mom." I answered filling a sand bucket. "I'm going across to Fred's, tell your mother if she's looking for me." He walked down the driveway just as Sandra arrived. She looked like a cheerleader in a white sweater, a short blue skirt and high-topped sneakers. We played some two-man kick ball making short kicks back and forth when she threw the ball into the sandbox. "Where's your dad, Bruz?" She asked.

"He went across the street to his friends house." I answered. "Come on," she said, "I'm going to teach you a new game. Come into the garage." We walked past my father's office and into the back door of the garage. The only light filtered through the small windows in the front overhead door. An old carpet was rolled up against the sidewall. Sandra sat down and patted the carpet next to her. "Sit here, Bruz, I'll explain the game to you." I sat next to her and waited for instructions. "Have you ever played 'showing sights' before?" She asked. I shook my head. "How do you play?" I asked.

"Well, I show you something," she pulled up her sweater and showed her belly button. "And you show me something." I pulled up my shirt and you could see my belly button. "That's right, you've got the idea. Want to play?"

"Sure. Do you always get to go first? How do you win?"

"Let's play a little while you'll figure it out. It's a simple game." She pulled her panties down and showed me her privates. I wanted to run but I was frozen on the carpet. "Isn't that pretty? Now, show me your pee-pee."

I didn't know what to do. I fumbled with the button on my shorts. It popped open. I wiggled them down.

"Are you kids in here?" My father came into the garage. He saw us on the carpet "Sandra, put yourself together and go on home." She ran out of the garage. "Pull your pants up young man and go into the kitchen we need to talk. I'll be right in." He stalked out of the garage. I held my shorts up and ran out of the garage into the house. No one was around. I ran into the kitchen. My father was going to kill me for showing sights. I couldn't stop to button my shorts, I needed to hide from my father.

I climbed under the sink and pulled the door closed behind me. It clicked. It was a big space. Only a box of soap and a small wastebasket was under there. I slid around behind the pipes and leaned against the back wall. I would be very quiet. Maybe they would never find me. In a few minutes I heard my father come in. "Bruz?" He called. I didn't answer. I heard him walk away.

"Hello! I'm home!" I heard my sister call out. Then I heard, "Oh hi Mom, where've you been?" "I was across at Aunt Bea's, she wasn't feeling well so I made her lunch and read to her. She fell asleep and I came home." I heard them come into the kitchen. Then I heard the crunch of my father's shoes on the tile floor.

"Hello, Ladies." He said, "Either of you see Bruzzy? We need to talk." Fear welled up in me. I squeezed back against the wall. I'd rather die in here than face my father. I remembered him hitting my big brother.

"What's the problem, sweetheart?" My mother asked.

"I caught him and Sandra with their pants down." And they both laughed. My sister Gen said, "that little Sandra is very wise for a first grader." My mother and father were still laughing.

I didn't understand. "Well, Bruz is somewhere. He'll get hungry and come out." "I'll never come out." I said to myself. "I'll die in here first."

Then my sister said, "I have some homework. I'll be in my room. Call me if you need help with supper." I heard her walk out.

"What's for supper, Mother?" My dad asked.

"There's lamb stew from yesterday. I made peach cobbler this morning and got some vanilla ice cream. I think it will fill you up." I heard my dad laugh. He didn't seem too worried about me. My mouth watered when my mom said peach cobbler.

"Well, I think I'll give Bruz another fifteen minutes to show up before I call the police." My dad said in a stern voice. I couldn't see him wink at my mom. What was I going to do? I didn't want to see any policeman. Maybe I should give myself up. I slid around the pipes, pushed the door open and wiggled out on to the kitchen floor. My mother and father watched. I looked at my father. "You ready to take your medicine, young man? Sit up here at the table and tell me what happened. I climbed up on the chair. "She said she wanted to teach me a new game, I followed her into the garage and she showed me her belly button so I showed her mine. Then she wanted to see my pee pee and I couldn't get my pants down and you walked in and spoiled the game, I didn't have a chance to win. I thought you were going to kill me so I hid." I started to cry.

My father hid his smile, "Well, Son, this is a good lesson for you. Never play a game unless you understand the rules. Especially playing with a woman. You'll discover that when you go into a dark place with a pretty girl the rules of the game change pretty fast. I recommend we forget all about this incident and put our minds on your mothers peach cobbler under a pile of vanilla ice cream. You go upstairs and wash so you're ready for supper."

I ran to my room. I couldn't believe I was still alive. I made myself a promise. I would never ever again in my whole life go into a dark place with any girl. Sorry to report, I wasn't able to keep that promise.

8

I held my mother's hand as she took me across School Street for today's guest appearance in kindergarten. Mr. Weller, the principal was standing by the gate. "Good morning, Mrs. Tyrrell, you're just the person I wanted to see. I have a problem and you can help me solve it."

"I'll be happy to give you a hand, Mr. Weller, if it's something I can do."

"Oh, you can do it all right. I hope you can make the time. You know our budget problems this year and I've just been told we need new books for the Glee Club and math books for the sixth grade, almost a thousand dollars, Mrs. Tyrrell, and we don't have any extra money at all."

My mother looked down at me, "Run along, Bruzzilah, I'll pick you up for lunch, I have to speak with Mr. Weller." I smiled and ran off to the big kindergarten room. I had an important game of dominoes with my friends.

"Can you come into the office for a few minutes, Mrs. Tyrrell? Maybe if we put our heads together we can figure this out. Fifteen minutes later, sitting in the office with Mr. Weller and his assistant my mother gave them a plan. "I've been thinking about a Christmas party for the school, all the kids, all the parents. We could make it outdoors on the front lawn I'll get some of the ladies to make finger food and some will bake cakes and pumpkin pies and we'll give Christmas presents to every kid in the school."

"We need to make money, Mrs. Tyrrell, not spend it."

"Certainly, Mr. Weller. Each family will buy a ticket. We'll charge two dollars and fifty cents. We'll spend fifty cents each for the presents. I'll buy the wrapping and tags. If I'm right we have 480 families in the school, so that would make a little less than what you need so I'll get three merchants to donate some merchandise for three raffles. The kids will sell the raffles for a quarter. If we sell two hundred tickets we'll have another 150 dollars and you can buy your books." She smiled and sat back.

"That's a wonderful idea but it's an awful lot of work, Mrs. Tyrrell, are you sure you want to take it on?"

"I'll get lots of help, the ladies of this school are workers but I do want one thing from you, Mr. Weller."

"Certainly, Mrs. Tyrrell, anything."

"I want to be Santa Claus. I want to give out all the gifts. The kids will line up and come across a dais to get their presents. I want to be Santa Claus and give them out."

Mr. Weller laughed, "I think you'll make the most wonderful Santa Claus who ever visited Benjamin Franklin Grammar School." My mom had the job.

When my mom had a job to do she did it. She did it better than anybody. She got many women to help make the food and wrap the presents. My sister got 18 kids from her class to sell raffle tickets and my mom got Sears in downtown Glendale to donate a washing machine and raised the price of that raffle to fifty cents. The Grand Central butcher gave her a Christmas turkey and the paint store came up with five gallons of enamel. My mom had great confidence in a successful ticket sale. The printer gave her the books at cost and she turned the project over to my sister to complete.

My dad was carving a leg of lamb at the dining room table. He put three slices of meat on the plate, a small mountain of mashed potatoes and filled the empty space with green peas. "Gravy, Son?" He asked my big brother. "Please, Dad, " Jay answered, "Can I have a little extra mint jelly?" My dad laughed, put of glob of green on the plate and handed it to Jay. "I'm going to work this Saturday for J.J. Newberry at the main store in LA.

I'm going to work weekends till I graduate after Christmas. It will be great experience. Saturdays I'm going to be stock boy and help out on the floor and Sunday we'll re-stock the store. I get twenty-five cents an hour…that's four bucks a week, I'm going to be a rich man!" My mother and father laughed, my sister reached over and patted Jay's hand. I felt very proud of my big brother.

"Wonderful, Son. I don't know about rich, but four dollars is four dollars. You'll have to spend forty cents on the trolley. Mom will make you a sandwich so you won't have to waste money on lunch. You may come home with nearly four dollars. I think that is a fine start to your career." Jay smiled.

"We're very proud of you, Jay, my mom said. "You said you wanted the job and you got the job. Very good. Maybe you can get me some Christmas paper for the school party. See if you can get me a break on twenty rolls of wrapping paper, some tags and Christmas seals. Would you?" Jay laughed out loud.

"Golly Mom, I haven't even met anyone and you're looking for discounts. I'll see what I can do. After all, a stock clerk is a big deal." Everyone at the table laughed. I wondered what was funny.

All the notes home had been sent, all the raffle books were delivered. The presents were wrapped in the paper Jay got at a bargain price, each tagged with the name of a lucky student and stuffed in a gunny-sack provided by my father. It was Saturday, December 22nd, 1928 and Mrs. Tyrrell's Christmas party was to be held on the lawn at Benjamin Franklin at one thirty in the afternoon. 475 tickets had been sold, the grass had been trimmed, cloth covered tables were arranged on the lawn. A foot high stage had been constructed and the big fir tree was hung with red and green decorations. It would be a party to remember. And hanging on the back of the door in my mother's room was her Santa Claus outfit. A beautiful outfit lined with white fur, the hat with a big white ball, a wig and a long white beard waited to turn Mrs. Tyrrell into Mr. Claus.

My mother led my sister and me across the street at half past eleven. Gen carried a big pot of Swedish meatballs and I had a sack of a thousand cookies Mom had baked.

The cafeteria people were taking care of food service and all the teachers were there to visit with the guests. Tables were covered with Christmas canes, and bowls of Christmas candy. Gen delivered her meatballs and I handed a lady the cookies. My mother was everywhere. Checking this, checking that. Gen and her sales group were meeting on the steps of the main entrance so I sat down on the front edge of the stage and watched the show.

The guests began to arrive. A car pulled up, the door swung open, kids and mothers spilled out while the daddys pulled around on School Street to park. No parking on Lake Street. The crowd grew. The noise grew. Gen's salespeople started to work. I could see money and tickets changing hands. Kids were licking candy canes, eating cookies and slices of cake while grownups had paper plates with meat balls and little franks and mushrooms. The food was being demolished. My Dad sat down next to me. "Hey Bruz, aren't you going to eat anything?" He said. "I only like my mother's stuff and it was all gone before I could get there. I'll save room for supper."

"Not a very good idea today, your mother's very busy. Come on, let's see what there is to eat." We walked over to the food. The place was jammed with parents, hungry kids, busy cafeteria people and a couple of local mutts wagging their tales looking for hand outs. My dad grabbed a couple of little franks and handed me one. We stood smiling and chewing on the tough little hot dog. My dad laughed. I loved how his eyes sparkled when he laughed. "Hey, look, there's the good humor man. Come on." We beat everyone to the curb. I got a chocolate sundae in a cup with a wooden spoon. My dad and I sat on the edge of the stage slowly eating the sundaes. I was feeling very happy. Time flashed away. We had to get off the stage because Mr. Weller was about to make an announcement. We joined the crowd forming around the stage. My dad scooped me up and put me on his shoulder.

"Welcome Ladies and Gentlemen, to the first Benjamin Franklin Christmas party. I want to thank Mrs. Tyrrell and all the ladies for this wonderful job. Genevieve Tyrrell reports that all the raffle tickets have been sold so what do you say if we have the drawings before the presents?"

Boos from all the kids. Loud applause from all the adults. My sister brought three wastebaskets to the principal. He put them in a row on a table, the paint, the turkey and the washing machine.

"First were going to see who wins the five gallons of paint from Alec's Paint Store on Ventura Boulevard. Thank you Mr. Burton for your generous donation. Mrs. Burton would you do the honor of selecting the winner. A little applause as a nice looking lady made her way up on the stage. "Now, stir those tickets around, dig deep and give me the winner." She handed him a ticket, he read the number, no on answered. He read the number again. Quiet. "Last chance to be a winner! No one answers this time we draw another number, please check your tickets for 3-7-1-6. "Oh! Oh!" A lady screamed, "It's me." It was the fifth grade teacher, Mrs. Skinner. "Well congratulations, Mrs. Skinner, you're a winner!" "I'm so happy, I really do need a new washer." She ran for the stage.

"That's wonderful, Mrs. Skinner, but you get five gallons of paint."

"Oh, well, Mr. Skinner will have to paint something." The crowd applauded. Weller finished the other drawings without incident and called for quiet.

"And now Ladies and Gentlemen, we're honored to have our friend from the North Pole here to visit us. Let's give a great big Glendale welcome to Santa Claus!!"

The double doors of the school main entrance opened and there was Santa Claus, a big bag slung over his shoulder. With everyone cheering, he made his way up to the stage, smiling and nodding. He put his big sack on the floor, stuck his hand in the bag and pulled out a package. He looked around at the crowd. "This present is for Tommy Tarpley!" he said, "Please come quickly for your gift." Tommy Tarpley came across the stage, took his gift, said "Thank you Santa." And stepped off the stage. And so it started. Over and over his hand went into the bag, out came a present up came a kid across the stage, took the gift, said "Thank you Santa Claus" and returned to his folks. Boys and girls came, "Thank you Santa Claus." They said. My mother was happy she had convinced the kids that she was Santa Claus. What a wonderful day.

37

Slowly the bag emptied. Finally the last gift was in his hand.

"Sandra Blaine." He said. I watched my girl friend cross the stage, take the present and say "Thank you Mrs. Tyrrell." The crowd laughed. My mother's heart sank.

She made the money Mr. Weller needed. Paid for the Glee Club's songbooks, paid for the sixth grade math books but she failed in her impression of Santa Claus. Still, for the next two years on the Saturday before Christmas, she would hand out presents to the kids.

Whether they thanked Santa Claus or Mrs. Tyrrell she was a very happy lady.

9

Something was shaking my shoulder. I opened my eyes. It was dark night. I blinked my eyes and made out my sisters face smiling down at me. "Wake up, Bruz, you want to see if Santa came?" She said. "It's dark, Gen, I'm sleepy."

"Come on, lets go see what's going on. Maybe we'll catch him decorating the tree." She smiled a big smile. I jumped out of bed. She took me by my hand; she put a finger to her lips to be quiet. She led me out on the balcony. We tiptoed up to the railing. There, in the bay window, my dad and mom were decorating a huge Christmas tree. A tall stepladder was open on the floor. I watched my dad hang silver and gold ornaments on the high branches of the tree. Gen sat on the floor letting her legs hang over the edge through the railing. Monkey see. Monkey do, I copied her. We sat together watching our parents bring Christmas to the house on Lake Street.

Two stockings hung over the fireplace. I figured Jay had outgrown the stocking age. I could make out a chocolate Santa in the top of one stocking. I hoped that was mine. I kept falling to sleep as the folks labored on the living room floor. Gen kept nudging me. My dad climbed up the ladder and put a beautiful Angel at the top of the tree and my mother clapped her hands, the job was done. My father folded the ladder and leaned it against a wall as my mother arrived with a pile of boxes. "These are for Jay, Bill, where should I put them." "Put Jay on the left, Bruz in the middle and Gen on the right, that's probably best." She made a nice pile of Jay's presents while my dad brought a second pile and put them on the right. They both left and returned with their hands full, big boxes, small boxes, round boxes and an orange bag, "Wow!" I thought, "Those are Bruzzy's presents!" They placed them under the tree in the middle and fell into the big living room chairs. "That's got it for another year, Dear, let's get some sleep."

Gen grabbed my hand, got me up and pushed me into my room. Kissed me on my head and was gone. I jumped into bed and lay there looking at the ceiling until the sun came up. I heard some noise. It must be my mother so I scrambled downstairs and approached the tree. I looked at the pile of packages I knew were for me. Very excited. I saw a round package. That had to be Tinker Toys. I played with them in school, now I would have my own.

"Merry Christmas, Darling." My mama said. "You're up bright and early this morning." I looked at her and smiled. I couldn't talk. I was too excited. "Merry Christmas, Merry Christmas!" Genevieve called coming down the stairs, "Happy Christmas to all!" She laughed. "Gen, you and your little brother go through your stockings while I get Jay and your father up. Then we can see what Santa Claus brought. I stood looking up at my stocking. It was high over my head. I couldn't reach it. I didn't think it would be a good idea to get a chair, Gen said she would be right back. "Here's a soup bowl for you, Bruz, we put all the stocking stuff in the bowl, then eat it." She laughed, handed me a bowl and my stuffed Christmas stocking. I sat right down on the floor. I pulled the chocolate Santa out and thought about biting off his head.

"Don't eat anything, Bruz and Gen, we have a huge breakfast after we open the presents." I looked up at Gen. She looked down at me. Her eyes said, "no eating only looking." A grumpy big brother came down the stairs. "Christ! I didn't get home till almost one o'clock this morning. I need my sleep."

"Oh! Shut up, Jay!" Gen said, "It's Christmas. Merry Christmas. Look at that pile of presents. You can sleep anytime." Jay started to laugh, Gen laughed, jumped up and kissed his cheek, "Here, have a brazil nut."

My dad arrived in his white pajamas and the bathrobe he got last Christmas. "Time to open presents!" He yelled, "Dottie get in here, Jay's going to open his presents." Jay sat on the floor as mom arrived, wiping her hands on a stripped dishtowel. I watched my dad get down on the floor, next to Jays pile. He picked up a box. "This is for Jay from Mother." He handed it to Jay.

"Thanks Mom, I'll save up my money this year so I can buy you a present next year. They've got some great beer glasses at Newberry's." Everybody laughed. What would mom want with beer glasses, I wondered. But I smiled anyway. Jay tore the wrapping off and opened the box. "Oh! Tissue paper, Just what I've always wanted, tissue paper."

His mother laughed at the standard Christmas joke, "Stop wasting time, the ham is almost ready." "Look. Three shirts, wow, they're swell. I could have used them this week; they're perfect for the floor. Thanks Mom, you are the greatest." He went through several packages, ties, hankies, two sweaters, socks, then Dad handed him a small present. Jay read the tag. "Merry Christmas, big brother. Bruzzy." I didn't buy anybody Christmas presents, this was a mistake. It was a key ring with Jay spelled out on a silver tab. "This is perfect, Bruz, how'd you know I needed a key ring. I have house keys, store keys and closet keys in the stock room. This is perfect." I didn't know what to say. Then mom piped up, "I helped Bruzzy shop we decided you would need a new key ring. You have a smart little brother." I didn't know what to say so I kept quiet. Jay reached over and patted my shoulder. Jay looked around, no more presents. "I guess that's it, folks, I need clothes and I got clothes. Father Christmas fills the bill."

"Hey, Dottie, isn't there another package for Jay in the hall closet, I thought I saw it there last night." My dad said smiling.

"Let me go check, dear, you stay right where you are."

We all looked at each other and my mother came back with a long box wrapped in silver foil with a big red ribbon. My mother handed the box to my father. My father checked the tag. "The tag says to our oldest son, Love, Mom and Dad. Hey Bruz, are you the oldest son?"

"No, I'm the baby." I laughed. "Right." Dad said, "So it must be for you, Jay." He handed him the box.

"Wow! That's heavy." Jay said putting the long package in his lap.

He took the silver foil off very carefully folding it over and over. He was holding a long blue box. He pulled off the top and peered into the box. "Holy shit." He said. My dad didn't say a word. My mom smiled. Jay reached in the box and pulled out a blue steel rifle. "Jeeze, Dad, a ten gauge shotgun. Exactly what I wanted. Fred is going to be blue with envy. I can't wait for deer season. Thank you. Thank you, Mom, Dad. This is great."

He heaved the gun to his shoulder and aimed at the Angel atop the tree. "Bam!" He said and laughed. "I told you he would hate that, Honey, I knew the suede jacket was what he wanted." The whole family laughed. My dad shook Jays hand. Jay pulled himself up and kissed my father, kissed my mother and carried his shotgun to the living room couch. He sat down. I could see tears in his eyes. I never forgot that Christmas.

My mother broke the silence. "I think we ought to have breakfast now and we can finish with the presents later. Anyone with a better suggestion?" No one spoke. I was going to do whatever I was told. I saw my brother kiss my father. That was the best Christmas present anyone could ask for. "Well then, Gen, come give me a hand. You guys go wash your hands, we're eating in the kitchen." My mother and sister left. We three men went upstairs. We got to the balcony. Jay said, "Want to carry my gun, Bruz?"

"Sure. Sure, if you let me."

"Just take it into my room, okay?" He handed me the big gun. It was the heaviest thing I ever held, but I wouldn't let myself drop it. I lugged it through his door and laid it on his bed. "Terrific, kid." He said and messed my hair. Why did everyone mess my hair, couldn't they just shake hands? "Go wash your hands Bruz, and go to the kitchen. You're big enough to appreciate Mom's Christmas breakfast this year." I ran off.

My dad sat at the head of the table, my mom at the foot, my sister sat alone on the stove side and Jay and I sat on the other side. I liked it like this. I liked sitting next to my big brother. I loved my sister, she was swell but there was something special about my brother Jay.

A big glass of fresh squeezed orange juice sat in front of each place, a roast ham filled the center of the table with two platters of sunny side eggs on either side. My dad served as he did in the dining room. My mom was the greatest cook in the world. I was full of ham and eggs when Gen put a big fruitcake in the middle of the table and dad gave a slab of dark cake to each of us. My slab was more a slice than a slab but it was a lot for a kid who would be four in a week. We finished eating. Everyone returned to the living room and fell into chairs. Except, Mom and Gen who did a quick clean of the kitchen before getting back to Christmas. Gen oood and awed through her presents. I was overwhelmed with a little wind up train with a round track and a station in the middle. Tinker toys, Chinese Checkers and a tiny catcher's mitt from my dad.

Finally it was mother's turn, she got the usual tea pot, a grill for her stove top, three hanks of string for her crocheting, a bottle of something and then dad stood up. "Dottie," he said, "Jay got the gun he's been wanting for years. Now he's big enough to handle it so he got it. You've been complaining about that poor old Essex and worrying every time we head for the beach. So to stop your complaining and worrying I got you a special present. Bruz bring your mother out to the front porch." I jumped up and grabbed my mom's hand. She was kind of out of it. I led her to the front door. Dad opened it, I pushed the screen door open and she came out on the porch. "A Clux a ma Laben!" She said, looking at a brand new 1928 four door Studebaker. My father laughed, "The top car of the year for the best wife and mother in the world." Jay, Gen, dad and me, all hugged her at once. Like I said, a Christmas I'd never forget.

10

I was four years old. I got three presents. My mom made a chocolate birthday cake with four candles. We had roast chicken for dinner. Mom served my birthday cake with vanilla ice cream for dessert. Jay graduated on Friday, Saturday he became a full time employee of J. J. Newberry. He worked six days a week, no longer an hourly employee he was paid the weekly sum of eighteen dollars. His future looked bright.

Christmas vacation was over. I went back to school, once more a guest of the kindergarten. Our teacher, Mrs. Miller, welcomed us back. She complimented my mother for the great Christmas party and all the kids clapped their hands. I felt like a big man. "Children," the teacher said, "In two weeks we begin the second semester of the year. Mr. Weller and I have decided that Bruz Tyrrell will become a member of this class, no longer a guest but a full-fledged Kindergarten student. Now, how about some kick ball outside!" I was dumbfounded. I belonged. Not a guest. A student. Wait till I tell my mom and dad. Won't they feel proud? Jay graduates from high school and I become a real student. 1929 will be a good year.

The Kindergarten decided to have an end of semester supper party. As usual they asked Mrs. Tyrrell to help. My mother planned a "help-your-self" buffet supper. Lettuce, tomato and cucumber salad, meat balls, boiled new potatoes and pickled beets, the main course with apple pie and cubed American cheese for desert. She got two of the mothers to help and was ready to feed the families of 32 kindergarten kids. Mrs. Miller got the Glee Club to sing and the principal wanted to stage a make-believe boxing match between two kindergarten boys. Naturally he told my mom, my mom told my dad and my dad offered my services. He would be the referee and I would fight Jimmy Fields, one of his roofers' sons in the Kindergarten class. Jimmy Fields was nearly six, nearly a head taller than me and a tough kid. I wanted no part of him.

"I don't want to fight Jimmy Fields, Mom. He's big and he's mean. He picks on the girls and pushes people around. I don't want to fight him."

"This is not a real fight, sweetheart, this is an exhibition. You'll wear big pillow gloves, even if he hits you it won't hurt. You'll look so cute in boxing shorts with your name printed on your tee shirt. It will be a lot of fun." She patted my long blonde curls.

Mom made French toast for breakfast. My sister was having cold cereal. Jay had already gone to work. My dad sat down. "I bet Big Jim a buck my kid would beat his next week. How about that Bruz?" I looked at him and lost my appetite. My mother spoke up, "Bet? There's no reason to bet, this isn't a fight it's a show. Bruz is four and that kid is nearly six. What kind of stupid bet is that?"

"It's all in fun, honey, but somebody has to win, why can't that be Bruz?"

"Ugh. Men! Men can be so stupid." I excused myself and went to school with Gen., I hated this fight. The kids talked constantly about the supper. All their folks were coming, half the class had sisters or brothers in the glee club but I knew my sister would be the best. Then the day of the supper arrived!

They dressed me in red shorts with a red tee shirt, B-R-U-Z printed on the chest; my opponent was in blue, J-I-M-M-Y J-R on his shirt. My father's friend Fred was my second and Jimmy's dad was his. My father was the referee. I wanted to be home in bed.

"Just keep your hands up in front of your face, Bruz," Fred was coaching me. "Keep knocking his hands away. When you see an opening punch him in the mouth!" I didn't have the slightest idea what he was talking about. Then I heard my father.

"Ladies and Gentlemen. Now, for the feature attraction. In this corner wearing the red shorts, Lake Street's own, Bruz Tyrrell!" The crowd cheered and applauded.

"And in the blue shorts, the king of Thompson Avenue, Jimmy Fields, Junior!" The crowd cheered and clapped, some one called out "GO get him, Jimmy!" He danced around his father and clapped his hands together. Fred pulled big gloves onto my hands. They felt heavy and very strange. Brown leather pillows on my hands. Stupid. The referee called us to the center of the ring. Fred pushed me ahead of him; Jimmy bounced right over and glared at me, like I was some kind of bad guy. I didn't like him. My father stepped between us, "Fight fair, no hitting below the belt, break when I ask you and don't hit after the bell. We'll fight three 1 minute rounds. Any questions?"

"I'm not mad at him, Daddy." I said.

"That's good, son, boxing is a game, you should never be mad."

"Come on let's get going!" Jimmy's second said.

"Right, the referee said, get back to your corners and wait for the bell. Come out fighting."

"I'm not going to fight him, Daddy, I'm not mad at him and this is dumb."

'I'll kick your ass!" Jimmy said. "Shut up!" His second said.

The audience stamped their feet.

"I'm not fighting." I crossed my arms. Mr. Weller came through the ropes. "Okay Bill, you tried. Bruz is right, he's not mad so let's skip the fight." My dad was speechless. Mr. Weller held up my hand and held up Jimmy's hand, "Let's give a nice round of applause for our stars. Jimmy Fields and Bruz Tyrrell, give them a hand." The people clapped while the Glee Club marched up on the Kindergarten stage. A piano played. They sang the "Pilgrim's Progress." My sister sang a solo in the second chorus, my family could be proud of one of their kids. Everyone thought it was a terrific party.

I kept a low profile around the house. I didn't want to be alone with my dad. I knew he wasn't very happy with me. Mom went along as if nothing happened. I was getting into bed when my brother came into the room. "I hear you were great at school the other night, Bruz, you really taught the old man a lesson. I'm sorry I was working, I would have loved to have been there."

"Dad is mad at me, he thinks I'm a coward. I told him right away I didn't want to fight. Why didn't he believe me?"

"Our dad is from the old school, kid, he is a tough guy and thinks his kids should be tough too. I've been putting up with it a lot longer than you. He is a terrific dad but he's very different from me. I guess we have Mama's genes." He laughed. He leaned over and kissed my cheek. "Go to sleep, little one, forget all about the fight. It's over. There'll be a new problem tomorrow." He messed my hair and walked out.

My brother was a psychic. I was watching some girls riding the merry go round at recess when somebody bumped into me. I turned. It was Jimmy Fields. "Hello chicken. How'd you like me to kick your ass?" I walked away. He followed. I went to Mrs. Miller, "Jimmy Fields is picking on me, Mrs. Miller. He bumped me and told me he would kick my ass."

"Don't use that language, Bruzzy, that's low class. You're from a high class family and shouldn't speak that way." I watched her walk over and talk to Jimmy. He glared at me as she chastised him. I couldn't understand what I had done to make him mad. I went back to watching the merry go round. The days went by, every time I was near Jimmy he would yell, "Chicken! Chicken!' I didn't pay attention. I went to Grand Central shopping with my mom. She was squeezing cantaloupes in the produce store and there was Jimmy Fields. "Sissy Tyrrell. Sissy Tyrrell." He yelled. The whole market turned around.

We were riding home in the new Studebaker. It still had that new car smell. "Mom, what am I going to do about Jimmy Fields? He keeps picking on me. Ever since I quit that dumb fight.

He bumps me, calls me a sissy and a chicken. I don't like that. How do I make him stop?"

"Punch him in the mouth. Make a tight fist and hit him as hard as you can in the face. Hit him first. The first word out of his mouth hit him. If he stands there hit him again, keep hitting him till he cries and he will never bother you again."

I looked out the car window wondering if I heard my mother right. She told me to hit him. My dad might say that, but my mom? Three days later the recess bell rang and I waited to go back to class. Somebody bumped my back. I turned around. It was Jimmy Fields.

"Sissy"... I hit him with my fist as hard as I could. His nose began to bleed. He shook his head and came at me. I hit as hard as I could right in the mouth, his lip turned bloody. I shoved him and he fell. The kids crowded around, they screamed, "Get him, Bruz. Get him. I jumped on him and hit him again. He started to cry.

"Now, you leave me alone, Jimmy Fields or I'll really kick your ass!" The kids were cheering. Suddenly they were silent. Mr. Weller was there peering down at us,

"Get off that boy, Bruzzy Tyrrell and go to my office." I sat on a chair in the principals' office feeling pretty proud of myself. I followed Mom's instructions and they worked. I had beat up on Jimmy Fields. Hot dog.

Mr. Weller walked in, my father not two steps behind. He motioned us into his office and sat behind his desk. "I won't have fighting in my schoolyard. Bruzzy, you have just been admitted to this school and you act like a hooligan, I don't know if I can let you stay."

"Just one minute, Mr. Weller, my son was protecting himself from a bully. Ever since that fake fight that kid has been pushing my kid around and not one soul in this school reprimanded him. Now my innocent little kid kicks the crap out of the bully and you're giving him hell? If you have so little understanding about kids maybe he doesn't want to be in your school and maybe you ought to count on the Fields to help you in your times of need."

48

"Is that true, Bruzzy?"

"He kept pushing me and bumping me. He called me sissy and chicken. Told me he would kick my ass…"

"Yes. Jimmy can be a little tough."

"That's all right, Mr. Weller, my mother told me what to do and she's right. I did what she told me and Jimmy Fields won't bother me again. I like your school. I don't want to go any place else. Please make my daddy happy so I can stay here."

"Sorry, Bill. I had no idea."

"Okay, Dan, but you should get a better reading on your kid's. They're all here longer than they are at home. Can Bruz be excused? He needs a little cleaning up."

"Right Bill. This won't happen again."

I took my father's hand and we walked home together. We didn't say a word. He took me into his bathroom and washed my face. Put iodine on a little cut on my hand, discovered a skinned place on my knee, and cleaned it up. "Get yourself a glass of milk and play in the back. I'm going in my office."

I was playing with a dump truck in the sand box when Big Jim Fields came barreling into the yard. "Bill Tyrrell!" he yelled "Get your ass out of that office!" The door swung open. My father, his sleeves rolled up, came out into the yard. "What can I do for you, Big Jim?" He asked.

"Your fucking kid broke my kid's nose for no reason and I'm going to kick your ass, Bill. Now how about that?" He took two steps toward my dad. My dad walked right toward him grabbed his shirt in one hand, his belt in the other and lifted him straight up in the air. He spun him around and threw him into the sand box.

"Now you son of a bitch, get your ass out of here. My kid beat up on your bully son and you're stupid enough not to even know it. Now go, before you really get hurt and by the way you might as well find yourself another job cause you don't work here anymore."

He grabbed the man's pants and lifted him off the sand. He walked him on his tippy toes up the driveway. The guy didn't say a word. Dad let go. He ran.

My dad came back up the drive, "Well, son, I guess the Tyrrells took care of the Fields. Right? Oh, when your mother gets home don't tell her about this. She hates fighting."

I looked at my father in awe. I guess the "old school" was pretty good, no matter what Jay thought.

11

Vacation! School was out. Time to join Ms. Miller's camp and play in the schoolyard all day. Summer was busy time for roofers. My dad and his men were away everyday. My mom was even paying his bills and keeping his books. Jay was never around, spending his time in the five and dime business. Away hunting every Sunday. I was getting my fill of rabbit, especially rabbit full of buckshot. Mom and Gen kept the house spotless, made great dinners and in their spare time, mom crocheted and Gen had her nose in a book. Suddenly it was August.

Dad started a new job, a brand new house up on the side of a mountain behind Hoover High. All his trucks, with two extra men had left early in the morning. My dad wanted to impress this new builder with his efficiency. I was home for lunch. We were in the kitchen, my mom making peanut butter and jelly sandwiches. There was a knock at the front door. I followed my mother to see who was knocking. She opened the door. It was Fred my dad's assistant; he held his hat in his hands.

"Bill's had an accident, Dot. The ladder slipped and caught his leg as it fell. He's got a bad break, the ambulance guys put it in a splint and took him to L.A. County Hospital."

"I'll get right over there, Fred. You go back to the job, make sure everyone keeps working. Bill worked very hard to get this client, don't let anything upset the job. Go. I'll go to the hospital."

"Don't worry, Dottie. I'll keep everything together. Tell Bill I'm worried about him." My mom was already getting her car keys. She grabbed me by the hand. "Come. Bubbalah, you'll stay with Auntie White till Gen gets home from the library." She took me across Lake Street left me on Auntie White's porch. I watched her drive away.

I knocked on the screen door. Auntie White wheeled her chair to the door, "Bruzzy? What's the matter? Where's your mom? Is something wrong?"

"My daddy broke his leg. He's in the hospital. Mom's gone to help him and Gen is at the library, so mom brought me here." I felt like crying, but Auntie White was old and sick, she didn't need a crying kid.

"Come in. Sit down, you poor child. Did you have lunch?"

"We were just making peanut butter and jelly when Fred came. I didn't get to eat."

"Sit, Honey. Sit in the big chair. I don't think I have anything, let me look in the icebox." I watched her roll away. She wasn't really my aunt. She was a friend of my Mother's. She was old and not well. My mom kind of took care of her.

"You like olives?" She called from the kitchen.

"I don't know! I never tasted them." I called back. She rolled her chair into the little living room. She had a plate filled with black marbles, shiny, rolling around on the plate as she traveled. "Olives are an acquired taste," She said. "My mother told me that HER mother told HER that when she first gave her olives. 'Eat eleven olives and you'll love them for life' she said and my mom loved olives the rest of her life. Same for me, I love olives. So, here's eleven olives, eat them, they'll put a little food in your tummy and maybe you'll love them for life too." I laughed. I sat on the old chair. It smelled sort of strange. I looked at the plate of black marbles in my lap. I wondered what acquired meant but I didn't want to bother Auntie White. She sat smiling at me. I picked up an olive. It was wet, kind of icky. I put it in my mouth. It didn't taste like anything. I bit. Ouch! There's a pit in it. I thought it was like a grape but it's like an apricot. I chewed on the olive meat and got the pit out of my mouth. It didn't taste bad. It wasn't sweet and it wasn't sour, it wasn't bad. I swallowed my first olive. Auntie White sat in her wheel chair and smiled at me. I didn't want to hurt her feelings so I put number two in my mouth. Carefully I bit it in half, took the pit from my mouth and put it on the plate.

I chewed. I noticed a flavor I'd missed with the first olive. It was a different taste. Not terrible. Three, four and five went down easily. I was enjoying the fruit. Vegetable? Auntie White sat giggling. Ten pits were in the plate. Only one olive remained. I was sorry. Slowly I bit the last olive in two, I put pit eleven on the plate. Slowly I chewed the meat, the oily taste was good, subtle, refreshing. Maybe she would give me another eleven. I swallowed. It was good. I liked olives. "I like olives, Auntie White, your mother was right." She laughed out loud. Someone knocked on the door.

"Hello! Auntie White? It's Genevieve, is Bruzzy with you?"

"Come in Gen, He's here." Gen came into the little house. She kissed Auntie White on the cheek. "I got home and saw the sandwiches in the kitchen. I knew something was wrong when Bruz wasn't at school. What's the matter? What's happened?"

"Dad broke his leg! Mom went to the hospital and left me here till you got home."

"Oh my god. Where's dad? How bad is it?"

"Fred said bad. Dad is at County Hospital. That's all I know."

"Thank you, Auntie White, for watching Bruz. I'd like to take him home. Can I do anything for you while I'm here?

"No, Darling, you go. Don't worry too much about your father until you have more information. Sometimes people worry for no reason."

We ate the peanut butter sandwiches. Gen read, I made a tinker toy bridge. Six-thirty Gen warmed some leftover stew from the Frigidaire. We sat at the kitchen table. We ate. We didn't talk. There was apple pie for desert. The car pulled into the driveway at eight fifteen. Mom was beat. She sat at the kitchen table and had some of the stew. We watched. She didn't talk. Finally she pushed her plate away and said,

"Gen, put the kettle on, I need a cup of tea." Gen got the kettle on the stove and sat back down. We looked at our mother.

"Your father is badly hurt. He has a compound fracture of his right leg just above the ankle. He'll be in the hospital for at least two weeks; it will take another month before it heals. The doctor has no idea how it will turn out. Your father is a very strong man; they're counting on that to pull him through. I'm going to the hospital everyday. I'll make breakfast for all of us then leave. I can be in your father's room at eleven thirty. I'll come home like today, a little after eight. I'm sorry to wreck your vacation, Gen, but you'll have to look after your little brother and make something for dinner. It will be tough but only for two weeks. If we can get your father home I'll take over. We'll get through this. We should keep smiling because it's a lot easier to get through this happy than sad. He isn't dead, which he easily could be, so let's be thankful for God's little blessings. Could you pour me some tea please?"

I was on the front porch. I could see my father sitting crooked in the back seat. My mother pulled the car into the drive. The engine stopped and she jumped out of the car. She pulled the back door open. My father handed her two things. She leaned them against the car. My father pushed his bad leg out the door. I saw the plaster cast and the white sock on his foot. He put one hand on the back of the driver's seat and one on the back seat and lowered himself to the floor. He slid forward till his good leg was on the ground and his cast hanging past the running board. My mom handed him the two things. He put them in his armpits, held on to their handles, put the tips on the ground and pushed himself up into a standing position. He swung his good leg along dragging the bad. He got to the front steps. As always, I was amazed at my father's strength. But now he faced three front steps. My sister was called. With mom on one side, Gen on the other, he put the fancy sticks on the first step and jumped up, jumped up again and again. He was standing on the porch, mom holding one arm, Gen holding the other. He got himself into the house, down into his chair swinging his bad leg up on the ottoman. "Christ!" He said as he relaxed in the chair. "Hey Bruz, Get me a root beer out of the fridge and give me a welcome home kiss!"

I ran to the kitchen, grabbed a root beer, snapped the top off in the opener. Ran to the living room and delivered the root beer and the kiss. My dad was home. My mom would fix him.

The first week home dad slept on a bed in the living room. The second week he figured out how to climb the steps. There was a lot of swearing but he figured it out. Dottie and Bill were back together. My mom was very happy when the doctor announced they were ready to remove the cast. They decided to take the cast off at home. So my father didn't have to go to the hospital. I watched the operation from my Christmas position on the balcony. Gen joined me. The cast went all the way up to the top of dad's leg. The doctor drew a red line about an inch off center down the cast. The doctor's assistant used a knife that looked like dad's straight razor to make a cut along the line. Over and over he ran the knife down the line. Then, what looked like metal shears; cut the cast open, exposing dad's leg to the air for the first time in six weeks. They were happy with how the limb had healed the bones seemed straight and strong.

But the wound made when the bone pierced the skin had not fully healed. There was a small bloody hole just above my father's ankle. I could see a frown on the doctor's face as he probed the wound. He took a sample of the bloody goo in the hole and put it in his bag.

"Well, Bill, we'll do some tests on the fluids we took from that wound, I don't think it's a big problem, you tore that leg up pretty good. Use the crutches for a couple of days and when you feel secure walk without them. You'll probably have a limp for a while but let's face those problems as we come to them. Right. Look on the bright side; you'll be rid of the crutches in a couple of days. Good luck. We're going back to work." He laughed, shook dad's hand, bowed to my mom and they left.

In two days my father put the crutches in the front closet and was limping around the house. Climbing the stairs, going out to his office, working with his men. It seemed as if the dark clouds were gone with blue skies in our future. Sunday night. Jay came home from hunting early and the whole family gathered around the dining room table for the first time in months.

We had corn on the cob. Mom went to a truck farm on Western Avenue and picked up six-dozen ears of country gentleman. Add some fresh tomatoes and some Spanish onions and you have a first class Sunday dinner.

Jay polished off a dozen ears, Dad polished off a dozen ears, I managed four. I didn't get a count on Mom and Gen. On Monday we got a phone call from the hospital. Tuesday morning my Mother and Father drove into Los Angeles and met with the doctor. My father had a low level infection in the wound. He would have to bathe it in Iodine and Mercurochrome. The doctor was sure my father was strong enough to get rid of the infection. My mother wasn't quite as sure. On the next Monday morning, Mom gave us all breakfast and my father went back to work. Genevieve and I joined our mother on the front porch. We waved goodbye to dad as his old Ford truck sputtered down the drive.

12

When my dad broke his leg and was lying in his hospital bed and Mom was commuting to L.A. County every day, my big sister decided it was time for me to learn to read. We had spent many hours on the floor with my blocks as she made a game of teaching me my ABC's. Then, when she accepted my alphabet dissertation, we concentrated on vocabulary. Like Dog, fog, log and cat, rat, sat and fat. I got very good at three letter block words. Now she took me out on the front porch, sat me on the top step, "You're going to read a real book." She was reading "Little Women," she handed me her book, read a paragraph aloud, pointed to the next one. "Read," she said. I fumbled and snorted, she pointed, pronounced, I mimicked and she pushed ahead. I began to recognize sounds and the words seemed to burn themselves into my memory. In a few days we were reading "Little Women." We continued, one book after another, while Dad was convalescing and Mom was cheering him on. By the time Dad went back to work, I could pick up one of Gen's books, read and understand what I was reading. I was starting first grade in a couple of weeks. Reading early would make me a star pupil. First grade, here I come.

School started. The teacher handed out baby books. She started making word sounds over and over. Most of the kids were lost. A few of us could read right through the book, but were stuck in with the rest of the class. Now here we were, in the middle of October and we still weren't reading. I began looking out the window at the blue birds.

The real world, the world my dad and mom lived in, was in trouble. Financial problem headlined every day's newspaper. The market's down! The markets down again. Money. Money. Money. Teachers whispered in the back of the room. Something bad was going on but nobody filled us kids in. We sat in the dark, worrying about what we didn't understand. Then the bottom fell out. It was October 24th. The New York Stock exchange crashed. The good times were gone. We all faced the end of the American dream.

My dad lost a couple of jobs; he cut his regular employees to four and sold his newest truck. I heard him complain to my mom about what a lousy deal he made. My brother came home with tales from downtown Los Angeles. Rumors that J.J. Newberry forecast a big lay off, store closings, but things kept stumbling along.

Christmas came. Holiday business was way off. Gen and I sat on the balcony and watched my mother trim the tree while my father sat on a kitchen chair and directed the operation. His leg wasn't getting any better. He had to sit most of the time. Fewer presents were under the tree. We had enough stuff anyway.

Christmas breakfast was digesting in our stomachs. Gen was upstairs reading one of the new books Santa had brought. I sat on the kitchen floor pushing a little car back and forth. My dad was talking to my mother.

"The bank that had my business account went under yesterday, Sweetheart. We had a lot of money in that account. I couldn't get it out. Our personal funds are in Bank of America; they tell me they're solid as a rock. We can get through this. We have enough money to keep living here. I couldn't sell the place for what we paid for it so maybe we're better off staying. I don't know. I'm a roofer, I know how to earn money, I know how to spend money but I don't know how to protect money. We live day-to-day. We've got a good car, Jay has a good job; we can feed Gen and Bruz. We'll be okay.

"Certainly, Darling, you shouldn't worry your head about things you have no control over. Let Mr. Hoover keep us afloat. The government will straighten everything out." So I finished the first grade, skipped second grade and would start the third grade in the fall. Genevieve graduated from Franklin with honors. She was moving on to Eleanor Joy Toll Junior High School; about a mile walk uphill from the house on Lake Street.

Jay's career at Newberry's was blooming. A couple of small stores closed. A few people were laid off or fired. They didn't fire Jay. They promoted Jay to Floorwalker, put him in charge of sixteen girls. His next step up would be assistant manager.

Right now he was in charge of the main floor at the large L.A. store and had his eye on one of the girls under his direction. If he got himself a girl where would he find the time to go out hunting? Who would keep the rabbit and deer population under control?

Nearly a year after the crash my dad realized we couldn't afford Lake Street anymore. He took an offer of $4,000 for our house. He made a deal with a builder friend to rent one of his houses on Hazel Street about eight blocks south of the Lake Street house. He got permission to build a small cabin where my brother would sleep, a hen house with a large chicken coop and rabbit hutches across the back fence. Dad realized he was growing weaker and weaker. He was making plans for something to do when roofing became too difficult. My mother stayed as perky as ever.

Soon it was Thanksgiving. We had Thursday and Friday off from school. My mom and dad were off to L.A. County hospital for my dad's checkup. Gen was working with her teacher so I had no reason to go home. I turned right on Lake Street and walked five blocks. I waited for the light to change at Sonora Avenue. I watched the traffic whiz by. Hazel Street was a block away on the right. I would investigate our new home. I crossed the Avenue; I was standing in an Esso station. It had two service islands and a garage. Handy.

There was a small house next to the gas station and then nothing. No sidewalks. A huge field of tall cattails, waving in the afternoon breeze, grew down the right side of the road. All the way down to the riverbed. There was one house across the street. A three-story white stucco building that looked very lonely among all the walnut trees that surrounded it. Hazel Street was in the middle of a huge Walnut orchard. There were no street signs on the corners. These were no-name avenues, I could see the Hazel Street Sign sticking up and then trees, no more streets, trees and cattails, no cars, only the sound of the wind. We moved eight blocks, going from civilization into the jungle.

Hazel Street was a macadam road with curbs but no sidewalks. Nice little clapboard houses built on big lots on both sides of the street.

They were basically the same design though each was painted in a different color. Throughout the neighborhood you made out these variations of color against the green background of a thousand trees. I stopped. I looked around. I smiled. I liked it. I liked it a lot.

Halfway up the block I figured out which was our house. It was empty, the shades pulled down. The yellow and black garage door was closed. I could see a little cabin under a huge walnut tree in the middle of the back yard. It was my father's building style, I was sure it was Jay's room. The lawn was on two levels with a little hill, I shook my head and hoped for slow growing grass. The hedges on the building line and down the driveway were as tall as me. They needed trimming badly. I knew I was in for some heavy work.

Directly across the street was a wide empty lot with two lines of walnut trees stretching off as far as you could see. We were in the city but it looked like the country.

Thanksgiving was turkey day. Dinner was planned for 2:30 so Mom was in the kitchen at six in the morning. Six thirty the bird slid into the pre-heated oven to cook for nine hours. My mom would carefully baste it every hour and a half. If someone could package that smell they would make their fortune. Sweet potatoes baked on the rack above the bird while apple and pumpkin pies were on the sideboard waiting for their moment in the sun. My brother's new girlfriend was coming for dinner. I would have to be on my good behavior.

Jay's girl arrived at 2:15. Jay proudly escorted her to dad's chair. Dad looked up at her, "You're a very pretty young lady," he said. "Please excuse me for not standing, I have this bum leg." He smiled. She smiled. Jay smiled.

"Dad, this is Kit Scheffic, we work together at Newberry's." My mother came out of the kitchen carrying a spoon, potholders stuffed in her apron pocket.

"Oh! You must be Kitty. Jay never stops talking about you, Kitty this and Kitty that. Come in the kitchen, Darling, let's get to know each other."

Kit laughed, took my mother's hand and disappeared into the kitchen. Jay stood near dad, his mouth hanging open.

Kitty sat next to my mother, Jay sat next to his girl and dad was doing his serving thing from the head. Gen and I filled out the table. "White or dark, Kitty?" My dad asked.

"A little of both please. Not a lot I'm not a big eater, even on holidays." My dad built a usual Tyrrell plate and handed it to Kitty. "Eat up, Kit, cant tell when we'll get a good meal again these days." My dad laughed. The table was very quiet. There was serious eating going on. My dad gave me the drumstick. I was in heaven chewing on the delicious turkey leg. My mom was the best cook in the world. "Katie lives at the beach," my brother spoke up, "Venice. They have a nice little house, three blocks from the ocean. Her father is gone, but her mom is a sweetheart, and she has two sisters one older and one younger but all grown ups. I love going there." Jay concentrated on the pile of stuffing on his plate. My sister, who had been very quiet, said, "Kit. Katie, Kitty, what do you like to be called. Seems Jay changes your name with every speech."

"The girls at the store call me Kitty, I prefer Katie, Katherine is my name. But I answer to whatever I hear."

"How would you like to be stuck with Genevieve? I hate my name, but it's the only name I've got. Gen isn't much better. I'd like to be an Anne, or Beth." I had never heard my sister complain. I loved Genevieve and Gen was so easy to say. I kept eating and stayed away from talking. The conversation went on, no one spoke to me. I hoped Jay found another girl. I didn't think much of this one. Dinner was over. The girls cleared the table and did the dishes. The family sat around the living room and talked about everything I wasn't interested in. Finally Jay asked to borrow the Essex and he took Kitty home. If I was lucky I'd never see her again.

13

Our move to Hazel Street was like a slow dissolve in the movies. Every couple of days a pile of tile would disappear. A strange crew would arrive and barrels of tar would roll down the driveway, off to somebody else's back yard. Two fancy ladies came. My mother showed them the dining room table, brought out her fancy company tablecloths that the ladies fingered. One lady wrote her a check put the cloths over her arm and walked out. Next day the table was gone. We were eating in the kitchen. I came home from school. One of the living room chairs wasn't there and the backyard swing was missing. Lake Street was drifting away.

It was Christmas morning. No tree. No presents. There was only my father's friend Fred and his friend Joe, who would make the move. My father's truck was in front, being loaded when a strange truck pulled up. Two men jumped out. My mother took them in the house. Soon Fred and Joe were loading my mother's bed on the Ford while the other men were putting my mother's dresser on their truck. Gen and I were in the way. "Don't stand there!" "Don't touch that!" "Mom?" I said. "I've been to Hazel Street, Gen and I could walk over there and be out of your way."

"That's a wonderful idea, Son. Take your sister and go. We'll be there in a couple of hours." We walked out into the sunny Christmas weather and walked to Hazel Street. We waited to cross Sonora Avenue. I pointed across the street. "You see all those walnut trees? We live in the middle of a big orchard. Isn't that great?" Gen looked at me like I was crazy. We crossed and walked on No-name Avenue to the corner. "Look Gen, nothing but cattails all the way to the river and Hazel Street is the last street. Look, the road ends. There's nothing but a fence. Isn't that great?"

"Yeah, great. Move from a mansion to a dump. Just great." My sister wasn't too happy.

"The house isn't a dump, it's beautiful, not as big as Lake Street but real cute, it's yellow and black, wait till you see it, you'll love it.

And maybe Dad and Mom will stop worrying about money. We can all live and be happy again." I gave her my biggest smile.

"Oh, Bruz, you're such a Pollyanna. Everything's great to you. Well everything isn't great, you'll see." We walked up Hazel Street. I watched Gen checking out the little houses. A handsome collie dog barked from his front porch, the lady sitting on the steps waved. Christmas trees were in most windows and the people were sitting out on their porches. It was a happy neighborhood. You never saw a person on Lake Street. Hazel Street was poor, but it was alive.

"There, there!" I screamed, "You see the yellow house with the black shutters? That's where we live! Isn't it cute?" I actually love this little house.

"Not bad," Gen said. "The lawn is cut and the hedge is trimmed."

I looked. "Someone took my job. That's my lawn, my hedge. My daddy said I was in charge of the lawn and the hedge." Gen laughed.

"You nut. Dad had somebody do it so Mom would be impressed when they drove up. You'll be stuck with it from now on. It's your job and you'll soon get tired of it."

"The front door is locked. Shall I look around back and see if we can get in?"

"Yeah. I'd like to see inside. The outside is kind of nice. It's a happy surprise."

"I told you so!" I yelled, running up the driveway. Jay's little house was terrific. The door swung open, it was a big room with exposed ceiling beams, a shiny wood floor, wood panels on the walls. Best bedroom Jay ever had, I said to myself. I closed the door.

I inspected the windows I could reach. The one that might work was behind a big geranium bush loaded down with huge red geraniums at Christmas time. I pulled the back screen door. It swung open. I was in the back porch, a nice big back porch. The back door was all little panes of glass. I grabbed the knob. It turned. The door was open!

63

I walked into a narrow room, just a little wider than a hallway. There was a hot water heater against the wall. The brown wooden door in front of me was the last obstacle. It opened into a large room that went all the way to the front door. A big bay window on the right, a glass front door on the left. This room was basically the whole house. I walked to the front door, turned the latch and pulled it open. Gen was sitting on the front steps. "Welcome to Hazel Street, my sister, and Merry Christmas to us all." I laughed. I was happy. I loved this little house. I didn't miss being rich at all.

Gen came in. "So this is the living room, no dining room, that's why the table went. Come through this arch. Look it's a hall." The hallway had three doors, one on each end and one in the middle. We opened the middle door. It was the bathroom. Not big but not small. It would work for the four of us. We opened the door on the end, "Oh!" Gen said, "This must be my room. Look at all those geraniums against the window. This is a nice room, my makeup table can go right there. This isn't going to be so bad, after all."

We opened the last door. It was the master bedroom; it was large enough not to feel small and had a big bay window in the front. Mom and Dad would love this room. We had to look fast because as soon as the bed arrived it would be off limits for kids. It never occurred to me to wonder where I was going to sleep, I was too happy with this little black and yellow house. We were inspecting the kitchen and the dining alcove when the movers arrived. Mom hustled into the kitchen. Took a look at the stove. Turned on the oven. Bent down to make sure there was a flame, opened a big bag she carried, removed the blue roasting pan and slid it into the oven. The bag held four big baking potatoes that went into the oven. There would be a Christmas dinner after all.

Fred and Joe carried the furniture in piece by piece. Mom directed them. The dining room rug went on the new living room floor. Dad's chair, the ottoman and the couch went on the carpet. Mom and Dad's bedroom was set up. Then Gen's bed, dressing table and bench went into the back room and my little bed went in too. Genevieve ran to her mother.

"Mom? Is Bruzzy sleeping in my room? I'm in Junior High, Mom, I can't share a room with my little brother. He's six years old next week. What will people think?"

"People will not think anything because we won't tell them you're sharing the room with your little brother. He will only be there till your father can get around to fixing up the back porch. Then Bruzzy will move. I hope you can put up with him for one or two months. Bruzzy will promise not to peek." I didn't have the slightest idea what I would peek at. I thought it would be great fun to be able to talk with my big sister at night, in the dark. That would be fun.

"Oh, I'm sorry Bruz, I guess I can put up with you till Dad builds your room. It might be fun sharing with you for a while." She messed my hair. No one had messed my hair for weeks and now she messed my hair. Oh well, she was my big sister and I loved her.

We sat in the room that would become the happiest room in the little house. It was round with eight windows. A comfortable bench was built in under the windows with padded seats and padded backs. This was the new dining room. Every day we would take our three meals in this room, learn each other's news, have family meetings and enjoy my mother's cooking. Mom would fill all the plates on the kitchen sink and deliver them to the round table. Dad lost his host's job, all he had to do was eat and talk. The family's most memorable hours were spent around this table.

Everyone was beat. The day had been a killer. Everything was in its place, our tummies were full, all eyes sleepy. The big Philco radio sat in a place of honor next to the hall archway, each living room chair facing it. Christmas music filled the room. It was a relic from our rich life that had ended only this morning. I was lying on the floor, looking at the ceiling, singing along with "Silent Night." We had never been so close a family in the big house. Here we were, crammed together and you could feel the love buzzing round the room. "Bruzahlah," My mother whispered. "Eight o'clock, time for bed." "Yes M'am." I got up went into my new room, put on my pajamas, went in the new bathroom, brushed my teeth wiggled into my little bed in the new bedroom in the new house. My mom came in.

She bent over and kissed me. "Sleep tight, my little baby boy. Christmas will be better next year." Christmas could never be better than today I thought, as I slipped off into dreamland.

14

I woke up very early. Sun was sneaking past the geraniums and filtering into the room I shared with my big sister. She was fast asleep just five feet away. I slipped out of bed, picked up my clothes, tip toed into the bathroom. I did my ablutions, dressed, pulled on my Keds and went out into the back yard. Jay wasn't in his room. He was spending a lot of time at Kitty's. The yard was quiet, no animals yet. I picked up a green walnut from the crab grass and threw it at a rabbit hutch. It sailed over the fence into the walnut grove. A bunch of quail squawked and flew up in the air. I walked up the drive. I planned to inspect the rest of Hazel Street. I hadn't seen anything beyond our little house. I walked up the street, I felt a slight incline; the street was on a hill. Nobody was out and about. Quiet. Peaceful. I walked to the corner, there, laid out in front of me, was the airport. It was huge. I looked far across the field at the big yellow stucco arrivals building, the tall control tower and metal hangars one after the other. Three Ford tri-motors were parked in front of the first hangar. Several small private planes were tied down here and there. Grand Central Air Terminal, the biggest airport in Southern California.

I looked left down the small two-lane road that had no street sign. The tall fence angled in forming a long parking lot. At the head of the lot, built inside the fence on airport property was a yellow clapboard house with a white door. A big sign on the roof advertised Fred Fuch's Flying School. No one was there. Breakfast suddenly crept into my head. I turned to go home. There on the lawn of the last house on the block were five boys, the oldest maybe twelve to the youngest who could have been four. "Hi," I said, "My name's Bruz Tyrrell, we just moved in yesterday. You live in the grey house?"

The tallest shook his head up and down. "I'm Larry Doyle," he pointed at his brothers, "that's Harry, that's Jerry, that's Johnny and the little guy is Albert, he don't talk much. You want to play catch?"

The front screen door swung open, a plump lady in a dirty bathrobe stepped out on the porch. "Breakfast kids, breakfast on the table."

Without a word the kids ran into the house, she looked at me, "I'm Dora Doyle, come back in a little while, my gang will be ready to play." She smiled. She closed the door. I headed down the hill. But I would return.

Everybody was up. Gen and Mom were making scrambled eggs, Dad sitting in the dining alcove waiting to eat. "Wash your hands, Sweetie." My mom called out. "Breakfast in a sec." I washed my hands and slid around to sit next to my dad. He patted my head.

"You want to come out to the valley with me, Bruz? We need to get some birds to fill that chicken coop." "Are we going in the truck?" I asked. "Yep. Got to get twenty or thirty chickens, they won't fit in the Studebaker." Mom put a plate of scrambled eggs and toast in front of him, ending the conversation.

Dad got us onto Ventura Boulevard and settled back for the long trip to Thousand Oaks. I sat tall and watched the sights fly by the big windshield. "Need gas." Dad said pulling into a station with nineteen-cent gas. The attendant came. "Two bucks worth." Dad said. "Yes sir." The attendant answered. The man pumped a little more than ten gallons into the old Ford. He wiped the windshield, dad handed him two bucks and we were back on Ventura headed for chickens. I fell asleep. The truck stopped, I woke up. We were at a farm. A chicken farm with chicken wire runs as far as your eye could see.

"Have a nice snooze, Bruzzy?" My dad asked. I nodded my head. My voice didn't work yet. Dad climbed out of the truck, I stood very close to him as a giant man wandered over. Dad stuck out his hand. The giant grabbed it. "Jeeze Bill, you've lost some weight. You dieting?" "Naw, Sam, broke my leg, been having a tough time. This depression sure isn't helping."

"Can't understand it. Nobody's got any money. How'm I supposed to sell chickens if nobody's got money? I'm counting on this FDR guy to change things; something has to get money back in circulation. I hope you came for chickens, Bill, give you a real good deal." I didn't have the slightest idea what they were talking about.

"I need some that are old enough to lay eggs, Jim, and some younger that will grow into laying. Got a good rooster, maybe a Rhode Island Red, I like red roosters." They both laughed. I didn't get the joke. Three crates that held ten chickens each were tied off on the flat bed. The big red rooster, in a crate of his own, tied to the crates of hens. My dad had a roll of money; he peeled off several bills and handed them to Sam. Sam counted and put the money in his pocket. My dad stuck his hand out, Sam said, "I got a couple of old turkeys out in back, Bill. Last turkeys on the place, the Tom's a mean old bastard but he's a fine bird, the hen is big, make a great thanksgiving. Give me two bucks and they're yours.

"How's our red rooster going to like Mr. Tom, Sam? See any problems?

"They'll work it out in a minute, they'll have great respect for each other."

"Okay, two bucks." He pulled out his roll, two bucks changed hands. "Oh, nearly forgot, throw on a bag of corn and a bag of mash. Starting a new chicken coop's a pain in the ass." My dad reached for his roll.

"No, no, Bill, foods on me, got to help an old friend out in times like these. I figure you'll be back in a couple of months. A few Sunday dinners and you're going to need more chickens.' He laughed.

"Smart ass." My father laughed. Everything loaded we drove back to Ventura heading back to Glendale. I opened my eyes. We were parked in the driveway on Hazel Street. I'd slept all the way.

"Good afternoon, Bruz, you were great company coming home, now that you're well rested give me a hand getting this bunch into the run. He tossed me up on the flat bed, he handed me an Asphalt knife. "Hook that on a rope and pull, careful it's sharp." I cut all the ropes. Without cutting myself. Gave the knife back to my dad, waiting for orders.

"Push the Tom over to the edge, we have to get him in there first, or there'll be no living with the bastard. Push it, that's right. Now come to me." He lifted me to the ground. "You go over and hold the chicken coop door open, I'll walk this box over." I ran. He pulled the crate off the truck it banged to the ground, the turkey threw its wings open, then relaxed. My father walked the crate to the chicken coop door. He placed it so when he opened the box the turkey could walk into the run. "Soon as the bird is in the coop slam the door, Bruz. If he gets loose there'll be hell to pay." I nodded. I didn't know what he meant. "I'll close the door when the Turkey is in the coop." I paid close attention. My dad cut the cord that held the door, the door swung open. The Tom stepped out of the crate. The bastard stopped cold. He looked at me with hate in his eyes. I swallowed.

"Move! Yikes! Yikes!" My dad screamed. The turkey fluttered his big wings, ran into the coop. I slammed the door sat down and laughed out loud. My mother and sister ran into the backyard. "Everything all right?" My mother called.

"Just moving a turkey, mother, go back to your chores." My dad answered, laughing. I looked at the big Tom. "BurrBle-BurrBle-BurrBle it screamed. It's black and white tail feathers fanned out wide; it strutted around the chicken run. I felt very happy! Mr. Tom was inside and I was outside.

Dad and I got Mrs. Turkey and all the chickens in the coop then we faced the rooster problem. Dad pulled the rooster crate to the gate, I held the gate. Dad cut the rope, the door swung open. The red rooster strutted right into the run. Dad closed the gate. We held our breaths. The rooster strutted across the run right up to the Tom. The rooster stood still. The turkey stood still. Face off! The Turkey pecked at the rooster. The rooster scratched dirt on the Tom's feet. The Tom gobbled, puffed his chest and strutted across the run, the rooster strutting right along, the red hens, the white hens and the speckled hens got out of their way. The Tom strutted to the gate, stopped, surveying his kingdom. His wife went to his side. The rooster strutted to the hen house door. He stood looking over his thirty wives. Peace settled in the chicken coop. The turkeys and the chickens were at home.

From that day on I was in charge of putting mash in the feeder, watering the flock, corn in the morning, corn in the afternoon. Check eggs in the morning. Re-check for eggs in the afternoon. I earned my Chicken degree in the Bill Tyrrell University of Fowl Knowledge

I walked up the street to the Doyle's. I stopped and looked at the little grey house with the dark grey shutters when the whole gang marched out the front door and Larry yelled, "C'mon, Bruz, we're going to the Flying School and check the weather. I fell in next to Jerry and marched to the Fred Fuchs' Flying School through the front door and up to a big dark brown machine that was typing words on yellow paper. Larry pointed at the machine. "It tells the news and the weather so Mister Fuchs knows if they can fly or not. Neat, huh?"

"But it doesn't sweep the floor, Larry." I turned around, Mister Fuchs was standing in the office doorway "The deal was, Larry, you could look at the machine after you swept the place out. Look around, is this place clean?" Larry hung his head, "No, Mister Fuchs, I thought we only had to sweep that one time. I'm sorry. Let's go, guys."

"I'll sweep out the place, Mister Fuchs, I'd like to see how that machine works. Where's the broom?"

"Who's the tow head, Larry?"

"Tow Head, I'm no tow head! I'm a blonde head. Don't call me a tow head; call me Bruzzy, I moved to Hazel Street yesterday. We used to live on Lake Street. Give me a broom I'll sweep out your place."

"Tow head means blonde head, Bruz. The sweeping job is Larry's, unless he wants to give it to you."

"I didn't take the job. I don't want no job, just wanted to see the machine, Bruz can sweep if he wants. We're going to play catch."

"We looked at the mans' machine, Larry, we owe him a sweeping…go catch, I'll be over later." Larry didn't answer. The Doyles ran out the front door leaving Mister Fuchs and me looking at each other.

"Well, Bruz, want the job?"

"Sure, Mister Fuchs, I love being around your airplanes, I like this place. I'll keep it clean if I can hang around." I looked up at the tall blonde flier.

"Brooms are in that closet, let's see what kind of job you do then we'll talk." He smiled. Walked out onto the airfield. I found the broom and a dustpan and went to work. I put all the sweepings into a wastebasket that held used yellow paper from the machine we came to see. I took it all out to a big barrel behind the school. I emptied it. I put the basket back under the table, the broom back in the closet. I surveyed the clean room.

"Nice job, Bruzzy. Want to do that three times a week? I'd sure appreciate it." Fuchs called from the back door. "Sure!" I said, "Maybe you'll show me one of your planes someday." He laughed walked over to me and messed my hair. "You're a good kid, Bruz, it'll be a pleasure having you around. Here's a nickel for the first time. From now on you're in charge of keeping the entrance hall clean. Remember a clean entrance hall makes students happy. Happy students make good business. So your sweeping could make my business successful and make you proud." He laughed. I would have laughed with him if I knew what he was talking about, instead I ran home to show my mom the shiny nickel I earned at my new job.

My mom was canning peaches. I ran into the kitchen. "Mom, mom, I got a job! I sweep out the flying school three times a week for Mr. Fuchs. He called me a tow head and he gave me a nickel, look!" I held up the shiny coin.

"That's wonderful son. But remember, you accepted a job. You have to do the job or tell Mr. Fuchs you can't work for him anymore. You must clean his place the three times you agreed to or until he asks you to leave. It's a contract, an agreement you must fulfill."

I stood, nodding my head, holding up the nickel. She took a Mason jar and put it on the shelf above the stove. Took my nickel, smiled, dropped it into the jar. "Now, we'll watch your money grow. Every nickel you get we'll put in this jar. We'll have a lot of fun watching you get rich." She bent over and kissed the top of my head. I wanted the nickel in my pocket but my mom was always right, at least that's what my dad said.

Tuesdays, Thursdays and Saturdays I swept the flying school entrance hall. I chatted with Mr. Fuchs, he told me flying stories that always ended when he tossed me a shiny nickel. The Mason jar was getting valuable. I walked to Franklin, Gen walked to Toll, Jay bought a 1929 Model "A" ford that made his trips to Venice much easier. Spring was just around the corner; I was still sleeping in my sister's room.

15

She was a small Plymouth Rock hen. She was my friend. She was fatter than the other hens, kind of oblong rather than round but she always followed me around the run, clucking deep in her throat. I called her "Bitty" and she answered to her name.

When I added mash to the feeders, I had to hold the sack and shake the brown meal into the flat boxes where the chickens took their meals. "Monster," my name for the fucking tom turkey that made my life miserable, would wait for my back to be turned then give me a shove with his wide chest. It never hurt but was a very uncomfortable experience. If Bitty saw him coming behind me she would scream, "Buck, buck, buck, be-DAW, Buck!" Warning me that I had a monster behind me. I couldn't figure out a way to get the bird off my back. He ran from my father but he persecuted me. I threw some corn around the run then grabbed my old Easter basket to collect the mornings' eggs.

I rummaged through the nests and found eight brown eggs and three white eggs. The small oval brown egg was from Bitty, I knew her eggs by heart. I cleaned the chicken do with the wide hoe, washed my hands and face in the faucet behind Jay's house, put the eggs in the Frigidaire and sat on the top step of the front porch.

I watched the kid across the street sweeping their front porch. I never met him. He went to Glendale Academy; he never seemed to be around in the afternoons. I crossed the street and called to him. "Hey, My name's Bruzzy. We've lived across the street for months how come you never come out to play?" He stopped sweeping, held his broom in his hand thinking. "I don't get home till four o'clock my mom likes me to stay indoors."

"What's your name? You play ball?"

"Floyd. Floyd Baumer. I don't know I never tried."

A loud whining noise came out of the garage. "My father is a cabinet maker, he works in the garage. I hang around in case he needs my help." Before I could answer, his mother came out the front door grabbed his arm flashing her fingers in his face, he looked at me but followed his mom into the house. Oh well, I thought, no figuring some people. I went inside.

Dad was sitting in his chair his bad leg up on the ottoman. Mom was cleaning the sore looking wound above his ankle. She dipped a cloth into denatured alcohol and carefully cleaned the sore. She painted it with iodine. My dad clenched his jaws not making a sound. She finished with a coat of Mercurochrome and started covering it with gauze.

"God damned it, Dottie, I can't stand long enough to build the cabinets for Bruz's room. Christ, that poor kid's been in a girl's room for months and I'm not half finished. I'd have to lay out at least a hundred dollars and I don't have that kind of dough. How the hell am I going to finish this job?" My mother bent over and kissed him on the mouth. "Don't bother yourself, Bill, you'll be better, you'll get it done. Bruz isn't complaining and Gen doesn't seem to notice, don't give yourself such a hard time."

"The guy across the street's a cabinet maker." I said, not realizing they didn't even know I was there. My mother jumped like she'd seen a ghost. Dad looked at me and laughed.

"Hey Bruz. You feed the chickens?" He said smiling.

"Yes sir, I got eight eggs this morning. They're in the fridge. I was talking to Floyd Baumer across the street. He helps his father. They build cabinets. Maybe he could give you a hand."

"You know these people, Dottie?" My dad sounded interested.

"The Shtimmers?" My mother asked. "The What?" Dad answered.

"Shtimmers, Shtimmers, deaf people. The mother and the father are deaf. The son is normal. They keep to themselves, very private."

"Well, hell, he's in business. I'll go talk to him. Come on Bruz." He pushed his hands on the arms of the big chair and stood up on his good leg, carefully putting his bad leg on the floor. He limped but moved right along. We crossed the street and walked up the Shtimmer's driveway. "Call your friend." My dad asked.

"Floyd! Hey, Floyd. My dad needs you!" I yelled. He came out the back door.

"Hi." He said. "We don't have many visitors."

"Hello, Floyd. I'm Bill Tyrrell, Bruz's dad, I need some help with a cabinet, Bruz says your dad's a cabinet maker, can you talk to him for me?"

"Sure, he's in the garage, come on." We walked to the garage. Floyd went in. In a minute the big doors swung open and Floyd's father came out. Floyd wiggled his fingers in front of him and he squeaked a mangled "alloo." Dad smiled. He offered his hand. Floyd's father reached out his hand. Two fingers were missing. I looked at his other hand, only four fingers on it. I quickly understood. The power saw. He couldn't hear the power saw running causing him to lose his fingers.

My dad spoke to Floyd. "Tell him I need two cabinets for my son's room I'm building in the back porch. I've got a bad leg, can't stand long enough to build them or get them installed. Does he have some time to help me out?"

"Floyd and his father did their hand signal thing and finally it was worked out. Mr. Baumer would build two plain cabinets, plain, nothing fancy. He'd install them where my father wanted. They worked out a barter deal, chickens, eggs, rabbits; the Baumers would get some good eating. I would get good plain cabinets. My dad would get the room off his back. The deal was done and I had a new friend. My mother became Mrs. Baumer's friend, teaching her to make peach cobbler and rabbit stew. All in all it was a good deal for all.

—

76

16

My mother and father were born in April, mom on the ninth, my dad on the tenth. Dad was fifty-one and mom was forty. She made a devil's food cake with white coconut icing for Dad's day. "For the love of my life" spelled out in blue on top. My dad laughed when he cut his cake, "Well, Dot, since life begins at forty, we've got a lot of happiness ahead. Give me a little kiss for my birthday." Mom held his cheeks in her hands and kissed him. I laughed and looked at my sister. She sniffed and blew her nose in a napkin. Girls! I thought.

Floyd Baumer and I became good friends. I would cross the street to see how my cabinets were proceeding. Mr. Baumer, stealing time here and there, out of his regular jobs to work on mine. We were playing Chinese checkers on his front porch. It was a warm Saturday morning. As usual, he beat me. "Hey, Floyd!" I said, "My dad's going to kill a chicken and a rabbit for you guys, want to go watch?" He shoved the game into its box, put the box on a chair, "Come on," he answered.

We walked up the driveway, my dad sharpened the hatchet he sometimes used to kill a chicken. Before he was hurt he would wring their necks, now he got tired so quickly, the hatchet was easier. He limped to the chopping block, next to the faucet behind my brother's house. We followed and stood by the chicken run fence. "Don't get too close kids. There'll be a lot of blood flying around. Your moms won't be too happy if you get all bloody." He went into the chicken coop. We watched him slowly force several chickens into the corner of the run. He held his arms wide "Shush, shush," he said over and over. Suddenly he grabbed the legs of a big white Leghorn. The bird squawked hanging upside down, flapped its wings to no avail. The chosen one for the Baumer's Sunday dinner.

He held the chicken upright, legs in one hand, petting the chicken's neck with the other. He got himself set at the block, stopped petting, took hold of the hatchet and laid the chicken's shoulder on the block.

As the chicken's head and neck relaxed on the block the hatchet did its job. Head flew one way. Body flew the other. The headless bird ran in circles blood spurting from its neck. Slower, slower circles till it toppled over. The chicken was gone. Dinner had arrived. "Tell your mom to dip it in warm water, the big feathers will come out easier." Floyd nodded his head; he was having trouble speaking. "You want to watch the rabbit or shall we go?" I asked. He shook his head back and forth, "Stay!" he croaked.

Chickens have feathers. Regular people can pluck feathers and clean a chicken for Sunday dinner. Rabbits have fur. They must be skinned and cleaned so regular people can enjoy the treat.

My dad selected a big doe that was very close to the size when rabbit meat gets tough to chew. He had raised rabbits since he was a kid in Pennsylvania; he knew when the time was right for rabbit stew. He held the rabbit by its hind legs, the rabbit stretched out its body. He petted the animal behind its ears. The ears moved forward. Using the edge of his flat hand he smacked the rabbits neck. A drop of blood showed on the rabbits nose. A "rabbit punch" illegal for boxers, legally made the doe ready for the pot. Skinning was an art. My father was the artist. He hung the rabbit head down on a special board. He used a very sharp knife a little larger than a paring knife. He cut off the rabbit's head letting all the blood drain on the ground. He split the skin at each of the knees, split the skin around the crotch making a flap at each knee. He removed the short front legs grabbed the two flaps and pulled the skin off the body. A pink skinned rabbit hung on the board. My dad cleaned out the insides, wrapped the rabbit and the chicken in newspaper and presented them to Floyd. "These will make delicious dinners, Floyd. I hope you and your folks enjoy. Take them home while I clean up this mess."

We ran across the street to Floyd's house. Mrs. Bauman was thrilled with the package. She gave us each an Oreo cookie and signed for us to play outside. We sat on the front steps. "Want to play hide and seek?" I offered. "Where?" He answered. "In the grove behind the big white house." I offered. "Don't want to walk around the block." He answered. "We can use our back gate and go through the trees." "Let's go!" He ran for my house, I followed. We ran past my dad, cleaning up his mess, through the gate into the trees.

We held our noses passing the rear of the tannery facing the avenue and ran into the forest of walnut trees behind the big white house. We picked a big old walnut tree hanging low to the ground loaded with green walnuts as home base. We played Scissors, Rock and Paper to decide who would be "it" first. One, two, three…I put out scissors, Floyd paper. He was "it." I ran off, he counted. "Five, Ten, Fifteen, twenty…"

I saw a big black limo in the driveway through the trees. The garage door was open. I ran through the trees looked into the empty garage. There was a big grease pit on the right; I could jump down there. Floyd would never find me. I looked around. No one. I climbed down into the pit. It was clean as a whistle, no grease no smear, just a box of Pennzoil on the floor. I sat on the box and waited. Boring. I looked around the pit. The minutes ticked away. There was a small door in the end of the pit. It was ajar. Not locked. I looked at it, I should sneak back and touch base, Floyd would never find me here. I crawled over and pulled the little door open. It was a big room. Boxes stacked all over the place. Shelves of bottles lined the back walls. What kind of place was this?

"Ally, ally, outs in free!" Floyd was yelling, giving up the search. "Ally, ally, outs in free!" I climbed out of the pit and ran back to home base. Floyd was standing there. "I looked everywhere, I couldn't find you." He complained.

"I was in the grease pit at the white house. I guess I cheated. You can win if you want." "Makes no difference, Bruz, it was fun. Let's go play Chinese Checkers on my porch. Mom worries about me."

"There's a little door to a big room in the grease pit at the white house. Lots of boxes stored in the room. Want to take a quick look?" "Is it scary?" "No. It's just a room with a small door in the grease pit, I just wonder what's in all those boxes."

"Okay, Let's take a quick look."

We jumped down into the grease pit. We didn't talk. I pointed at the small door. Floyd nodded his head. I grabbed it with my fingers. It was heavy. I pulled.

The door swung open, the hinges squealed loudly. We waited to see if anyone came out of the house. All quiet. I bent over and crept through into the dark room. I could see some light coming through the shelves, probably a grate in the garage floor. Floyd came in. He looked around nervously. "I don't like this place. Let's get out of here!" He turned back as the door swung shut. He pushed. Nothing. He felt around the door for a handle, a knob. Nothing. "We're stuck in here, Bruz!" He said, a tear in his voice.

I heard my dad's voice in my head. "If you're ever stuck in a bad place, never panic. Think!" "Don't be scared, Floyd, there's plenty of air. Let's make sure we can't get the door open. If we can't, then we'll just wait. My dad will find us." I was certain my dad would come. It was just a matter of time.

I saw a pile of short fat candles on the shelf next to a box of kitchen matches. I lit a candle. We inspected the door. It was smooth, nothing but a white mottled surface. We were stuck in this room till somebody from the outside let us out. We investigated our cell. Every box was filled with bottles full of white liquid; the shelves were filled with tall, fat bottles of brown liquid. Suddenly Floyd blurted out, "This is alcohol! This stuff is against the law! These people are bootleggers, we're in a lot of trouble."

"We don't know that, Floyd, we're kids, what do we know about bootleggers? We were playing hide and seek and got locked in here by mistake. Let's just wait until my dad shows up, he'll get us out of this mess." Floyd shook his head. He wasn't buying my story.

We found a notebook and some pencils. The front pages were full of numbers, some names and addresses, but the book was only half full. We sat on a couple of boxes and played Tic Tac Toe, trying to forget about our situation. Time passed. "You know how to play Hangman?" Floyd spoke, breaking a long silence. "Show me." I answered. He taught me Hangman. I wasn't the greatest at word games. Floyd was older than me and his school made them read a lot of books. So, I was being hanged over and over. But the time went by.

"My mother is going to kill me." Floyd stuttered. "She doesn't want me to leave our property and here I am trapped under some bootlegger's garage. Boy, I'm going to be locked in my room for a week."

I thought that was pretty funny, "You're worrying about being locked in your room by your Mom when we're already locked in a gangster's garage. Let's worry about getting out of here, then worry about your bedroom."

"At least there's a bunch of books in my bedroom. I'd at least have something to do. Stead of beating you all the time."

"Best thing we can do is concentrate on our fathers finding us. They might kill us and we won't have any problems." Floyd looked at me, a smile flickering across his face. He nearly laughed when the door swung open.

"Hey, you kids, get your butts out of there right now. Come on move!" Floyd ran out. I was right behind him. Our fathers were standing on the edge of the grease pit. "Don't say a word, Bruz. Just keep quiet. You too, Floyd, get up here and stand with us." My dad said in his mad, talk to the roofers, voice. I ran up and held his leg. Floyd stood next to his dad who was signing a mile a minute. My dad messed my hair. I relaxed.

"So, they gunna keep they're mouths shut?" The man who let us out asked. "These kids won't say a word, Mr. Antonelli, but I think you should consider a change of scenery. Now, if it's okay with you we'll leave you with your problems."

"Yeah, yeah. Go. Go now before I change my mind." My dad grabbed my shoulder and we limped off into the walnut grove, Floyd and his father right behind. My father stopped and stood me next to Floyd. "You kids forget all about this. Not a word to a soul. You are very lucky to be alive. Someday you'll tell me all about it but right now mum is the word. It's after five let's get home. I need to sit in my chair."

"After five!' I screamed, "I'm late! I'm supposed to sweep the flying school! I'll lose my job! Dad, I have to go sweep. Okay?"

"Go, Bruz, can't lose a job in a depression."

"See you Floyd!" I yelled running through the trees toward Sonora Avenue. Fred Fuchs would be looking for me. I couldn't let my hero down!

I ran across the parking lot. I could see the tall flier standing in the front door. He walked toward me. I ran up to him and stopped. "Sorry, I'm late, Mr. Fuchs."

"Better late than never, Bruz. What happened? I've got a big pre-flight class at six and the place is a mess. I was sure you'd be here."

"I got locked in a garage. My dad got me out. I can't talk about it. Mum's the word."

He laughed. "Go sweep up, your nickels on the desk when you're done. I have to go prepare five and six for the pre-flight demo. See you Tuesday." I got to work. Swept the entrance hall, cleaned up the class room, straightened the chairs, wiped off the desk, put my tools back in the closet and picked up my nickel. I looked at the shiny Indian Head, checked the buffalo on the back. It was dated 1929. Going out of circulation into the Mason jar atop my mother's stove. I wondered what was for dinner.

17

Airway Street ended at the tall wire fence that closed off the east-west runways of the airport. The walnut grove ended at the fence, there weren't any houses, no streets, only the airport. The huge green airport spread before us like a desert leaving us nowhere to roam. The five Doyle boys, Floyd and me stood facing this dead end.

"You know right across that field is a water-hole where kids swim naked and roast frog's legs over an open fire. Ever taste a frog's leg? They're mighty good eating." Larry Doyle was tempting his younger followers.

"I wouldn't go cross that airport to find a gold mine. I don't need frog's legs, however good they taste." I said.

"Who said anything about crossing the airport. We go under the airport. Through a private tunnel that opens right on the water hole. We could be there in ten minutes. You interested?" The Doyle devil made me do it.

"Not me!" Floyd shouted. "I just got off the shit list. No, I'll just go home. You guys have fun. Coming Bruz?"

"I'm thinking, Floyd, you go. No sense scaring your parents again so soon. I'm going to think about it." Floyd waved, headed back to Hazel Street.

"You guys done this before?" They shook their heads. "Jerry. Have you done it?" He shook his head up and down. "Okay Larry, what's the secret? How do we get to this wonderful land of oz?"

Larry pointed down. Pointed at the sewer. "We slide into the storm sewer. We walk through a big pipe that ends right at the water hole. We climb down a little pile of rocks and we're there. Want to make a test crossing?"

"Yeah, first show me how you get in the sewer." Larry lay down in the street parallel to the slot under the curb; he wiggled himself through the slot and stood with his face looking out from under the street. It didn't look hard. I could do it. I watched each Doyle slide into the sewer; I laid down, wiggled through, got my feet down to meet the floor and stood up under the Grand Central Airport.

Larry led the way. We walked to the end of the sewer entrance. You had to walk with your legs apart to keep your feet out of the little stream of water that flowed into the big round pipe that drained storm water under the airport. We marched like soldiers through the pipe. Nothing out of the ordinary happened. Larry climbed down on the pile of stones and got to the ground. I reached the end of the sewer and saw the waterhole for the first time. It was beautiful. Weeping willows and pepper trees surrounded a small blue lake. Three naked boys were swimming. An old tire hung from an overhanging branch. Kids would swing out and fall into the water. It looked very deep. No one waded in, they all dived off the edge. I was in trouble. I couldn't swim.

"Come on, Bruz, climb down. I'll show you the place." I got on my knees slid over the edge of the big pipe and reached the stones. It was going to be harder going home than coming. I'd worry about that later. I ran over and joined the Doyles. The lake was bigger from the ground. The trees were thicker and taller. It was a great place. There wasn't a girl in sight. "No girls?" I said.

"Men only," Larry snorted, "Can't have girls around when you're swimming bare ass." I guess I should have figured that out for myself. I watched four guys dressed in swimming trunks roasting pork chops over a fire built in half of a large trashcan. "Where'd they get pork chops, Larry"

"Kid's bring all kinds of things, I don't know where they get them. Pork chops are cheap, maybe they bought them." We walked around the lake. A long grassy hill raised on the far side. Piles of clothes dotted the grass, bicycles laid on the ground here and there.

"Want to sit on the grass and watch the swimmers?" Larry asked.

"Sure," I answered. "Swell place, I just can't understand why there are no adults around."

"No roads. You can't get here in a car. It's hike over the hills, ride the bike trails from Griffith Park. It's a boy's place and I hope it stays that way."

"Wow, it sure is great. I wish I could swim."

"You can't swim? You better learn before school's out. Summer is waterhole time. You're going to be very lonely if you're not in that water." I sat shaking my head.

I managed to get myself back in the storm sewer pipe. March back to the Airway Street end, climb out, brush myself off and walk home. A 1929 Model A soft top coupe was parked in front of my house. We had company. I ran home and saw my big brother sitting on the front steps talking with my sister Gen.

"Hey Jay!! What're you doing home?"

"Christ, youngster, you've grown a foot. Come give your big brother a hug." I ran over and jumped in his lap. Gen laughed out loud. "Hear you've been giving the old man trouble. Go easy he's not in the greatest shape."

"I was only playing hide and seek. I didn't know we had bad guys in the neighborhood." He laughed and messed my hair. "You know how to swim?"

"Yeah. Fact is I'm a pretty good swimmer. I'll teach you how Sunday morning. Katie's off on a church thing, I'll be home till Sunday."

"Great! Great! Then I can swim in this great waterhole across the airport. It's a swell place. Boys only. No girls. Naked swimming. Outdoor cooking. No adults. But no shallow water, a guy has to swim. You'll really teach me Sunday?"

"I promise you. You'll learn to swim the same way I did. You'll be swimming Sunday night and you'll never forget." I don't know why he laughed.

"Is that your car?" I asked. He nodded. "It sure is neat. "Does the top come down?" He nodded. "Could I drive it?" He laughed.

"Not tomorrow but soon. California says you have to be sixteen, but maybe we'll cheat a little." He laughed again. I loved to hear him laugh. It sounded swell."

Gen got up. "I have to help with supper. I'll go give mom a hand. Bruz go wash up at the faucet by Jay's house. Dads taking a bath." I nodded.

"C'mon, Bruz, I have to check out my place before dinner."

The whole Tyrrell clan sat around the dinner table for the first time in months. Mom made boiled chicken. I loved boiled chicken. I always got a drumstick and a wing in a big bowl with soup, potatoes, carrots, celery, and white onions. So good!

My brother was talking. "I have this little room in this lady's house about six blocks from the store. I park in her driveway. I give her twelve bucks a month; I'd spend that for gas commuting from here. She couldn't make it without me. Not too many people have steady jobs. I'm pretty lucky. My boss tells me I'm going to get transferred into the main office and get some kind of executive job; he says Mr. Newberry really thinks I have potential. I just nod my head. I'll do what they tell me till I can get my own place, then you watch my smoke.

"We're very proud of you son," Mom said, "you've done so well for yourself with no help from us at all."

"Nonsense, mom, you and dad raised me. You taught me how to get along with others, how to work hard and not bitch, you gave me the foundation to be successful. I love you for it."

"Too bad I won't be around to see you president of J.J. Newberry son, but you're building yourself a good life. You and Katie seem to get along, you should bring her around more often so we get to know her." My dad looked tired.

"I know, dad, but she's got a lot of family responsibilities. Her mom's not well. They're short of cash. They have to give the church money for her sister the nun. We're going to get married in a couple of years when times get better. We both will be making good money then and I can help her with her problems. If I ever get my own place she'll be worth her weight in gold."

"I'm sorry I'm broke, Jay, and can't give you a hand. I lost all my money but didn't have any of the fun. The stock market screwed me, even though I never bet a buck on their products and the banks have let my assets slip away. I was a very rich man, now I don't have a pot to piss in."

"Bill! Don't talk like that. Bruzzy's at the table. How would you like him to repeat that in school?" My mother protecting her baby.

"You don't worry about Bruzzy. He's the brainy one in this family. If anyone in the Tyrrell clan is ever going to be rich, I'd put my money on Bruzzy. The kid reads something, he can tell it to you word for word. His teachers say he's got a photographic memory, he's a year ahead of himself in school and he never studies a single thing. He is either the biggest charlatan that's ever come along or he's a genius. I bet on genius." The whole family laughed. If my father said I was smart, then I must be smart because my dad was never wrong.

Jay reached over and messed my hair. Mama kissed me on the neck. My sister patted my face. "Well," I said, "I don't know about rich but every teacher I have says she hopes I'm as smart as my sister Gen and there's no way I'm that smart."

"This has been such a lovely dinner. I have the greatest family in the world. Now how about having the greatest peach cobbler in the world and I've got vanilla ice cream just for Jaywha."

"Christ! It's nice to be home." My big brother had spoken.

Pop's Willow Lake is a man-made pond about the size of two football fields. It had a shallow end that got deeper and deeper the further you went into the lake. Jay drove, his best friend Fred Fultz sat up in front, I was squeezed into the back. We pulled into an almost empty parking lot; it was Sunday morning most people were in church. The admission was fifteen cents for grown ups, ten cents for kids. The cashier stamped a purple date on the back of our hands making us official swimmers for the day. We pulled off our clothes in the changing room. Put on our bathing suits, stuck our clothes in little lockers hanging the keys around our necks. "Come on," Jay said, "Time to drown my little brother." They laughed, so I joined in, not too sure it was funny. I followed the two big men to the shallow end. We waded into the cool water. We stopped when the water was up to my waist. Jay told me to bend over, "Put your face in the water and stroke pretending to swim, each time you stroke with your right arm turn your head out of the water and breathe. Go ahead, try that." I pretended to swim, I breathed when I stroked with my right arm. I did that over and over, I thought it was dumb. Jay and Fred were laughing and talking, I was stroking and breathing. "Dumb."

"Okay, kid, let's move this along." My big brother grabbed me, "Lay flat in the water." He said, one hand on my belly, one hand on my back. "Now kick your feet, stroke and breath I'll hold you up so you don't sink." I kicked, I stroked, I breathed and we moved in a big circle in the shallow end of the pond. "Good," Jay kept saying. Kick, stroke, breath, I could feel his hand going deeper in the water, now it was under me, not touching, I was still swimming. I faltered for a second and his hand was back on my tummy, then I was swimming myself again. I was getting pooped.

"Okay, Bruz. Take a break. You're a quick study. You're swimming already. Fred and I are going for a swim; you play here in the shallow water, rest up. When we come back you're going to swim in the deep water."

"Really? In the deep water? Then I could swim in the water hole. Go ahead, I'll play right here." I watched them swim away, both powerful swimmers, they moved easily through the water getting smaller and smaller as they swam away. I played around, I sat on the bottom letting the water push me around. I counted seven other swimmers in the lake. Pop's wasn't making a profit this morning. I dreamed about swinging off the Willow tree plopping into the water hole with the other kids. "I'm so lucky to have Jay to teach me." I thought watching a rowboat coming closer and closer to where I was sitting. Suddenly I realized my brother was rowing the boat, Fred Fultz sitting in the front seat. They coasted up next to me.

"You pretty well rested Bruz? Jay called. "If you're ready, we'll try the deep water."

"Time to see if you'll drown!" Fred called out laughing. "I'd show him!" I thought.

"Climb in the back and sit on the edge of the boat." Jay gave instructions. I slid over the side of the boat, got my feet on the bottom and sat on the back edge. I wondered what Jay had in mind. He turned the boat around heading for the middle of the lake, the deep part of the lake. I looked at the lifeguard stand. Empty. I looked where we were heading. No one was swimming there. I knew I wasn't in trouble my brother would take care of me. "You still pooped, Bruz?" Jay asked, putting the oars up on the sides. "No. No, I'm good."

"Then swim!" Jay pushed me into Pop's Willow Lake. I saw a bunch of bubbles. I kicked my feet. I came straight up to the surface. I breathed. I started doing what I learned in the shallow water. I was swimming behind the boat. Jay was standing, watching while Fred pulled on the oars. I swam and I swam and I swam. I swam forever. Finally, Jay reached over and pulled me into the boat. "Well, young man, you're a swimmer. How about that?"

"You pushed me in! You pushed me in the water. What if I couldn't swim?"

89

"But you did swim, just like I swam when your dad threw me in. You're a swimmer, kid, you'll never forget and we will never have to worry about you drowning. There's only one more thing for you to learn. Interested?" I shook my head yes sitting on the back edge of the boat. Fred beached the boat. We jumped out. "See those diving boards over there, you're going to learn the easy way into the water. It's scary but you can't get hurt." We walked to the diving board, Jay walked me up the steps. "This is the one meter board, Bruz, three feet over the water, all you have to do is jump off and swim back here. Okay?" I nodded ran up the board, jumped, came to the surface and swam back to the diving board. Fred and Jay gave me a hand. I walked tall. I climbed up on the board.

"This time it's harder. You're going to dive in. Head first. No big deal. Stand on the edge of the board, lean over as far as you can, put your arms out in front of you, touch your hands together and fall into the water. Don't forget to swim back."

I walked out to the edge. I looked at the water. I wasn't afraid. I knew I could swim. I bent over, held out my arms. Put my hands together and fell into the water. I went in headfirst. I went deep into the lake. I looked up, kicked my way to the surface, stuck my head in the air and breathed. I swam back, ran up on the board, ran to the edge, bent over and dived. I loved it. I did it five times. Then Jay yelled, "Hold it." I stopped. Jay and Fred were laughing. "Okay, Water Rat, just one more thing and you'll always be safe in your waterhole. Want to try one more thing?"

"More diving?" I screamed.

"Just jumping. Diving off this board takes some time. See that tower? That's ten meters tall. Thirty feet. Guys who know how to dive off that say it's thirty feet up and a hundred feet down. Jump off a couple of times and you won't be afraid of heights. Willing?"

"Yeah, yeah. You come up with me first time, okay?"

"I'll be right behind you, little Bro."

It really was a tower. Built of dark brown four by fours. It had a hand over hand ladder with flat rungs almost too far apart for my six going on seven legs. I climbed, Jay right behind me. He put his hand on my butt and shoved me up onto the platform. I looked around. You could see the Hollywood Hills one way the Sierras the other. We were way up in the air. I looked down at the water. It sure looked like a hundred feet. "The first time I did this," Jay said, "I ran jumped off and hit the water with my feet, you do the same, okay."

I leaned against the fence. "Did dad tell you that?"

"No. Fred's dad brought us. He taught us to jump off the tower. We were older than you. You want to try or shall we climb down?"

"I'll jump. Be like the swing off the big willow tree at the water hole. I'll jump right now." I ran and jumped out into the air. I was flying without wings. It felt wonderful. I crashed into the water. My legs stung. I kept going down and down then my feet hit the sandy bottom. I pushed off the bottom, kicked my legs and broke the surface. I screamed in sheer delight. I swam out of the lake. I could see Jay and Fred laughing atop the tall tower. I climbed back up. Got my knee on the platform and stood up. I looked at Jay and Fred. "One more time for luck!" I said and was airborne on my second trip to the water. I swam for shore; I could see Fred preparing to dive. He did a perfect jack knife and popped out of the water right next to me. "Watch your brother, he's good at this." Fred garbled, water running out his mouth. My brother came off the tower in a perfect swan dive; he entered the water without even a splash. My brother was a diver, what else didn't I know about him?

I slept all the way home. We got there in time for our three o'clock dinner. Fred stayed. The booth was crowded but friendly. Jay and Fred bragged about me until I was red in the face. We had corned beef and cabbage. I loved to chop up the cabbage and mix it with the potatoes. Mom called it bubble and squeak, I thought that was funny but didn't understand the connotations. My dad said, "Bruz. You're a swimmer now. Work on it, be a good swimmer, like Jay. You can never tell when it might come in handy."

"Well, Fred," my mother said, "you're the guest at this table, there's apple pie or peach cobbler, there's vanilla ice cream and Neapolitan. What can I give you?"

18

"Next week's the last week of school for us, Floyd, when's your vacation start?" We were playing a game of Pick Up Sticks Floyd was studying his move. "Friday." He said.

"Friday?" I answered. "You get a week more vacation than us? What a gyp. Just cause you go to an academy and I go to a school. Maybe I should go to an academy."

"That would cost your dad tuition. I don't think he has the money. Besides, I'd rather be with regular kids than the rich ones in my school. My dad has to work so hard to keep me there. I don't understand."

"My dad broke his leg and the man at the bank lost his money and they took two of his trucks and now he stays home and mom's always asking how are things and he grumbles and I can't move into my room until your father finishes my cabinets and your father has to work to pay your tuition so he doesn't finish my cabinets and you'd rather go to my school so your father didn't have to work so hard. It's a real mess isn't it?"

Floyd flicked a Pick Up stick off the pile. He was ahead of me again. He stood up. "Come on, Bruz. Let's go see how he's doing with your cabinets." I followed him to the garage. The doors were open. His father was sanding something he was working on. Mr. Baumer waved at me. I smiled. He started signing with Floyd. Floyd signed back and laughed.

"My dad's finishing up your cabinets right now. Says he can install them tomorrow if that's all right with your dad." I waved at Mr. Baumer and said "thank you" so he could read my lips. "I'll go ask my father." He nodded.

"Want to come?" Floyd shook his head. "I'll put away the pick-up Sticks. You go ahead, I'll be on the porch."

I could hear a hammer banging behind Jay's house. I walked around the back. My dad was building a big cage. He was screening it in. It had a long screen door that swung up and hooked to the top with a lot of little boxes against the back wall. "What kind of chicken coop is that, dad?" I asked. "It's not a chicken coop, Bruz, it's a pigeon coop. I haven't kept pigeons since I was a kid. Our friend in Thousand Oaks has a bunch of pigeons he needs to give away so I'm going to take them. Pigeons can be very tasty."

"Mr. Baumer wants to install the cabinets in my room tomorrow. That okay with you?"

"I thought he forgot all about us. Tell him I'll welcome him with open arms."

"Floyd says he took a long time because he has to do extra work to pay for the academy. Floyd wants to come to our school but his parents want him with the rich kids. I don't understand." I shook my head.

"Deaf people are handicapped. If their children are well they worry they will suddenly lose their hearing or something else bad will happen so they try to give them a better life. Many times they're wrong but they keep trying to be good to their offspring."

"I think it's dumb."

My father laughed out loud. "Oh, Bruz, you are some piece of work. Go tell Baumer he's welcome tomorrow. Maybe you'll sleep in your own room tomorrow night." It was my turn to laugh.

I got home from school at three thirty. I went in the back door to see how far along Mr. Baumer had gotten. It was quiet. No noise. No one working, something wrong I surmised. I pulled the door open. The room was finished the cabinets in place. My bed was against the wall. I opened a cabinet. My clothes were all there. My Keds lay on the floor. My room was done. I was out of my sister's room. I could sleep in my shorts. I went in the house. My mom was in the kitchen. I walked in.

"Your room is done. I moved all your stuff in there. You're all out of Gen's room. Happy?" I hugged my mom and kissed her. "Happy!" I said.

"The Witches Tales" was a scary story on the Red Network at seven-thirty. My dad loved the show. Mom sat listening, her crochet needle clicking as she made little circular things that would eventually be my sisters bedspread. I lay on the floor, scared out of my wits trying to keep from running away as doors creaked open and screams poured out of the speaker. My big sister sat on the floor, her hand resting on my back, trying to help me get through the experience. I was thinking about sleeping in my new room.

"Eight o'clock, Bruz. Bedtime. School tomorrow." My mother said as the opening theme of "Manhattan Merry-go-round" filled our little living room. I jumped up, ran into the bathroom, tinkled and brushed my teeth. I kissed my dad, my mom and my big sister. I was ready for bed. Ready to be alone, in my own room. I closed the back door the radio sound went away. I entered my newly finished bedroom lit by moonlight coming through the trees. I felt a little tingle in my stomach, thrilled to have my own space again. Plunk! Something hit the roof. I turned on the little mahogany lamp atop a tiny bed stand. I could see my father's artistic hand in both. I jumped out of my clothes and stood in my shorts ready for bed. Plunk! Something hit the roof. I pulled the covers up to my nose burrowed down into familiar territory.

My mother came in. "I have to kiss my baby goodnight his first night in his new room." I felt warm and safe. My mom bent over and kissed my head. Plunk! Something hit the roof again. Mom looked up at the slanted ceiling, "Must be nuts falling off the tree. You won't hear that once you're asleep." She kissed me again and tip toed out as if I was already asleep. I turned over and drifted away.

I was freezing. I was hemmed in, quarts of vanilla on one side, Neapolitan on the other. I was being frozen to death by the ice cream I loved. I opened my eyes. I was in my new room. A cold breeze blew in through the screened windows. I needed another blanket. The small clock's green letters read 3:15.

I mustn't wake my mom. What should I do? I got up ran in my shorts out the back door across the yard into my brother's room. A yellow blanket lay folded at the foot of his bed. I grabbed it, ran back to my cold room, threw Jay's blanket on the bed and crawled in. In two minutes, warm as toast, I fell fast asleep.

When I got home from school next day the yellow blanket was folded at the foot of my bed. Jay's turn to freeze I laughed to myself. I didn't have to worry about Jay. He got a promotion. He worked out of the main offices in LA. They put him in charge of all the stores in Los Angeles County. Big job. Keep the shelves filled with products that sold. Make sure the stores were cleaned; make sure they made money. Jay wouldn't be sleeping in his bed in the back yard. He would be someplace fixing problems or in Venice with his girl. I would miss my big brother.

19

School was out! I ran home. Ran through the walnut grove, in our back gate, into my bedroom on the back porch. I pulled off my shoes, pulled off my socks; I threw them in the bottom of Mr. Baumer's cabinet. Barefoot. I wouldn't put my shoes on until Labor Day! I took the white envelope the teacher had given me addressed to Mrs. William Tyrrell. She looked at it then at me. "Sit in your father's place. There's apple pie and milk to celebrate the last day of school." I jumped up into the breakfast nook and went to work on the treat. My mom's apple pie was the best apple pie in the whole country. "MMM, good, mom."

"You have a very nice report card young man, just like your sister's, all A's one B+. There's a note from the principal. You're to report to Mrs. Nelson in the third grade in September, you've skipped second grade. You should be very pleased with yourself." I didn't answer. I didn't do anything special in the first grade I couldn't figure out why they were skipping me, all my friends would be in the second grade. Why couldn't I stay in the second grade too?

"Wait till your father hears about this, he'll really think you're a genius then." I took a long drink of the cold milk. I could still play with my friends at recess, I thought. "Hey, mom. What's a genius, anyway?" She laughed and messed my hair.

Larry led the way into the storm sewer. I'd been walking without shoes for a week. The souls of my feet were getting like leather. I didn't have to walk with my legs spread to avoid the little river of water that always trickled through the sewer pipe. I splashed along in the cool water. I loved it. We climbed down the rocks pulled off our clothes, stored them in the rocks and headed, bare ass naked for the waterhole.

"Remember it's deep Bruz. No wading. You have to swim. I laughed at him and dove into the water. I swam out to some guys who had a big inner tube and joined the group. Larry came puffing up and grabbed the tube. "I thought you couldn't swim?" Shaking water off his head.

"My brother taught me. He's a great swimmer. He taught me how to float, how to tread water, how to swim and how to dive. He dove off the tower and didn't even make a splash!"

"Wow!" Larry retorted. "Wish I had a brother like that. I'm stuck with all little brothers. I have to teach them to swim. I learned at the Y." We swam all day. I swung off the willow tree. Jumped in the water from a low hanging limb. Practiced swimming underwater holding my breath, then I had to leave. Time to sweep out the Flying School. I dried in two minutes under a hot California sun. Got dressed. Climbed the rocks to the sewer and splashed my way back across the airport's east-west runways. I got to Fuchs' Flying School at three-thirty. It was nearly five o'clock when I put my nickel in my pocket and headed for home. The Macadam streets were hot from the sun so I moved right along, my feet sticking in the melted tar. I could see my dad standing in the driveway, waiting for me, the lawn mower parked in the middle of the lawn. I figured I was about to win the honor of finishing mowing the lawn. My dad had run out of strength. I waved to him as I saw a big brown dog running at me from the lot next door to Floyds. The dog looked strange, saliva running from its mouth as he came growling toward me. I was never afraid of dogs, I though I would give it a pet and he would run along. It leaped at me. I swung my fist and hit it on the side of its head. I landed on my back, the dog on top of me snapping and growling. From nowhere my father appeared. He grabbed the dog's hind legs and spun around like a hammer thrower. He flung the dog into the sky; the dog squealed flew through the air and crashed into the curb at the edge of our driveway. His head cracked against the curb. It didn't make a sound. It just lay there.

I didn't know what to do. I wasn't scared. I all happened too quickly for me to be scared. My dad looked as if he was hurting. I jumped up. "Thanks, Dad, you saved my life! I said. "I saw that mutt across the street yesterday. I knew there was something wrong with him. I should have shot the poor son-of-a-bitch." I laughed.

"My leg's killing me, Son. Let me borrow your shoulder. I'm going to lean on you pretty hard, you have to last to the front stoop. Want to give it a go?"

"Sure, Dad. I won't let you fall." I walked over and stood next to him. He put his big hand on my shoulder and gripped. It hurt. I said nothing. "Now, just walk slowly with me, you're my right leg so for god's sake don't give away." We walked; he leaned, one foot, two feet. He was very heavy. I was having a hard time being a right leg. We got up the driveway. I could feel sweat running down my back. "Just a little farther, Bruz. Just across the lawn. I'll sit on the top step." I nodded, saving my strength. He leaned. I stood tall. He turned and sat on the step lowering himself with his left arm. "God damn!" He said.

I'd done it. I had helped my dad. My dad, who always helped me. He whistled out his breath. "You're a lot stronger than you look young man. I'm in your debt."

"You saved me, Dad. That dog was going to kill me. You killed it. I was only a crutch."

"Okay, Crutch. Put the lawn mower in the garage. Then drag that dead dog into the trees behind Baumer's. Let me sit here a while till my leg comes back to life. Oh, and don't tell your mother."

The dog was ugly. Blood ran from his mouth. He didn't look so big lying dead in the driveway. I grabbed his hind legs and pulled him across the street making a line of blood on the black top. There was three feet of lawn next to Floyd's driveway; I dragged the dog along the grass. Floyd stuck his head out the door, "Want some help, Bruz?"

"Sure Floyd, that'd be great."

"Your dad threw that dog thirty feet in the air. He must be very strong. My mom saw that dog in our lot she wouldn't let me go out." Floyd rambled.

"Dad says to drag this animal deep into the grove. He says the animals back there will eat it. Think you can pull that long?"

"Let's try." We pulled and we rested. We went deeper and deeper into the trees. Suddenly we ran into three men. One was stringing wires through the trees the other two were watching what the third was doing. "Hey kids, where're you dragging that dog?"

"My dad says if we get this dog deep into the grove other animals will eat it."

"True," the man answered. Let us handle that. Okay? We're going to do a radio program here tonight. That guy with the wires is a telephone man. He's doing the hook up. We don't want some smelly dog lying around. Let us get rid of it. Okay?"

"Sure, sure." I answered. "Who's going to be on the radio?"

"Ever hear of Roy Rogers and the Riders of the Purple Sage? They're going to do a radio series all summer long right in this walnut grove. Tell the neighborhood people we need an audience."

"How about kids?" Floyd spoke up, "Can kids come?"

"Sure. But you have to be quiet. And clap when a song ends. Eight o'clock. Get here seven thirty. Now let's take care of our dead friend here."

We got back to Hazel Street in a couple of minutes. Dragging that big dog made it feel like a long way. Floyd went into his house. He had to convince his mom and dad to let him go to the radio show. My dad was still sitting on the porch. He looked a lot better. I told him about Roy Rogers on the radio in the walnut grove. He said I could go. I ran up to the corner and told Mrs. Doyle. Jerry had to go to bed but the other four could come.

I was standing in Floyd's driveway waiting for the Doyles to come down the hill. Floyd came out the back door in a heavy winter sweater. "You're going to sweat in that outfit, Floyd."

"My mother worries about me. I'll take it off when we sit down." Floyd had much different parents than I had.

"So where's the cowboy singer?" Larry Doyle yelled halfway down the block.

"Come on. We'll show you" Floyd yelled back. We walked into the grove. Little red flashlights were taped to the trees to show the path when it got dark. The show would be over at eight-thirty; it'd still be twilight when we left. They were being very cautious.

They had built a big bon-fire in the center of the small clearing. Six musicians were warming up their instruments. They played guitars, a banjo and a big bass fiddle. People from the neighborhood came into the clearing. Twenty or thirty people leaned against trees, or sat cross-legged on the ground. A couple of smart people brought blankets and pillows. It was Saturday night in the Walnut Grove. And the show was free.

About five minutes to eight one of the men who got rid of the dog stood up by the fire. He was wearing leather chaps with pointy black boots, a plaid shirt and a leather vest. His cowboy hat hung on a string down his back. "Ladies and Gentlemen, thank you for coming here tonight to hear one of the country's up and coming music groups. 'Roy Rogers and the Riders of the Purple Sage.' We're going to be doing this radio show for the next thirteen Saturdays at eight. I hope you'll tell your friends and if you can't make it, tune to KFWB to see how it sounds over the air.

It was a great show. We were spellbound. Roy Rogers was a young cowboy with a great voice. You could bet we would be in the walnut grove for the next thirteen Saturdays. We walked out of the trees at a quarter to nine, laughing and chortling. We'd had a swell time. Larry was walking up the hill toward his house. He was singing, "Keep a moving Dan, He's a devil not a man and he paints the burning sand with water. Cool, clear water!" Roy Rogers didn't have a worry in the world.

20

The school playground was closed. There was no money for summer time activities. Glendale's moms and dads didn't have enough to pay for the summer school. No money. No playground. The playground was closed. All the ballplayers sat along the curb on School Street. One of the kids said there was a big lot on Western Avenue. Too far someone answered. Larry Doyle spoke up.

"There's a huge lot where Lake Street ends. It's full of cattails but we could cut them down and make a ball field. Then we wouldn't have to play on macadam, we'd have a dirt field. Let us check it out, you guys come up tomorrow morning and we'll clear the space. Everyone agreed, running off to their homes not wanting to waste a vacation day. The five Doyles and I walked up to the cattails. We stood and surveyed the tall, grey frankfurter-like flowers waving in the breeze as far as you could see. Everybody looked. Nobody spoke.

"You guys wait here. I'll go get our hedge clippers so we can mark off where we'll put the field." I didn't wait for an answer I ran to my dad's garage, grabbed the clippers, a shovel and the hoe. I yelled at Floyd, playing on his porch, to come and help. The Doyles were sitting on the curb waiting for me. I threw down the tools walked to where Larry was sitting. "Let's start right here. We'll cut down one cattail after the other and make a line for where the field starts, Okay?" Nobody argued, I guess I was the boss, maybe because it was my hedge clippers. I cut the first stalk close to the ground. Jerry threw it into the street. Two inches of thick round stalk stuck up out of the ground. We stood around the stalk looking at it. "You can't play ball with those things sticking up all over the field you'd hurt your feet." Harry yelled. "Be like playing a pin ball game!" Little Jerry laughed. "You have to pull them up!" Floyd's voice was coming from the street.

"Wait a minute," I shouted, "We're just making a line to lay-out the field, we'll have to pull the plants up, roots and all, Let's see how big the field will be, my dad will help us pull them up."

I cut the plants down in a straight line until Larry could make a hundred strides into the field of plants. Larry and I sat down the jungle standing all around us. Suddenly we had company. A Garter snake slithered up; stood tall on his tail, his slanted eyes glittering at us, before we could do anything he slipped off into the maze of stalks. "Boy, that snake would make a great belt. I bet there are a thousand snakes in here. You want a snake belt, Bruz?" I shivered. "I've got a belt, thank you." We marked off a hundred yards on no name street, then a hundred yards back into the jungle. We were connecting our first line with the second line when we ran into an unfinished house hidden deep inside the waving cattails.

"Some poor bastard tried to build a house. I guess the depression got him." "You think somebody owns this place? Maybe they can throw us out after we've busted our butts on the field?" I didn't want to work hard for nothing. "He didn't finish the place, so he must have lost all his money. There're only two walls up. I don't think it'll be a problem, let's keep going."

We sat on the curb. We had laid out a plot the size of two football fields, filled with stalks standing taller than any one of us. But, dumb kids wanting a place to play ball weren't afraid of a little hard work. Harry and Johnny had been watching Larry and me marking the field. Sitting on the curb, the rest of us watched them grab the next stalk. They pulled. Nothing happened. They rocked the stalk back and forth. They pulled, grunting loudly. The stalk moved up a tiny bit. "We can't get a hold of the thing, our hands slip, it's in too tight." Johnny said. My dad limped across the street.

"What're you kids up to now?" He said. I answered. The school playground is closed. No money. There's no place to play ball. We thought we could clear this field so we'd have someplace to play. The stalks are too deep, we can't get them to move." My dad walked over to Johnny, he grabbed the base of the stalk and pulled it out of the ground. A big ball of dirt clinging to it's roots.

"That's a bitch. You kids aren't strong enough yet to pull those suckers up. Let me go back to my bench, I have an idea. Might let you get rid of this jungle." He messed my hair. I watched the kids watch him limp away as if they were watching super man.

103

We sat on the curb talking about the swimming hole. Poor Floyd felt left out but he hung on every word as one story segued into another. Larry was talking about me flying off the Willow tree when my dad reappeared. He was carrying four long pieces of one by two. "I think this will do the trick. Larry, Bruz, come over here." He handed me two pieces of one by two. I could see they were attached with a long fence hinge. We stood by a tall cattail. Dad gave instructions. "Bruz," he said, "You hold the hinge end, Larry you're stronger than he is so you'll control the pull. Just open it like a pair of pliers. Put it about a foot from the ground and close it on the stalk. Squeeze it so it cuts into the stalk a bit. Then you and Bruz bend over, hold the wood tight and pull with your whole body. Want to give it a try?" All the kids gathered around. I opened the gadget and placed it around the stalk about a foot off the ground. Larry squeezed it shut biting into the stalk. We were bent over holding each end. "On three!" Larry said. "One, two three!" We pulled, the stalk pulled back, we kept pulling finally out the stalk came, roots and all. My dad's invention did its job.

"Floyd," My dad said, "Run up to our house and tell Mrs. Tyrrell to make a pail of 'Kool Ade' and bring back a couple of cups. Floyd nodded and ran up the street. My dad was full of directions, he told us to work for half an hour then take half an hour off. Larry and I were one pulling team; Harry and Johnny were the other. All the rest piled the stalks in the road to be thrown away later. In the first half hour we got good enough to pull up a stalk every three minutes. Seventeen stalks lay in the street when we took our first Kool Ade break. Cold grape Kool Ade. My favorite. My dad left us at work, we kept at it, half hour on, half hour off. Floyd got a Kool Ade replacement and two clean cups. We had displaced four Garter snakes, and a tiny cottontail, probably out on his first walk when his forest went away.

Five more times we pulled for half an hour. We were bushed. Two hundred cattail stalks littered the street. We had cleared twenty square yards. Not much, but a start. Tomorrow we would have a lot more kids. We dragged ourselves up the hill. Floyd went in his house I could hear his mother speaking gibberish. Poor Floyd got himself dirty. He was in deep trouble.

I put the tools back in the garage. My dad was working on the pigeon coop. "That looks great dad, when you get the birds." He looked at me, shook his head, "Next week, I think. Can't rush things when they're free. Now, you, Young Man get out of those clothes and stand on the grass over there." Get out of your clothes, my father said. Get out of my clothes I did. No questions. I stood on the grass in my all together. Dad walked around my brother's house holding the hose. I knew what was coming. I was all dirty but I was going to be clean in a minute. He turned the nozzle water spurted out. He sprayed me, the cold water made me scream but it felt wonderful, cattail fuzz, mud, dirt, sweat rolled off of me. My mother was standing in the back door laughing; the water kept coming and coming. Finally, it stopped.

"You can't get any cleaner than that, son. Go in the bathroom, towel off and dress for dinner. You've had a tough day." I laughed, running into the house. I had a swell family. I lived in a house full of love.

"So, Bruz. I hear you're building a ball field." My big sister said, sitting in the dining nook eating supper. "I'm not, all the kids are. And dad is helping us. We would be nowhere without him. We're the muscle, he's the brains." Mom was serving her stuffed cabbage with boiled potatoes and we had a pitcher of iced tea. I couldn't stop drinking.

"Well," my sister continued, "I had to walk up to Grand Central and buy a whole box of Kool Ade so you guys would have something to drink tomorrow. You owe me."

"And that box was fifty cents, Bruzalah, fifty cents is a lot of money for a ball field." My mother smiled.

"Take it out of my mason jar. There must be fifty cents in there; I've been working since we moved. The kids need the field, no school field this year so we need a field."

"We're teasing, Bruz." My dad's calm voice. "You'll have your field. I made two more pullers this afternoon. Tomorrow you can have four teams.

Make four new teams, let today's teams just clean up, they put in a hard day today and you've got a lot more work to do. Let's enjoy mother's stuffed cabbage and forget about cattails for the evening."

Nobody had to tell me to go to bed that evening. After dinner I collected the eggs I'd missed pulling cattails. I put them in the fridge, brushed my teeth. I was asleep before the first "plunk" of the evening.

Ten kids showed up the next morning. The eight biggest got to be the pulling teams, the rest of us the cleaner uppers. Buckets of Kool Ade came from my house and from Floyd's mother. When she figured out how he got dirty she was sorry she yelled at him and made up by making Kool Ade. By lunchtime we had half the space cleared. The deeper we got into the field the easier the stalks came up. The dirt was much sandier so the pulling was much easier. Everybody went home for lunch. We would go back to work at 2 o'clock. Floyd and I walked up the hill together. "Your dad have a rake in the garage, Floyd?" He nodded yes. "Bring it with you, I'll bring my dad's we have to rake the field, get rid of all those holes."

My mother made me a peanut butter and jelly sandwich. I ate it with a glass of milk, kissed her, grabbed the rake and went back down the hill. I was the first one back so I raked a little area, the ground flattened out, the holes disappeared but my feet sunk into the dirt as I raked. I hoped the whole field wouldn't be like this, you couldn't field a grounder off soft ground. A problem we would have to face later. Seemed like this might be a bigger job than we planned for.

As cattails piled up in the street, the snakes ran to find a new home and the rabbits ran in circles. Our ball field materialized. The only problem we had was that it wasn't a ball field it was only a field. Floyd and I had raked nearly half the big lot; the more we raked the more we realized the field would have to be rolled. This could be the ball field killer.

A tall bright twelve year old stood where he thought home plate would be, swinging a make believe bat. "You know if I was batting and I fouled off the pitch the ball would go right into that grove of cattails and we would never find it.

Anybody think about a backstop?" My little six going on seven head spun. Problems. Problems. I was getting very tired of this project and I had to go sweep out the Flying School.

"I have to go do a job. Let's all go back to work on this tomorrow morning. We'll work out all the problems then. We all agreed. I walked up the hill with Floyd; he put the rake in our garage as I went on up the hill to Fuchs' School. As I passed the fence leading to the schools front door I saw a very big roller parked against the school wall. I had never noticed it before. Was this a gift from the gods? I walked into the school. Fred Fuchs was sitting at the reception desk filling out some forms.

"Hey, Bruz," Fred said, "You look like you've been working someplace else. I thought I was your exclusive employer." I wondered what he meant by that? "The school hasn't any money. They closed the playground. There's no place for us to play ball so we're building a ball field." He looked at me and laughed.

"You kids building a ball field? That's a huge job. It takes machines and men. How're you doing?"

"We got a space 100 yards square. We're almost finished pulling out the cattails but one of the kids thinks we need a backstop and I've been raking up after the cattail pulling but the ground needs to be rolled. I think we might be in trouble."

"How many kids are working?"

"Twenty-one today. Do you own that roller outside?" I didn't believe I said that.

"No. It's the airport's. They have to roll the dirt each side of the runways to keep it firm in case a plane rolls off the concrete. Why?"

"Well, if you owned it, maybe you'd lend it to us. We could roll it down Hazel Street and roll that field so we could play ball on it." He laughed again.

"Bruz, that thing weighs a ton. Twenty kids roll it downhill on Hazel Street, that thing will roll right into the Los Angeles River!"

"Oh well. I just wondered. I have to get to work now. I have to wash and clean up before supper."

"One second. That field is at the end of Hazel Street where all the cattails are?"

"Yes. We've pulled up most of the cattails. Tomorrow they'll all be gone. We've raked most of the field and I have to try and convince my dad to build a backstop so we don't lose our ball if we foul it off."

"You kids will be there working tomorrow?"

"Yes sir."

"Okay. Go to work, I'll see what I can do."

I was pooped. I cleaned up the school got my nickel and walked down the hill. I walked down the driveway looked into the garage to see if dad's rake was there. It was. I walked into the yard; my father came out of the chicken coop carrying my egg basket.

"I collected your eggs, you're far too busy for such a menial task."

"Thanks dad, my ass is dragging."

"Language, language, young man. Take your ass into the bathtub. Hot. Soak, then you'll be able to work again tomorrow."

"Yes sir. If you say so. I'm really pooped."

"You'll feel much better after a hot bath." He patted my backside and moved toward the house. I guess I was going to take a bath.

As always my dad was right. I felt much better after the bath. Our house smelled of mom's dinner.

Ox tail soup. "Ox tails were 5 cents a pound today. I know it's hot for soup but I couldn't resist. There're onions and carrots, celery and potatoes in that bowl. It's a one-bowl meal, easy to serve, easy to clean up. Enjoy." My mom made the sale, no complaints from the customers at her table.

I looked at my father. He was eating slowly, enjoying his wife's cooking. Good time to ask about a backstop. "Dad?" I said. He looked at me. "And what do you need now, young man?" His eyes glittered.

"One of the big kids, a good ball player, says if we foul off a pitch we might lose our ball in the cattails behind home plate." He interrupted. "And you want me to build a back stop. Right?'

The wind went right out of my sails. I had gone too far. All I could muster was, "Uh huh."

"First, I'd need some help. This gamey leg is worthless. Let's say Fred and Willie will give me a hand. I don't have the money for two by fours and one by sixes and chicken wire. Could you kids come up with that?" He gave me a big smile. He figured he had me.

"I don't know who owns it but there's a house somebody was building in the cattails. The foundation and crawl space is there. Two walls of two by fours are up. The floor is there. Maybe you could use that?" He looked very interested. "Mother, I'm going to run over to Fred's after dinner. Is that okay?"

"Certainly Honey. Let's finish our dinner."

Dad left right after dinner. Gen helped mom clean up. I crashed into my bed, enjoying the fresh breeze coming through the screen.

Twenty-six kids showed up at the field. A couple of fifteen year olds, towering over us little kids. Four big guys made quick work of the few cattails that still stood in the playing area. We had four rakes and we traded off raking the playing field for the second time. It was level but it was soft.

An old Ford flat bed pulled up to the curb. My dad's friends Fred and Willie climbed out. I recognized the truck that once belonged to my father. They came over to me, the kids crowded around.

"Hey, Bruz. Show us that building with the two by fours. Let's see if we can make a backstop out of them." I saw my dad limping across the field. "Here comes my dad, Uncle Fred, let's wait for him, okay."

"Mornin' Bill!" Fred cried out, "Come on let's look at the house." My dad puffed up and I led the three men into the cattails. About twenty yards into the waving maze you could see the house. The three men walked over. Fred climbed into the building. He pushed a couple of two by fours. He bent down and inspected the floor. He jumped down. The three men held a short meeting. My dad walked over, "Well, Bruz, there's enough material there to build you your backstop and pay Fred and Willie for their time. They're going to pull the place apart right now if you kids agree." The kids yelled, "Yes!" A couple screamed, "go to it." I was very happy with my dad. We left the men to work and got out of the cattails.

A big red truck pulled in behind the Ford, a red and blue light flashing atop its cabin. A tall skinny guy in overalls got out. He walked toward the crowd of kids standing around my dad. A red "TWA" printed on his chest. "I'm looking for Mr. Ty-rell." He said in a Texas twang.

"I'm Bill Tyrrell, but I think you're looking for my son."

"Not Bill. Bruz, this order says I'm to see Bruz Tyrrell."

I stepped forward, the tall guy looked down at the little kid. He smiled. "My boss says I'm to see you, we're supposed to roll this field until you're satisfied with the job. You Bruz?"

"Yes sir. We sure would appreciate it if you could make this field hard enough so we can play ball on it." He knelt down, sifted some soil through his hands. "Yeah, a couple of rolls will do it. Same kind of dirt as the runways." He said standing up. "Okay guys," he yelled, time to go to work!"

The back doors of the red truck swung open. A ramp slid out and clanged on the street. Four more big guys pushed the huge roller down the ramp over the curb and onto the field. They kept rolling right along, got to the cattails reset the roller, got to the cattails reset again. The big square getting smaller each time they rolled around the field. We all stood and watched our mouths hanging open.

They were almost finished rolling the field when a fancy sedan stopped next to the red truck. A man in suit and tie got out. He came over to us kids and spoke to the group.

"Is everything working out all right?"

I answered. "Yes sir, thank you so much for helping us. They closed the schoolyard and we didn't have a place to play. Now you've given us a great ball field, I haven't any idea how we can pay you back but if you need us for something all you have to do is ask."

He laughed. "We all work for TWA," He was laughing, "We heard you kids were in trouble and it's a slow day in the airline business. Maybe you'll remember when you grow up and fly Transcontinental and Western Air." He laughed walked over said something to his men. He saw my dad laying out the backstop and walked over. My dad shook his hand, they laughed together and the suit got back in the fancy car and drove away. The big roller guy tapped my shoulder. "I think we're done. The field is very firm, if you sprinkle it down every once in a while it'll stay firm. Can you try it out before we go?"

The two big kids had a hard ball and a couple of fielder's mitts. One guy stood near my dad the other ran fifty feet out. They threw grounders to each other. The field was great. Better than the tar surface at school. This was like a real baseball field. We all applauded as the TWA men rolled the roller back into the truck, waved goodbye and went back to the real world. By the end of the day we had a backstop, a long bench on the first base line, a long bench on the third base line.

All the kids were looking at the job my father and his friends did on the backstop when Mr. Baumer and Floyd showed up. Floyd's arms were full of bases while his father carried a white with black edges home plate and a big tape measure. My dad said, "Baumer has the finishing touches. Let's finish it then we can all go home happy."

Floyd signed to his father who laughed and nodded his head. He lined up Home Plate and drove long wooden shafts through holes in the plate into the ground. It was a permanent installation. He measured the base line for softball, put in a base then continued the line for a hardball base. He finished the fields. A softball field and a hard ball field all in one place. Perfect!

I was eating breakfast when Larry yelled in the front door, "Come on, Bruz. Let's play catch on the field." Floyd joined us. We walked down toward the ball field. There was a softball game already underway. A couple of kids who had helped build the field were playing. All the rest were strangers. We played catch in right field for while. It wasn't any fun, the fielders kept yelling at us to get out of the way. Finally we went swimming in the water hole. At supper my dad asked me how we enjoyed our ball field. "A bunch of kids got there early and were playing softball. They kept yelling at us to get off the field and stop ruining their game. We went swimming."

"Too bad. But you can't put a lock on an open field."

We tried again the next day. The softball teams must have gotten there before eight. We had never seen them before. We played catch. We didn't listen to their insults. We were having fun. Several cars came rolling up and parked. A lot of big kids, high school kids, walked on the field. One of the biggest stood on home plate and yelled. "Okay you kids. Games over! Get off the field, time for a real baseball game." All the smaller players complained. Let them finish their game then they could play hardball. No deal. The big guys shoved the little guys off and started to warm up. The softball players walked away toward Lake Street. We sat down on the first base line bench to watch the game.

The big mouthed guy yelled, "Hey, you kids, get off that bench. It's for players only."

"You go to hell!" I screamed. "My dad built this bench. He built it with our lumber. We cleared this field so everybody could play. You have no right to take this field. The softball players were here first. You should have waited for them to finish. You don't own this field. We'll sit here if we want to!"

"Yeah, and I'll kick your ass into the fucking river if you don't get the fuck out of here right now. Move it. Get out!" I stood there glaring. "Come on Bruz. That's a mean guy he'll really kick your ass. Not worth it." Larry said, dragging me away from the bench. Unhappily, we walked up the street. I went into the back yard. My dad was still at the pigeon coop. "What's up, Son? You don't look very happy. Lose your ball game?"

"There are no ball games. The big kids won't let us play. Won't even let us sit on your bench and watch. One guy said he was going to kick my ass if I didn't shut up. I'm sorry we ever built that field. We worked hard and haven't gotten to play at all. None of the guys that built it get to play. It's a big gyp."

My dad didn't say a word. He limped into the garage. He came out carrying a hardball bat. "Come on, Bruz. We're going to take our field back." He limped down the street. You could hear the ball players yelling, laughing, cursing. My dad walked straight through the game right up to home plate. He pushed the batter aside and pounded his bat on the plate. "This game is over. Get your asses off my ball field before I kick the shit out of all you assholes!"

Everybody stopped. Quiet. Big mouth walked up to my dad, "Okay, old man, fuck off." My dad stamped his bat down on the kid's toes; he fell screaming to the ground. "I'll count to ten then I'll start swinging this bat." I was amazed! They ran for their cars, zoomed away. We were alone on the field. "Come on, Bruz, let's go talk to the cops."

I held my dad's hand as we walked into the local precinct on San Fernando Road. My dad led me up to a tall desk. A cop said hello. "I would like to talk with the Lieutenant. I don't have an appointment. This is a community problem. My name is Bill Tyrrell, this is my son, Louis."

The cop picked up a phone; I couldn't hear what he said. "You the roofer?" He asked my dad. "Uh huh." Dad answered. "Third door on the left, Mr. Tyrrell." The cop pointed.

Dad knocked. "Door's open!" A voice said from inside. We walked in. A big guy, his collar open leaned on his desk. "God damn, Bill. Long time no see."

"Jesus, Joe, don't you get any older?"

"Going on forty-five. Twenty years on the force, may even retire, not much chance for captain in this economy. Maybe I could try roofing again, huh? I wasn't too bad."

"You were a great part timer Joe, but the roofing business is dead. Who needs a roof when it isn't raining? Nobody has money for roofs these days. My kid, Bruzzy, here, and I have a problem with a baseball field. He told him the story. Joe kept nodding. He got angry when he heard about the big kids. Finally he scratched his head.

"We could make it part of our community athletic program. We would put a cop there to supervise the schedule. We could give your kid the first game, let's say, three times a week for all his work. We would love to have the facility. Most of the school playgrounds are closed because of the depression. We could really use a good ball field.

And so the 'Hazel Street Diamond' was born. I played there three times a week until we moved to Dryden Street many years later. Things work out when you have a dad with friends.

114

21

The little three by four foot building where Patrolman Carpenter sat at a miniature desk to supervise the games on the Hazel Street Diamond was painted dark blue. The white front door supported a bulletin board that showed schedules, teams competing and rules you had to follow or be expelled. Large glass windows filled the other two walls. A big white card was hung on the board. "End of Season," it read, "Diamond closed August 31, Saturday and Sunday games arranged by special request. RDC, GPD"

Our softball team, The Hazel Nuts was made up of ten kids who had built the field. Larry Doyle was captain. We weren't very good, but we had a lot of fun. We played Tuesday, Thursday and Saturday, eight o'clock in the morning. By ten thirty most of us slid down into the sewer and went for a swim in the old waterhole. Five o'clock I would be at Fred Fuchs' Flying school doing my janitorial duties, depositing my nickel in the Mason jar before supper in the dining nook. Every time there were twenty nickels in the jar my mom changed them for a dollar bill that she folded and put in the bottom of the jar. The nickels piled up.

My dad got 36 pigeons from Thousand Oaks. Every afternoon they would fly around the walnut groves, then come back to the pen behind my brother's room. My dad's infection got a little worse every day. He would sit longer in his chair, the gamey leg up on the ottoman but he was strong enough to bring home ten white leghorns, five Rhode Island reds and six Plymouth Rock hens. My chicken job didn't get easier. Still, it was a fabulous summer.

I put my shoes back on Tuesday morning, September eighth. I found new jeans and a plaid "Gaucho" shirt my mother had made from a remnant of cloth with large squares of blue and green plaid, folded neatly on my bed. I had long pants and a new shirt that fit me. I was proud to go back to school.

I walked to school carrying my lunch. I found Room 109 where the third grade met and pushed into the room. I looked around. I didn't know a soul.

Everyone was milling around, talking, making friends. I made my way towards the teacher. A very pretty young woman they were calling Miss Banker.

"Hi Bruz." A voice came from behind me. I turned. A very pretty blonde girl was smiling at me. I didn't know her at all. "Hi. Do I know you?"

She laughed. "Intimately." She said.

A flash went off in my brain. Sandra! I remembered the girl in my dad's garage. I hid in the pot closet. Oh, my! I pulled myself together. "Sandra!" I said. "How could I ever forget you?"

"You must be pretty smart. I'm nearly two years older than you and here we are in the same class." She stuck her hand out. Very grown up. "Friends?" She said.

"Please find seats, people, this is the third grade, I'm Miss Banker, please sit in alphabetical order by last name." "See you later, Friend," I said and headed for the last row where the "T's" usually sat. Sandra's name was Blaine, front row material. In five minutes we had worked out the seating plan and my first day in the third grade had begun.

I tried very hard to be grown up, but every thing was new and so different than first grade. The teacher kept putting books on our desks. A geography book, an English book, a Math book and a book entitled "Black Beauty." I wondered what that was about.

"We will use all the books on your desk this semester. When I looked at the list of students assigned to my class I tried to pick out a book you might like to read. Each of you will be responsible to turn in a book report on what you read two weeks before this class ends. At that time we will discuss your work and I'll give a gold star to the best report and discussion to a girl and a boy. If you don't like the title I've picked for you trade it with someone else who is dissatisfied. Okay? Now pick up the geography book. Let's see what you remember from second grade." I held up my hand. "Yes, Louis?"

"Bruz. My names Bruz, I didn't go to second grade."

"I know, er, Bruz. You just turn to California, read for the next ten minutes while we discuss New York. The principal told me you could join the discussion then." All the kids were looking at me. I opened the book. I could do that.

Lunch time. I sat on the steps of the kindergarten. I felt safe there. I opened my bag. I could smell the peanut butter. "Can I sit here?" My stomach flopped. It was Sandra. My friend. "Sure, sit down. It's a free country." She gave me a sick smile.

"I was very impressed. Where did you learn so much about California?" I opened my sandwich. "I don't know much about California. I was born here but so are a lot of people."

"But you gave the right answers to all the teacher's questions?"

"She only asked me about what she told me to read. Nothing hard about that." I took a bite of my mother's strawberry jelly and peanut butter. Delicious.

"You must have a photographic memory! That's why you skipped the second grade. I have a tough time with geography. Maybe you'll help me once in a while?"

"Sure. As long as we don't do it in the garage." She laughed. I didn't see what was so funny.

I walked through our back gate. Nobody was in the back yard. I went into the house. My mom called. "That you, Bruz?" She was in the kitchen peeling beets. I kissed her cheek. "You're carrying a book?" She took it from me. "Yeah. 'Black Beauty' I have to do a book report before the end of the term. I have to read the whole thing. I don't know if I like third grade."

"It's a wonderful story. You have months to read it. Your sister will help you with the report. You'll do very well in the third grade. Make any new friends?"

"Remember Sandra from Lake Street? She's in the class. We ate lunch together."

"Well she's a little mature for you, Bruz. Best you stick to boys."

"No she's okay. I'm going to help her with geography. But not in the garage." The car pulled into the driveway. A door slammed. My father came up the front steps. "Dotty!" He called. "What are these bags out here?"

"Bags?" My mother answered heading for the porch. I followed close behind. We went out on the porch. Dad was rummaging through a bag. "Food." He said. "Produce and canned goods. Where'd this come from?"

"I guess I didn't hear them when they came. The County, once a month, twelve dollars worth of food, no charge."

"A hand out? We don't need handouts. We can afford to buy what we need." My dad was sore. I backed down the stairs.

"Bill darling. Come down off your high horse. If I can get twelve dollars from the County each month, that's twelve dollars cash we can hang on to. You're not able to work right now, we have to try and conserve what we have."

"Well, I don't like it, there's lots of folks much worse off than we are. I don't like it."

"Fine, then don't eat it because I'm going to protect this family. We don't have the slightest idea what tomorrow's going to bring. So just you forget about where this food comes from and we'll get along just fine."

"All right, sweetheart, all right. I just thought."

"Bill, Darling, let me do the household thinking, you go out back and take care of your birds. What did the Doctor say?"

"Only that I'm worse and there's nothing they can do about it. Same shit. I'm going to let the pigeons out. Coming, Bruz?"

I swept out the Flying School, put my nickel in the Mason jar and watched my mother unload the County bags. There was a lot of stuff. Twelve bucks was a pile of money in 1931. Two heads of lettuce and two purple cabbages came out of a bag. There was a bag of tomatoes and a bag of potatoes, six cans of corn, six cans of peas, twelve cans of pink salmon, twelve flat cans of tuna fish, two loaves of white bread and two of wheat. It was a never ending well. My mother was very happy when everything was finally put away.

"One thing is sure, Honey, we're going to keep eating this month."

"Why is dad upset?"

"It's a man thing, sweetheart. He feels he's not doing his job taking care of his family. He doesn't realize he's sick. This depression is not his fault but we're in it and we're going to get through it. I don't care if we have to steal food from the Jap farms; this family is going to get through this mess. You have my solemn word on that, my boy."

I didn't know what mess she was talking about; I was living a very happy life.

"Go help your father with his birds, Son, try to spend a little extra time with him. He loves to have you around."

"Sure. Dad going someplace?"

"No. No. You just help him out. His leg hurts him. Maybe a little extra hand from you will make him feel better." I jumped down. "I'll go see how I can help." I headed for the back yard. My mother called after me, "Send your sister in. She's reading on the back steps. It's nearly dinner time."

My dad was standing by the pigeon coop searching the sky.

"Can I help you with something, Dad. Mom says I should try to help you out."

"You take care of the chickens, you mow the lawn, trim the hedge, sweep out the flying school, build ball fields and go to school. I think your plate is pretty well filled up, young man. If you want to hang around and shoot the bull, okay, but you do enough work around here." He messed my hair.

All of a sudden pigeons surrounded us. They all tried to get in their home at once. They sat on the edge of Jay's house, along the top of the chicken run. One sat on dad's shoulder, I chased one off my head. My dad was laughing out loud. When he got them all into the cage he lifted the last off his shoulder placed it in a nest and closed the swinging door. "They're a bunch of great birds. It's a shame we have to eat them."

22

"Father Juniper Sierra founded all the missions in Southern California. Everyone knows that." Sandra insisted that I call her Sandy. We studied together every lunch period on the kindergarten steps. I was good at geography and English and she was a math whiz. We were friends. I didn't think of her as a girl, she was my friend, just like Floyd or Larry. She even started eating peanut butter sandwiches and my mom would put an extra piece of apple pie in my bag for "Sandra." Miss Banker said we were her best students. I started walking her to the corner instead of cutting across the schoolyard when going home. Third grade was great.

My mom was elected President of the P.T.A. She started to walk to school with me a couple of times a week. I loved it. If it was cold she would put her shawl around me and we would walk shoulder to shoulder down Lake Street. My mom never said a dumb thing. She always spoke to me as if I were her equal, a grown up. She never talked down or belittled anything I did. She made me feel I could do anything.

"Do you like Sandra, Bruzzilah?" She asked one morning. "Sure." I said. "She's very smart. She helps me with math. That's my worst subject. I help her with English and geography. They're easy."

"One thing I want you to remember when you're friendly with a girl. Always treat them the way you would want your sister to be treated." I looked at my mom. I treat her like I treat all my friends. I thought. I could see she wanted to hear me answer.

"Sure, Mom, she's my good friend. We eat lunch together, we study together, and we're good friends. She's the smartest girl in the class just like Gen. but; she's not my sister. So how should I treat her?"

"With respect. Treat all your girl friends with respect, just like you would want Gen's friends to treat her.

Remember that and I'll feel like I raised a good man." We walked into school. Mom went into the principal's office. I went to my class. I couldn't figure out what she was talking about. I would ask Sandy.

"We just haven't any money for Christmas, Dottie, we can hardly pay for paper and pencils. I'd love to have our celebration but we can't afford it." The principal shook his head.

"We could have a very simple party." My mom insisted. "Serve lemonade and cookies. No food. We could give the kids Christmas stockings with candy canes and hard candy. Maybe have the Glee Club sing 'God rest ye, Merry Gentlemen' and 'Silent Night.' We could all sing along. I know several merchants who would give us something we could raffle off. We could print ten-cent tickets, sell dollar books. The whole thing could cost less than two hundred dollars. We have to try to keep something normal for our kids. Everyone in this school could scrape up a dollar."

"Let us discuss it, Dottie. I see your point about normal. You feel out the merchants, I'll talk to the board."

I was leaning on my broom watching yellow paper spill out of the Tele-type in the flying school lobby. I was trying to figure out what my mom's problem was with my friendship for Sandy. She didn't tell me how to get along with Jerry or Floyd. Maybe it was because they were boys and she was a girl.

"You look like you have the weight of the world on your shoulders, Bruz. Can I help you so you can get on with the floor?"

"You have a girl friend, Mr. Fuchs?" I asked. "I study with a girl at school. She's smart. I help her and she helps me and my mom tells me I should treat her like I want my sister to be treated, I should respect her. I don't know what she wants from me." He laughed out loud. I looked at him. Did I say something funny?

"First, Bruz, you've been around here for a long time, how about calling me Fred from now on?"

122

"My dad says I have to call grown ups 'mister.' Kids have to know their place."

"Listen to me, Bruz. Your dad was probably born in the last century. You and I are from a younger generation. We can relax the rules a bit, call me Fred."

"Okay, Fred, what am I supposed to do about Sandy? I don't know what my mom is talking about. Respect? She's my friend!"

"Right, Bruz. I recommend you forget all about what your mom is talking about. Treat her like you treat everyone. Just be her friend. You'll have plenty of time to figure out the boy and girl stuff later on. Your mom told you how she feels, let some time go by, grow up a little and you'll understand where she's coming from. Right now, sweep this joint out so you can get home in time for supper. First things first." He laughed. So I laughed. Fred was funny. I swept out the "joint" got my nickel and went home for supper. I would ask Sandy what she thought.

The sun was high overhead in a cloudless blue sky. Sandy's lunch was spread out on the kindergarten step. She looked through her math book. Miss Banker had warned us about a test after lunch. "I know she's going to test us on long division." Sandy said flipping through pages. "You get along with your mom and dad?" I asked out of the blue. She stopped flipping pages and looked at me.

"My mom and dad are lawyers. They share an office on Brand Boulevard. Dad does real estate, wills, contracts and mom is a divorce lawyer. She has a lot of clients; my dad and mom make good money. This depression hasn't hit our house yet. We're a lot luckier than most." I was impressed; too bad my dad was a roofer instead of a lawyer.

"You go home to an empty house?"

"No. We have a Japanese houseboy. He really is a man. I don't know why they call him a boy. He does everything, cooks, cleans, watches out for me till my folks come home.

He lives in an apartment over the garage. Dad had it built right after you moved away."

"My father's friend, Fred Fultz, lives in a little house right across the street from you."

"I know Fred, he takes care of our front yard and the garden in the back. Nice man."

"My dad's friend is a roofer." I said. She laughed.

"I know, but nobody is fixing roofs and he has to eat so he works as a gardener, Dummy."

"I guess I just don't understand what's going on. Fred's a roofer but he's mowing your lawn, my dad's a roofer but he's raising chickens and rabbits and my friend Larry doesn't have a dad at all. It's confusing isn't it?"

"My dad says it's the times. There aren't many jobs around so people have to do anything they can to keep food on the table. He says it's going to be bad for years. You know your old house is empty? Nobody lives there. I'm lucky my parents keep getting work."

"My mom says I should treat you like I want my sister to be treated. I should respect you. You're my best friend; I like having lunch with you every day. Why do I have to treat you different than my friend Floyd or Larry Doyle?"

"Because I'm a girl, Stupid. Girls and boys are different. Your mother is a girl so she wants you to treat me like your father treats her. I don't care how you treat me because I like you. You're smarter than me and I can learn a lot from you and you're fun to talk to. So let's just stay friends. Let the grown ups worry about us if they want. I'm Sandy and you're Bruz and we're friends. Okay?" She stuck out her hand. I shook it. We both laughed. "Now, what's one hundred divided by four?" She asked.

"Hey Bruz!" Four Doyles were coming down the hill calling me. I was sitting on the front porch waiting for supper. The Doyles stopped by the driveway, "Want to go for a short hike? Larry joined the Toll Glee Club. They practice today. We don't have anything to do."

"I'll ask my dad." I ran to the garage door. My dad was sharpening a knife on a grinder wheel. I waited for him to finish. He wiped the knife off with an oily rag.

"Thanksgiving's right around the corner Bruz, I've got me a turkey to kill."

"The Doyles are going for a short hike. Can I go with them?"

"Be very careful crossing Riverside Drive. Get home by five-thirty, you're mother will have supper at six."

"Thanks dad." I ran down the driveway and we headed down to the river. The ball field was closed. We made our way through the cattails down a long sandy slope into the riverbed; jumped over the river and climbed up to Riverside Drive. We walked along the shoulder to the first bridge. There was a flashing yellow light at the bridge. Not a car in sight. We looked both ways then ran across the wide roadway. We were in a grassy meadow, the hills rising up in front of us. Three paths started up the hill, I knew the third path turned right at the top of the hill and looped around the front edge of the ridge and back to where we started. I led the way up the path.

"We've hiked this path before," Johnny Doyle piped up, "It comes right back here. We won't get lost this time."

"Supper's in an hour, I don't have time to get lost. It's a good trail." I said, reaching the top of the rise and heading right across the hills. Yucca trees were still blooming along the trail, the rocks glistening in the dark earth path.

"What's black and white and read all over?" Jerry yelled out.

"The Los Angeles Examiner!" Albert laughed.

We came down a little hill the path ran along the edge of a cliff that angled maybe forty-five degrees down to the grass meadow along the side of Riverside Drive. "Careful, everyone, you could break your ass falling down there." I yelled, the Doyles laughed.

Suddenly the path ended at a small gulch two or three feet wide. A rainstorm must have washed away the path since the last time we were up here. "Albert! You're the smallest. Can you jump across there?" He came up and looked. "Sure," he said, "I can jump twice that far." I stepped aside. "Okay, go ahead." He took three steps back ran and jumped across the missing path. He walked ahead a few feet and waited. "Come on!" He shouted. Johnny jumped. Jerry jumped. Harry stood appraising the space, took three steps back, a deep breath and jumped. He joined the rest of the Doyles a few feet up the path. I took a couple of steps back and jumped. I landed on the path and the path fell away leaving me standing in space. I grabbed for a Yucca bush on the hillside, missed and tumbled down the hill. I tried to dig my feet in and slow myself but the ground was too hard. I began to roll over. I stuck my palm out and pushed myself upright again. I hit a small rock. My pants tore. I could see blood on my leg. I hit against a small fir tree near the shoulder of Riverside drive. It stopped me cold. My head was spinning. For some reason I jumped to my feet and ran in circles around the little fir tree until I realized what I was doing and stood still. I took inventory. Two hands, ten fingers, one of them bleeding, two arms, I swung them out, two arms working. I shook my buzzing head; a bell rang in my brain. I had taken a good knock on my noggin but all the pieces seemed operable. I got across Riverside, down into the riverbed. I walked along the water running in the middle until I saw the grade that took me home to Hazel Street. I jumped across the river, through the cattails across the Hazel Street Diamond up the hill to my house. I ran down the driveway. "Daddy, Daddy," I screamed, "I fell off the cliff. I think I'm dead." I ran right into him. He caught me by the shoulders.

"Take it easy, old man, you're far from dead. Let me get a look at you. What hurts?"

"Everything," I cried "My knees, my butt, my shoulder." "Stand still and be quiet, let's not get your mother involved." He pulled off my shirt. My shoulder stopped hurting. "Your shirt's full of nettles, your shoulder is going to itch. Let me wash you off." I stood outside my brother's room. Both knees were torn in my jeans. Mom's going to kill me I thought. My left knee was bleeding but I was beginning to feel better. Dad came back with washcloths and towels and Mercurochrome and iodine. He gently cleaned me up. Put medicine on my cuts and bruises, petted and comforted me like I was a baby. I loved it. He handed me one of Jay's tee shirts. "Put this on, go in and tell your mother you fell on a hike get in a hot tub and soak. Don't frighten your mother. Understand?" He gave me a hug and kissed me on my neck. He'd never kissed me there before. I put my hand over the place and went to face my mother.

"Well, young man, you seem to have had an accident. What happened?"

"We were hiking, I fell down a little hill, and dad fixed me up. He says I should take a hot bath." She hugged me, "I see, I'm glad you weren't killed. Go jump in the tub."

I was relaxing in the hot water, lying back soaking my broken body, when the front door bell rang. I heard Harry Doyle scream. "Is Bruzzy all right? He fell off a cliff! He was running around in circles, all bloody, is he dead?"

"Bruz is just fine. He's in the bathtub. He'll see you boys tomorrow. Go on home now you might be late for supper."

I came into the kitchen. Dad and Gen were at the table, mom at the stove. I sat in my place. No one said a word. I hurt all over but I knew it was the kind of hurt that improved day by day and would soon be better. I was happy to be alive.

My mom put plates in front of us; she put a piece of toast on each plate. She brought the pot off the stove and stood by my father.

"This is a special night, Bruz had a humpty-dumpty fall and dad put him all together again." She spooned out a creamy pink liquid on my dad's toast, "and in honor of the fall we're having a new dish for dinner, courtesy of Los Angeles County and a recipe in the Times. Creamed Salmon on toast."

My dad put a fork full in his mouth. "Dottie, my darling, you could make horse manure taste delicious." We all laughed. I liked Creamed Salmon on toast but I loved my family.

(By the way, he didn't say "manure.")

23

I read aloud sitting on my front porch. "White star in the forehead, one white foot on the off side, the little knot just in that place. It must be Black Beauty! Why Beauty! Beauty! Do you know me?" I smiled. Black Beauty was home.

"Who you talking to?" It was Floyd. He snuck up on me.

"I like reading aloud to myself, it's fun. You want to think I'm crazy, go right ahead." He smiled. "I've read 'Black Beauty' a couple of times, one of my favorites. Ann Sewell writes good books."

"There's a couple of more pages. Then I have to write a book report." He nodded, "We do three book reports a term, every six weeks. Been doing it since I entered the academy. Book reports are fun." Floyd was in his world; I'd rather feed the chickens.

"I have to turn the report in next Friday. I'm going to work on it this afternoon." I said.

"Put in a lot of material from the book, teachers like that, they think you really understand if you quote the book a lot." By suppertime I was half through, I used a lot of quotes and told the story of the horse. I thought it was pretty good. Gen came into the kitchen. She read over my shoulder. "Good, Bruz. Quotes always help a story along. Your report is just a little short, write a couple of paragraphs on how much you liked the book and use a couple of quotes, then I think your Miss Banker will give you a good mark."

Gen's comments gave me a lot of confidence so Monday at lunch I showed it to Sandy.

"Too many quotes, Bruz. Not enough of your own thoughts. Miss Banker really wants to know what you're thinking, how the book effected you rather than more of Sewell's words."

Put in a final paragraph about what you really thought of the book, that ought to get you an A." I wrote the paragraph, copied the whole thing over in my best handwriting and turned it in on Wednesday morning, two days before Christmas vacation.

Thursday afternoon I was looking out the window, half a day tomorrow then the Christmas party and vacation time. No school till next year.

"Oh, Bruz!" Miss Banker called from her desk. "Would you stay after class, I'd like to discuss something with you."

"Yes Miss Banker." I said, all the kids looking at me. The bell rang. The kids filed out. Sandy winked at me and patted my arm. Miss Banker walked back to my desk and leaned against the one across the aisle. "Did anyone help you with this book report?" The teacher asked.

"Yes," I answered. "My friend Floyd goes to Glendale Academy, he told me they do three book reports a year and that his teachers like having book quotes in the report. My sister read it and told me to add how much I liked the book and Sandy said you wanted to know how it affected me so I wrote the part about me riding the black horse in the lot behind our house. I know that had nothing to do with Sewell but Sandy's very smart so I did what she thought would give me an A." Miss Banker laughed.

"You are some piece of work, Bruzzy. I didn't know what to do. Your report was so different from everyone else in the class, so mature and well thought out, I thought you had someone else write it but I see you were following instructions from experts, I was going to give you a D but I didn't want to spoil your record. Now I'm giving you an A. Thank you for being so clear in your answers. Run along home now. I'll see you tomorrow." I never told anyone why I was kept after class; it was Miss Banker's and my secret. Sandy saw my A and sang, "I told you so, I told you so!"

Mom's Christmas party began at noon. The big fir tree on the lawn was brightly decorated. Three ply was laid on the lawn for the ceremonies and gift giving. Tables were here and there around the big yard with ample supplies of lemonade and cookies. My mom had gotten a radio, a Mix Master, an ice cream maker and a wood drill with a set of auger bits from her local merchant friends. The kids were out of school. Many parents were already drinking lemonade but the grass wasn't as crowded as it had been for the last two years and no one was buying raffle tickets. The kids had sold a lot before the party but people usually bought most of the tickets on the last day. The depression had really taken over. Nobody was spending a dime. My dad was sitting on the front steps of the school. I ran over. "Want some cookies and lemonade, dad? I'll go get it."

"No thanks Bruz, come sit here next to me, I want to have a talk with you." I sat next to him and looked at his face. He looked worried, the laugh lines around his eyes looked like a maze of wrinkles. His bright eyes dull and damp. I had never seen him like this. He put his hand on my shoulder.

"I'm going to have to go away sometime this year. Your big brother is basically out of the house so that means you're going to be the man. I want you to promise me you'll help your mom as much as you can. Go to the market for her; make your own schedule for mowing the lawn and clipping the hedge. Don't let the house run down. If something needs to be fixed go to your Uncle Fred and ask him. Don't do anything that might upset your mom, study, get good marks and find a little job somewhere to make a little money. Newspapers or magazines, something you can have fun doing. And don't forget about me, remember we were buddies, remember that your mother and I love you and want the best for you. Help Gen if she needs it, don't fight with your sister and watch out for her when she starts meeting boys. That's a big responsibility for such a little boy but I know you can do it. You're smart and capable. You'll be a big success at anything you try. Now go get us some of that lemonade and cookies and we'll forget all about what we talked about until I leave, okay big boy?

He hugged me to him and kissed my neck again. I didn't know whether to laugh or cry. I kissed his cheek, his rough beard scratching my face. My dad was going away but I wasn't going to cry.

We ate our cookies and lemonade and watched all the people wandering around. Kids trying to pedal their raffle books while most people just shook their heads. Not a very merry Christmas. The placed perked up when the Glee Club sang the carols. Everybody sang along. My mom arrived in her Santa Claus get-up, the kids lined up and got their Christmas stocking, they were all very happy. Each one held on to the fancy stocking filled with all kinds of candy, a little doll in the girls' stocking, a jackknife in the boys. My brother had conned JJ Newberry into supplying the stockings, candy and toys at cost. Good Christmas memories for the kids even if the grown ups were nearly broke. Nearly three years of depression. How much longer, I wondered.

"We lost a little money Dottie, but the kids were very happy. It was a good idea, I hope you didn't work too hard." The principal thanked my mom. She smiled. Her Santa Claus career was at an end. We walked home, my dad limping along, me in the middle holding my mom and dad's hand. We waited for the light to change at the corner of Lake and Sonora, my dad leaned over and kissed my mom. She laughed. "I needed some strength to make it home, Dottie. That kiss is all I need."

"You devil!" Mom said and we laughed all the way up Hazel Street.

The little tree was on top of the radio. The base wrapped in fake green grass, our stockings taped to the front of the cabinet. Not a very good replacement for the big fireplace at Lake Street. But it was Christmas and everyone was supposed to be merry. We each got a wrapped present. Genevieve got the lovely new dress she would need for her solo with the Toll Glee Club. I got two new shirts, both gaucho cut, both plaids. I was very happy.

We had ham and eggs for breakfast; our twenty hens still delivering every morning. The Plymouth Rocks outlaying the Leghorns. The turkey was in the oven. Heavenly smells filled the small house.

A bowl of mixed nuts and mom's nutcracker sat on the radio, guarding the little tree. My dad sat in his big chair reading the paper. It was Christmas. It smelled like Christmas. It looked like Christmas but for some reason it wasn't the joyous day we had enjoyed on past Christmases. Dinner saved the day. The big turkey in the middle of the table, the baked sweet potatoes on a platter, a bowl of shimmering cranberry sauce and mom's ubiquitous carrots and peas. My dad took the long carving knife and prepared to carve the bird.

"I think we aught to give thanks for old tom here. He's been a good gobbler in the chicken coop since we moved in and here he is, the star at Christmas dinner. Bruz you get the drumstick because that was the leg he always kicked you with. Now there are only chickens in the coop."

We all enjoyed eating tom. He was tender and sweet and I ate all the meat off his drumstick. We had pumpkin pie and apple cider for desert. It was the last Christmas dinner our little family would enjoy together.

I always had to go back to school on my birthday. January second, 1932 was no different. Third grade, second semester started off as the first semester had ended. I shared a turkey sandwich with Sandy on the kindergarten steps. Miss Banker selected "The Call of the Wild" for my next book report. Sandy got Jane Austen's "Pride and Prejudice." It would be an interesting second semester.

My mom made an angel food cake for my birthday. She put white icing with blue letters and roses on the top. "Happy 7th Birthday to Bruzzy" it read with eight blue candles all around. I took a deep breath and blew them out. The family applauded.

"Very good, Bruz." Gen said. "Now you'll get your wish." I hoped so. I wished our family could stay the same forever, that dad would skip his trip and stay home with us. Mom gave me a piece of cake and a box wrapped in Christmas paper. I always got cheated, my birthday being so close to Christmas. My sister was born in the middle of June, far away from Christmas. She always got more presents than I did. I took the present just the same. It was a new pair of Keds. Black, high top Keds. Terrific.

133

And so I was an old man of seven, my tummy was full, I had new shirts, new shoes, I looked forward to 1932 with confidence.

24

Miss Banker was calling the roll, each student saying "here" when they heard their name. The door near the teacher's desk swung open. A tall skinny kid came into the room. He stopped just inside the door. He was a study in black and white, his white hair and white face above his black shirt, pants and shoes looked like a painting.

"How can I help you, young man?" The teacher asked in her pleasant voice.

"I'm new," Black and White answered. "The principal told me to report to Miss Banker's class. Am I in the right place?" His voice wavered. He was a little frightened.

"That's Miss Banker and this is her class, you're in the right place." I spoke up out of turn. Miss Banker gave me a dirty look.

"Yes, you are in the right place. Are you Bobby Hessong? They said you'd be here at ten, you're very early." Miss Banker gave him her dazzling smile.

"My step dad drove me over, he wasn't supposed to be home. We just moved into the neighborhood. I'm early, I hope I can stay." Miss Banker laughed.

"You go sit next to your new friend with his big mouth. That's Bruz Tyrrell; I'll do your paperwork at lunchtime. He shook his head and came to the desk next to me at the back of the room. I had a new friend. All the kids buzzed and watched him move across the room. "Quiet down, Boys and Girls. Take your English book and read from page 137 to 145. Then we'll discuss what you've read. Bobby sit with Bruz and read with him. I'll have your books together after lunch."

I slid over, my skinny new friend sat next to me. I pointed to the top of the page he nodded. We read the assignment together.

It was lunchtime before all the class had finished. We met Sandy by the kindergarten steps. "This is Bobby, Sandy."

"I know, I was in class when he stumbled in. Hi Bobby, you joining us for lunch?"

"I guess." He stammered. "I don't have any lunch, my mom gave me a quarter for the cafeteria." He looked scared again. I calmed him down. "Our cafeteria only sells fruit, milk and soft drinks. You can share my lunch, my mom always gives me too much anyway."

Bobby Hessong smiled. We sat on the steps. I gave him one of the peanut butter and jelly sandwiches my mom put in the sack. He looked at the sandwich as if he'd never seen food before. "Go ahead, eat it, Bobby I have another one right here." Sandy laughed. "Where'd you come from, Bob?" She asked.

"We lived in Pasadena. My dad died last year and my mom married another guy. He bought a farm on Western and we moved in last week. My brother is twelve; he's going to Toll, and my step dad brought me here. We aren't very organized yet."

"I know that place." Sandy said. "Big white clapboard house. I loved the rocking chairs on the front porch. You guys grow lettuce and tomatoes. I saw a lot of Japanese working the field. Must be fun to live on a farm."

"I've only been there a week. We miss Pasadena. Lived there all our lives. I don't really know my step dad. He's only been around a couple of months and he never had any kids of his own. He's a cowboy from Texas, but he loves California. He thinks our farm's going to make a lot of money. But mom likes him, she didn't like living alone."

I could see Bobby was going to need a friend and made up my mind I would be the guy. I walked him home after school. Sandy was right. It was a big white house. His mother was rocking on the front porch, her skirt way up showing her bare legs.

She pulled it down quickly when she saw Bobby and me coming up the drive. The place was huge. I was flabbergasted. Bobby ran across the porch and kissed his mother hello, she didn't seem too happy about it.

"How'd you like your new school, Bobby?" She asked.

"Okay." Bobby answered, "This is Bruz Tyrrell, he's my new friend. He gave me a sandwich for lunch and we shared the best apple pie I've ever eaten. His mom is a swell cook. He lives on Hazel Street. His friend Sandy, she's a girl, had lunch with us too. They study together. They're going to be my friends."

"That's nice, Honey. Why don't you show your friend the farm. I'm sure he has to get home. His mother will be worried."

"Come on, Bruz, this really is a keen place to live." He walked. I followed. I noticed, out of the corner of my eye, that she pulled her skirt up as we left. She must like fresh air. The property went all the way up the hill to the railroad. A big siding was right on their property. The land was empty across the tracks. A huge lot that ended at San Fernando Road. Then he showed me my favorite feature of the Nichol's household. Nichols was Bobby's mom's new name. Garth Nichols was his stepfather. I stood in the middle of a long driveway and looked up at the tall water tower. A huge water tank sat on the top, a room below the tank with a balcony around the whole structure. Flight after flight of stairs led to the ground. I wanted to run right up those stairs and see what was in that secret room. Imagine, a water tower right in your back yard. Bobby Hessong was a lucky kid.

I gazed at the tower and dreamed of sleeping in that little room beneath the water tank. Some one yelling at Bobby brought me back to the present. A big guy, dressed in black, was cutting diagonally across the Nichol's estate. "That's Frank. He's my big brother. He goes to Toll, gets home later than me." I watched him come. He didn't go greet his mom, just came straight to his brother.

"Man, I don't like Toll half as much as Pasadena. The teachers aren't friendly; the other kids don't seem to care for me. I wish we could move back home."

"This is home now, Frank. Get used to it. We have a new family and a new home. Mom is happy so we should try and be happy." Bobby was smarter than his big brother.

"Hi, Frank. My name's Bruz, I'm Bobby's new friend from Benjamin Franklin. You sing at all?" He looked at me like I was crazy, but he answered. "I was an alto in the Pasadena glee club. I liked that a lot."

"Toll's got a great glee club. Audition for it. My sister is soprano soloist, she'll help you make friends. Then you can be happy here." He looked at me. He shook his head up and down. "I'm going to try that, kid, what's your sister's name?"

"Gen. Really Genevieve. Tyrrell. You'll meet her; I'm going to tell her to watch out for you 'cause you're my new friend's brother. I got to go now in case my mom's home. I'll tell her I'm coming here tomorrow so you can really show me around, okay?"

"Sure." Bobby said. "If I bring lunch can I eat with you and Sandy tomorrow, Bruz?"

"Yeah, that'd be great. You good at anything like geography or English, we kind of make lunchtime a study period. You up for that?"

"Sure, you guys are fun. See you tomorrow." Frank waved as I angled across the big lot heading for Flower Street and my route home. There was no traffic light at Sonora and Flower. I had to wait for traffic to slow down so I could get across the street. I walked in the front door and yelled "hello!" My mom came out of the kitchen. "You're late, Sweetheart, did you have to stay after school?"

"Sorry, mom, I met a new boy today, he was kind of scared since he just moved in.

Lives in that farm on Western, I went home with him so I'm late. Sorry."

"Your dad was looking for you. He has some problem with his pigeons. Go give him a hand, okay, Honey?" I went straight through the house out the back door across the yard to the pigeon coop behind Jay's room. My dad was standing there looking at his birds.

"Hey, Bruz. You're late. I need some help. We have to tag the birds. They're going to compete in a meet tomorrow, the tags tell who they belong to if they get lost. I need you to hold them so I can get this tag on their legs. Willing?"

He had little red "U"s that held a flat piece of Bakelite on the pigeon's leg. Each tag was printed in black ink. WT1, WT2 meaning the bird was William Tyrrell's, 1 was his best bird and so on. We tagged thirty-six birds. We were late for dinner.

We were having creamed salmon on toast. We had it quite often since the big bags appeared on the front porch. We had all decided we liked it, so Mom wouldn't feel bad serving it. Even my dad ate it without comment. We were enjoying our main course when my father remembered tomorrow's competition. "Bruz," he said. "Please come right home from school tomorrow, I have to take the pigeons to Santa Monica at noon, leave them and drive home. They'll be released at 2:30. You can be home by three in case I have a break down or a flat tire. You can time the bird's return. We have to time the first three birds and the last three birds. If we win we get a year's supply of food. We could really use that. So come straight home, take the clock off our bedside table and keep track of the time if I'm not here. Understand?" I nodded. I hoped he would get home. But I nodded.

A disappointed Bobby Hessong sat on the kindergarten steps, "I guess your father's pigeon race is more important than meeting the Sapporros at the farm. We can do that tomorrow. The birds are flying today."

"Sorry, Bobby. I have to help my dad. He's not well. My mom says I have to give him a hand."

"So let's work on our math and have lunch, fellows. No sense wasting time." Sandy was always right.

I got home at five minutes to three. Mom wasn't home. I grabbed the clock off their nightstand. I didn't have to knock to enter the private room. I put the clock, a pencil and a notebook from school on an empty tar barrel and sat down on the ground. It was quiet, a cluck, cluck from the chicken coop every once in a while and a swish of wind through the walnut trees. Then dad's car was in the driveway, the motor stopped, the door slammed and he limped around Jay's house.

"Hi, Bruz. I got caught in traffic, I had to get gas but seems I've beaten our birds home. They should be here any minute if we have any chance of winning this thing." I didn't answer. I watched the bright blue sky. Nothing. Dad put his arms behind his back, leaning so he had a clear view above. Cluck, cluck, some hen complained squeezing out an egg.

I saw a pigeon; it wasn't high in the sky it was flying low through the walnut grove. It came right over the fence and landed atop the pigeon cage. My dad grabbed the bird, "3:07:27," he said. I opened the notebook and scratched 3:07:27.

"Bird, number three, Bruz. Put that in the book." Dad said, putting Mister three into the cage as two pigeons came out of the sun. "Dad!" I yelled, "Two more up there."

They dived down and sat on my dad's arm. "3:08:17. Bruz, a tie. We have to wait for the last three, I don't know how they score but we have to follow the rules. Bird 27 and Bird one tied at 3:08:17. Mark that in your book. And now we wait."

Actually birds kept arriving landing on my father's shoulders, his hands and arms. He took them in his hand gave them a kiss on the beak and put them in the pen. In five minutes thirty-four birds were home.

Thirty-five came over the fence. "3:14:12 Bruz, Bird 12." Then one right behind the other. The last two birds landed on the fence. "3:14:22 and 3:14:27 close enough for Irishmen. Bird 35 and Bird 7 last. Mark that down. I have to call in and report all birds home and how they finished. Saturday they will tell us how we placed." He limped off toward the phone in the kitchen. I sat down on the tar barrel. Pooped. I didn't do a thing but I was pooped. I went to collect the eggs to keep myself awake. I crossed my fingers. I wanted my dad to win.

Bobby's mother was sitting on her rocking chair as we approached the big white house. I wondered if she sat there all day, I thought all moms were always busy like mine. Mrs. Nichols was different. Her skirt was up around her thighs, she just left it there, I guess I was part of the family now. "I'm going to take Bruz to meet the Sapporros. Can we go up in the water tower?"

"Be careful of the stairs. If you fall down you'll kill yourselves. Tell Mrs. Sapporro I could use some tomatoes for supper."

"Okay, Mom, Come on, Bruz." We walked around the back of the house past the water tower and followed a path outlined with yellow bricks. We passed two small houses painted white with blue shutters. They looked like doll houses. Big people couldn't live there. As we passed the houses you could see garden after green garden, big square gardens with pathways between them, I stopped and stared at the sight, there must have been thirty gardens, three wide and ten deep, probably the size of two football fields, several men and women hoeing, raking, watering. A small man pushed a wheelbarrow piled high with heads of lettuce. Here was a country truck farm not ten blocks from where I went to school. Amazing. Bobby enjoyed watching my reaction to this painting come to life. He was very proud of this beautifully laid out farm his stepfather owned. A tiny Japanese lady, her hair tied up in a yellow bandana waved at us. We met her in the path between two gardens. "Hello, Bobby. This your new friend from school?" I looked at the little lady; she spoke English with no accent. Sounded just like my mother.

"This is Bruz Tyrrell, Mrs. Sapporro, he wanted to see your farm. I told him it was beautiful." She smiled. I didn't know what to say. Mrs. Sapporro spoke. "Nice to meet you, Bruz. I saw your eyes open when you heard me speak. I'm Japanese but I was born in that little blue house. I went to Benjamin Franklin, just like you kids, then to Toll and I graduated from Hoover. My parents wanted me to have a good education so I could run the farm. They call me Nisei. That means I was born in the United States. I learned the Japanese farming methods from my mom and dad and even though they're gone, we keep operating the way they taught us." I was at a loss for words. She was treating us as if we were her equals, not two kids in the third grade. I stammered, "Well you sure do a good job. This place is like a picture of what farms should look like." She laughed.

"Come over to the wheelbarrow, Bruz, I'll give you a couple of heads of lettuce. Your mom can make a salad for supper."

I carried the sack of lettuce and followed Bobby back to the water tower. He stood on the first step. "Leave the lettuce here. It's a hard climb." I put the bag behind the steps and followed Bobby up. One flight, two flights, three flights. I looked down. We were way up in the air and only halfway to the balcony. Maybe this wasn't such a hot idea.

"Pay attention, Bruz," Bobby cautioned, "If you slip, you'll break your ass." I held the railing and paid attention. Up, up we climbed and then we were on the balcony. Safe. We walked all around the water tower, each view spectacular. From the top of the stairs you saw straight across the property, across San Fernando Road, the beautiful homes of the well-to-do people in the hills above town and into the mountains that glowed purple in the crisp clear afternoon. To the north was the geometrical loveliness of Mrs. Sapporro's farm, the houses that lined the streets that fed right into downtown Burbank. You could even make out no-man's land, the little bridge that separated Glendale and Burbank that neither city claimed. The space flourished in late June as the sales center of illegal fireworks that destroyed the peace on the Fourth of July. "Hey, Bobby! You think your mom would let us sleep up here sometime. Wouldn't it be great to be up here after dark? The views. The stars. Ask her sometime. Okay?"

142

"I'll ask, but don't get your hopes up. She's very nervous about this place. First time she let me up here without Frank. Let's go down now, I'm not too keen about heights."

My mom loved Mrs. Sapporro's present. We were having lamb stew and a big lettuce salad for supper. My dad was very happy, chewing on a piece of meat for a change. "Well, Bruz" my sister broke the silence, "this lettuce is the best I've ever eaten. I'm glad you met the Hessongs. By the way, I met Frank in Glee Club this afternoon; he's a very good singer. Mrs. Levine didn't even think about it, she put him right in the group. We had a long chat. He's a very nice boy."

"Mom, could I sleep over at Bobby's, up in the water tower room, if his mother will let us?"

"Ask me when she invites you, I'll have an answer for you then." My dad laughed.

"Meanwhile, Dottie, can I have some more stew. I fell in love with your stew before I fell for you."

"Oh, Bill. You devil!" She laughed and filled his plate. Gen looked at me and smiled. I nodded my head. Life was great when your folks were in love.

25

Memorial Day, May 31, 1932. The unofficial beginning of summer was the official opening day of the water hole. Jerry Doyle rolled into the sewer. Harry Doyle squeezed through. Albert had grown a foot but easily entered the underground pathway to fun. Larry got down on the street and slid toward the sewer. He didn't fit. He was too big to get into the sewer; too big for the water hole. He stood up, looked at his brothers and shook his head. "Sorry guys, I'm in charge, if I can't go, the Doyles can't go."

I got down on the street rolled into the sewer. I didn't fit. I was too fat to get into the sewer. Mom's cooking and my eating had cancelled a lot of summertime fun. I sat on the street and listened to the Doyles laugh.

"Today's Memorial Day, Griffith Park pool opens today." I said.

"Yeah." Larry answered. "Costs a dime, I think Albert and Jerry can get in free, but the rest of us need a dime. I don't think my mom has thirty cents."

"We could walk in the river, probably a mile to where the zoo road goes up to the park. We'd only have to climb out and get across Riverside. Let's ask if we can get the money."

"We'll need swimming trunks, we can't go bare ass in Griffith Park Pool." Jerry said and we all laughed. We walked home, the Doyles stopping to ask their mother, I went down the hill. My father was in the garage. The doors hung open; he was working at the bench. "Hey dad, we want to go to the Griffith Park Pool it costs a dime, could I take two nickels out of the Mason jar?"

He reached into his pocket. He found two dimes. "Here, swim and buy yourself some candy. Mom wouldn't like it if you went into the savings." He smiled. I grabbed the dimes. He mussed my hair. I ran and got into my trunks, put the two dimes in the pocket and sat down on the curb waiting for the Doyle tribe.

They came slouching along, heads down looking at the ground, not a happy sight. "My Mom didn't have thirty cents. She had two dimes. Not enough. Want to play ball?"

"My dad gave me two dimes, that's enough for all of us. Get your trunks and let's get going before the sun goes down."

We crossed the Hazel Street Diamond. Four cops were raking the field. The new season would begin on Saturday. We went through the cattails and down the long grade into the riverbed. We turned left and headed for the pool. It was an easier walk than the sewer pipe but not as adventurous. The city had built flood control walls where the river bent. Some were short, some long with sandy grades filing the spaces between the new walls. We were halfway to the pool when the river began a long bend to the left. A huge control wall was built all along the side facing the pool. "I hope that wall ends before we get to the pool. No way we can get over that." I said.

"Let's wait and see. We have about half a mile to go." Larry said. The sand was warm on the soles of our bare feet; there was only a tiny trickle of water in the middle of the river. Building floodwalls in this dry river was really dumb. We could see the end of the wall right where we wanted to get out of the riverbed. We climbed up the sandy hill to Riverside Drive. The pool was on the point of land between Riverside and the zoo entrance. There were very few cars. We were careful, everybody held hands and we ran across the Drive. The pool cashier let the young boys in free. We paid our four dimes and the cashier stamped our hands. My hand had a red May 31 in the middle of my palm. We were all in our trunks so we threw our shirts on a chair and went right into the pool. It was wonderful! The sun beat down. It was very hot for the last day of May. The hot concrete walks burned the bottoms of our feet. After all, this was the first day we all went barefoot, our feet weren't leather yet. It was swell as long as we stayed in the pool.

I thought it was about four in the afternoon. I looked up at the beacon on a hill in Griffith Park. It went on at five o'clock. My mom had made me promise that when that light went on, wherever I was, I had to go home. The light blinked on!

"Hey, Larry, I've got to go. You can stay if you want but my Mom wants me home now."

"You know the way, Bruz. We don't have to leave for another half hour, okay?"

"Yeah. See you!" I grabbed my shirt and walked out of the pool, across the grass to Riverside and watched for my chance to cross. The street was burning hot, my feet screamed as I ran across, I ran down the hill into the river, the sand was burning, I jumped along. I walked in the trickle of water, my feet still too hot. I couldn't get out of the river cause I wouldn't know where I was or how to find home so I gritted my teeth and kept walking. It hurt. I finally decided to get out of the river and find my way home. I looked for a way out but there was a flood wall that I didn't noticed coming to the pool. I was trapped in the riverbed. The hot sun fired the sand that burned my new bare feet. I gritted my teeth harder and trotted toward home. I saw a puddle of standing water, I ran to it and stood letting my poor feet cool off. I didn't want to go back on the hot sand but I had to mind my mother and get myself home. I looked back over my shoulder; the Griffith Park beacon was flashing its light beam. I was in a lot of trouble. I jumped along, covering three or four feet at a time keeping my feet on the sand for as little time as I could to get myself airborne again. I was never religious, but my burning feet made me ask God to give me a hand. I promised to be good if he helped me out of this riverbed. I saw the end of the wall and ran up the long hill out of the river. I ran right into a walnut grove. Our walnut grove! I was beyond the Grand Central runways, the ground was shaded and cool. I headed into the grove, knowing I would wind up on Hazel Street right by my house. I dodged green nuts lying all along my route. When I stepped on one it cracked and gave my sore foot a pinch. Not as bad as the burning sand. I passed the bon fire ashes where Roy Rogers sang last summer. I was almost home. I passed Floyd's house, his dad working in the garage. I stood at the edge of Hazel Street wondering how hot that tar was going to be, my cool front lawn just across the street. I stepped into the street. It wasn't hot; maybe there was a god after all. Our front lawn was divine; I stood still for a couple of minutes enjoying the cool grass. I went into our house and stood on the living room carpet. Heaven.

"Is that you, Bruzalah?" My mother called from the kitchen, "Did you enjoy your swim, Sweetheart? Get washed up, supper's almost on the table."

Every day was hot. The sun, hanging large in the constant blue sky, burned down on Southern California. Ninety degrees. Ninety-five degrees. Good thing we didn't have humidity. We could live with the dry heat. Sandy and I sat on the warm kindergarten steps. She was telling me about Mr. Darcy in the book she was reading. I wasn't much into love stuff. Bobby came along so we worked on sentence structure out of his English book. Two weeks left of school, my book revue was finished, ready to be handed in. I loved Jack London even though I never noticed his sentence structure. Miss Banker came along. She said we should get out of the sun. Go to the auditorium, it was cool in there. The place was crowded. We found three seats and went back to work. Bobby kept starring at Sandy. I didn't like that. But Sandy paid him no attention.

"Two's company, three's a crowd." My mother often said. I was beginning to believe her. There were only two more weeks of school.

Today the temperature reached a hundred and three degrees. It was hot. Something was going on with this strange weather. I walked home. The lawn needed mowing. I'd do it Saturday after the ball game. My dad was in the garage. I walked in. He had all his roofing tools out on the workbench; he wrapped each one in an old towel and put it in a gunnysack.

"Got a job, Dad?" I asked.

"Fred's going to buy them. I'm never going to roof again with this game leg. Might as well let some one have the use of them, unless you're going to be a roofer?" He smiled.

"Me?" I said, "I'm going to catch for the New York Yankees. I'm pretty good with your old catcher's mitt, Dad."

"Well, Bruz, consider that glove yours. My present. If you want to play for the Yankees you're going to have to work harder at baseball than anything else. Baseball with the Yankees isn't a game, Son, it's a religion. You want to be Bill Dickey you have to make baseball your life, not just spring and summer but everyday. I don't think you want to work that hard, but it's up to you. You can hit, you can catch. All you have to do is grow up very lucky, cause a lot of guys can hit and catch and only three hundred guys get the chance to play in the majors. Now if you think you're one of the 300 best ballplayers in America than you work for it. If you don't think you're that good think about being a roofer." He messed my hair and laughed out loud. "Got to do something about that hair." I held his hand as we walked into the house for supper. Mom was serving rabbit stew.

We sat ourselves down at the table. The clock on the shelf said five to six. The clock started to dance around the shelf. It fell off on the floor. The house was shaking.

"Everybody out in the yard quick!" My dad said, sliding out of his seat. Walnuts falling on the roof sounded like a machine gun shooting. We got outside. Everything was shaking. The ground was rippling. Nothing stood still. A loud roar filled the air. EARTHQUAKE!

The garage door swung open. It ripped right off its hinges. The rooster was crowing, the chickens jumping against the wire fence trying to get away from the shaking earth.

"Bruz, let the pigeons out!" My dad yelled. The house rumbled, a window in the dining nook crashed and fell out on the back lawn. I pulled opened the pigeon pen. They burst into the air, flying straight up into the sky.

We stood in the middle of the back yard, green walnuts bouncing off us. The walnut tree swung back and forth as if it was in a strong windstorm. There wasn't any wind, only the strange roaring sound. The big walnut tree in the next backyard made a loud cracking noise falling across our hedge into our driveway. A branch knocked the tin drain off our roof. It lay under the tree in our driveway.

148

I watched the gate to the chicken coop shake back and forth. A chicken, its foot caught in the wire clucked wildly as it was shaken by the quake.

A crack appeared in the driveway where the tree had fallen. The crack came right across the back yard, my father stepping away as the earth gaped open, green walnuts falling into the long hole in the ground. And then it was over.

Quiet. I ran over and freed the chicken. It ran around in circles and flopped over. I went to my dad. The crack in the ground had closed. We stood in the backyard in a daze.

"Can we have our dinner now, Bill?" my mother asked.

"There might be an aftershock, that was a pretty good quake, I think we should just stay here for a while." Before his sentence was through the roar began again. The back screen door ripped right off of the house, the window in Jay's room shattered. Nuts kept falling. Gen's bedroom window cracked but stayed in the frame. The earth quivered and rippled. Slowly it quieted down. A little noise, a couple of shakes. A nut fell, but it was over.

Quiet. I had lived through my first earthquake. We were lucky our house was barely scratched.

My dad limped for his rabbits, I ran along by his side. The big white house on Sonora was on fire, smoke pouring out of its roof, sirens coming in the distance. Three of dad's rabbits lay stiff in death on the floor of their hutch. Rabbits, scared to death. Uneatable.

I gave the nervous chickens some water and threw some fresh corn on the ground. They forgot the quake and scratched in the earth. Things had fallen inside the house. Mom straightened everything out, as best she could. Uncle Fred would fix the windows and doors. We were lucky our house was livable. Seven o'clock the Tyrrell family was eating delicious rabbit stew only disturbed by the breezes coming through the broken windows. It was just getting dark when we heard a big disturbance in the back yard.

Our pigeons had returned. They settled into their nests, I hadn't closed the door of the cage. The Pigeons would never leave as long as Bill Tyrrell was alive.

The school was a mess. Walls were down. The glass in the principal's office all destroyed. Something had shorted the electricity. There wasn't any light. They closed the school for a week. We came back, finished the last week. The school was closed for repairs. The schoolyard closed. School was over, no happy ending for the third grade. Our report cards would be in the mail.

"Don't let the door hit you in the ass!" The old janitor made a joke as he locked the big front doors.

My dad couldn't seem to get himself back together after the quake. His leg pained him. He saw double images once in a while. He had a temperature. Aspirin made it go away. It would return. Aspirin made it go away again. He felt lousy.

Genevieve's twelfth birthday was June twenty-second. Mom made a chocolate cake with pink icing. She decorated it with red roses and put long green leaves down the side of the cake. It was a masterpiece. Mom made Gen's favorite dinner. Pot roast with mashed potatoes and peas. Pot roast was an expensive cut of meat in the depths of the depression but my mom was friends with the Grand Central butcher and he gave her a special birthday price. My mother's pot roast had thick brown gravy that made mashed potatoes so delicious you could never get enough.

Gen got three presents, not one of them wrapped in Christmas paper. June was a much better birthday month than January. My dad put on a happy face for his only daughter but we all knew he was hurting. He picked at his food. Gen blew out the thirteen candles. Dad clapped his hands twice and headed for his chair. In five minutes, with his bad leg on the ottoman he made little snoring sounds. He was fast asleep. My dad never slept in his chair. Something was definitely wrong with our father. I was scared. My mom called the doctor. She would take him to the doctor tomorrow.

She gently shook her husband. "Wake up, sweetheart. You have a nice bed to sleep in. Come, darling, let me help you."

He didn't say anything. He got his bad leg off the ottoman and my little mother pulled her sleepy husband upright. He put his hand on her shoulder and they moved off together into their inner sanctum. I looked at Genevieve. Genevieve looked at me. We sadly shook our heads, worried about the changes threatening our happy home.

26

Gen and I watched dad get himself into the car. My mother drove. She rolled her window down, "We should be home this afternoon, don't worry if we're a little late."

"Okay, Mom, we'll be fine." My sister answered. The car backed down the drive into the street. We followed along. We watched it go up the hill and turn left on Flower Street. We didn't have the slightest idea our father would never come home.

Genevieve was sitting on the front steps reading, Floyd was teaching me how to play rummy on his front porch when the Studebaker came down the hill. We could see mom was alone. I ran across the street as she pulled into the driveway. We waited for our mom to get out of the car. She walked over to us, "Come in the kitchen. I'll tell you what happened while I get supper on the table." She walked past us up the front steps and into the house. We followed her to the kitchen. She opened the fridge, took out the pot roast pan put it on the stove and lit a small flame. "We'll eat in half an hour," she said, "Sit in the nook. I'll tell you about your father." Gen sat in dad's seat; I sat in mom's. Mom stood in the middle of the kitchen.

"Your father has a bad infection. He's had an infection in his leg for years but now it's gotten much worse. They think there's a sack of puss against the bone. First they're going to clean up the whole wound. There isn't any new medicine that will help him, they only hope if they can clean the wound it will heal itself. They didn't give me much hope. He's in the hospital. The doctors will start on him tomorrow. We'll just have to wait and see." She uncovered the pot roast, took a wooden spoon and pushed things around, raised the flame and recovered the pot.

"Is he going to die?" I asked, my tummy trembling.

"Everybody dies, son." She said. "Your father's not in the best of shape. He's been fighting this for nearly three years. My mother used to say 'the old must die, the young can die.'"

Your dad isn't old but he's not young either. We can only hope that he's strong enough to fight off this infection. When he does, he'll come home to us. So it's up to us to keep happy, keep the house in good shape, feed his pigeons and the chickens and the rabbits so he has a happy home to come back to. And that's what we'll do. You both agree?"

We both shook our heads. She kissed Gen on the cheek, mussed my hair and kissed me. "Your father said we have to do something about your hair. Your too old for long curls. So, young man, this weekend we're going to play barber shop. And you're the only customer." She laughed. I giggled and Gen smiled. My mom was a trooper, she wouldn't let our happy home disappear without a fight. She was a winner.

Everyday mom would visit dad. Everyday she gave us a report. "Better." Smiles all around. "Not good." Head shakes. Frowns.

Sunday afternoon she put newspapers down on the back lawn. She brought the chair from her dressing table and put it in the middle of the papers. She sat me in the chair, wrapped me in a sheet, stood back and stared at my head. Gen sat on the back steps waiting for the show to begin. I saw her best seamstress scissors in her hand. She put an open brown paper bag on the newspapers. She lifted a curl from the top of my head measured about an inch of straight hair snipped off the curl and dropped it into the brown bag. Lift. Snip. Drop. Suddenly my curls were all in the bag my head a mass of straight shaggy hair. I wasn't me anymore. I didn't say a word. Sat straight and quiet.

She ran dad's comb through the straight hair over and over, combing it this way and that way. Finally she spoke. "Walk over to the faucet behind Jay's room, please." I walked. I got to the faucet. "Biddie" my pet hen started to cluck. She recognized me with all my hair gone. All was not lost. A bottle of mom's shampoo was on the ground next to the faucet. "Bend over," she said, turning on the water. "Put your head in the water." It was cold. I didn't say a word. She poured shampoo on my head and used her hands to make my head full of little bubbles. She massaged my scalp and pushed my head back in the water till all the soap was gone.

"Stand up." I stood up. She took a soft towel and rubbed my head till it was dry. She took the towel away and my sister clapped her hands.

"Bravo, Mom, you've made a man of him." They both laughed. "Go look at yourself in the bathroom mirror. See what you think." I ran off. They were still laughing. I turned the light on in the bathroom; I looked at the face in the mirror. I didn't know who he was, but his hair looked terrific. Tight little blonde curls all over his head, like a blonde cap. I loved it. I'd never change it for the world. "Well?" My mother said from the door.

"I love it! I love it. I'll never change it, thank you Mom, you're the best."

"Ladies and Gentlemen, welcome to the final night of the Democratic National Convention here in the great city of Chicago."

Mom, Gen and I sat in our living room listening to history being made. The Democrats had nominated Franklin Delano Roosevelt, the Governor of New York to be the next president of the United States. The Texan, John Nance Garner, Speaker of the House would be the vice president. My dad was rooting for this ticket. He thought they would end the depression. Too bad he wasn't here to listen.

The summer melted away. Mom visited dad every day. Everyday we got a report. FDR campaigned every day, every day the radio would blare the news. More and more it looked like a landslide for Roosevelt. "You think they'll change the name of Hoover High?" I asked my sister. She laughed. Jay's birthday was the twenty-ninth of August. He would be old enough to vote for FDR if he was a Democrat. We didn't pay much attention to politics in our house in the thirties. But Jay was too busy working, we never saw him, he was all over LA county helping keep Newberry's in business.

Mom reported on her day's visit with our father. "The doctors at County can't do anything more for your father, they are transferring him to a nursing home near here on San Fernando Road. I'm afraid we have to prepare ourselves for bad news.

I've been offered a job at Grand Central Market. Saleslady and cashier in the variety store. I'm going to work. I need something to take my mind off your dad. I can visit him on my lunch break, it's just a few blocks from the market." I didn't know what to say. Was my mother saying my dad was dying? She's going to work and dad is dying? I didn't understand. I knew that next week I started fourth grade. That I was getting through a lousy summer. It would be fun to be back with Sandy and Bobby Hessong. I hoped they would like my new hair. All the kids on the block did. Fred Fuchs thought it was "classy" and would be comfortable in a pilots' helmet. I wondered how mom's job would affect life on Hazel Street. I would find out very soon.

Mom went right to work at Grand Central. I walked up Sonora to San Fernando Road and went in the back door of the big building. The Variety Store was right in the center of the market. I could see my mom talking to a customer. She looked great in the blue and white uniform, her red hair piled high atop her head. She rang up a sale and another customer took her away. She worked constantly. I didn't get a chance to even tell her I was there. I went home. I crossed Sonora at the light on Airway and walked down Sonora next to the airport fence. A Ford Tri-motor was about to take off. I stood at the fence behind the big ugly tin machine feeling the wind from its propellers blowing past me. Harder and harder the wind blew. I hung on to the fence until the machine started rolling down the runway on its takeoff. The wind died as the plane sailed up into the air. It was such a unique experience you could sell tickets. I stood behind hundreds of planes in the years I spent living on Hazel Street.

School started the day after Labor Day. I was assigned to the fourth grade in room one eleven with Mrs. Hurley. I pushed open the door and searched the room for Sandy. I saw Bobby Hessong up near the teacher's desk but no Sandra. "Nice hair, Bruz." One of the girls called out. "Where are those gorgeous curls?" Another chimed in.

"In a brown paper bag." I said. "I think my mother kept them, I'll ask her if you want." The girls laughed. Bobby walked up. "Missed you all summer, Bruz, you have fun?"

"Worse summer of my life. My dad got sick. He's still in the hospital. I didn't do anything but help my mom worry."

"Hey, Bobby, whose this good looking guy?" It was Sandy. I looked at her and laughed.

"You know." Bobby answered. "Bruzzy Tyrrell, like Samson he's lost his hair. I hope he kept his strength." Sandy kissed me on the cheek. "Well Mr. Tyrrell you look downright delicious. We're going to have to rethink this friends thing." I smiled. I couldn't answer. I didn't know what she was talking about. Bobby seemed to understand cause he laughed. Luckily Mrs. Hurley came in and slapped her ruler on the desk for attention. "Anyone not in the fourth grade is in the wrong room. All fourth graders sit down in alphabetical order.

"Goodbye Sandy, goodbye Bobby, I'm always in the back."

"See you later, Good Looking," Sandy laughed. Bobby shook his head and headed for H territory. I was in the back row. I was always the back row. I was used to it. It had its advantages.

Mrs. Hurley was a big woman, both up and down, fore and aft. Five foot ten at least and probably a hundred and eighty pounds, most of her weight in her bosoms. She had a big bush of black hair and wore large round glasses with dark black frames. She had a nice friendly face and a voice that could shatter glass. This would be an interesting year.

"Are you all seated comfortably?" She asked. Many nods. A few yeses. "Well good. Now we're going to change it all around. I plan to seat you in order of your grades in third grade. The top student will sit in the first desk in the first row, the second best student in the second desk and so on. So let's play the game. Will Sandra Blaine please sit in the first desk?" The class laughed.

"And what's funny about that?" Mrs. Hurley lost a little charm.

"I'm already in the first desk. I'm Sandy Blaine." The kids laughed again, Mrs. Hurley joining in. "Yes, that is funny."

She looked at the boy in the second desk, "I suppose you're Louis Tyrrell?"

"No M'am, Charley Black."

"Well Charley Black, go to the rear of the room till I call your name. Louis Tyrrell, sit here."

"Bruzzy Tyrrell, Louis is my grandfather." I stood up.

"Here, Louis, this desk."

"Bruzzy." I said.

"I can't use a nickname in class, Mr. Tyrrell, what did they call you last year?

"Bruzzy." I said.

"And in second grade?'

"Nothing."

"They called you nothing in the second grade?" The kids began to titter.

"I didn't go to second grade."

"You skipped second grade? And you're second in class in the third grade?"

"I guess so. You want me to sit next to Sandy?"

"Okay, Bruzzy, sit next to Sandra." The kids fell out of their seats. I walked to the front of the room and sat next to my best friend. Fourth grade was going to be just fine.

Lunchtime, Sandy and I sat on our favorite steps; Bobby stood waiting for an invitation to join us. He had a large red apple in his hand. "Sit down, Bobby," Sandy said, "We have to make some plans." I put my two peanut butter and jelly sandwiches on the top step, Sandy had her lunch in her lap.

"Where's your lunch, Bobby?" I asked. He held up the apple.

"That's all your going to eat?" Sandy said.

"My mom's not too organized, not too good at lunch making. She told me to take an apple and buy some milk, then, didn't have any money to give me. My step father is away on business today and she's broke." He kind of shrugged his shoulders.

I handed him a sandwich. "Sit. Eat. Let's hear Sandy's plans."

"First, let me ask you a question." She looked at me. "You think Mrs. Hurley will keep this seating arrangement all semester?"

"I think she'll keep it all year. She's trying to prove something to herself. She thinks the slower students will improve and compete with the smarter ones. She wants to see us move back and someone move forward. Make studying feel like a game so we all improve."

"Well, that's an interesting opinion. I know I want to stay number one so here's what I think we should do. First week, Bobby and I will keep notes on everything we discuss in class and you'll write down questions about what's being discussed. We'll trade off each job the next week so we'll write down everything that happens. Then when Mrs. Hurley decides to give us a test, we'll study all our notes, answer the questions and be prepared to score high marks. The three of us can be at the top of the class if we work hard enough."

"I'm a lousy student, Sandy, I just squeak by, you guys don't need me I'll just slow you down." He shook his head. Took a big bite of his sandwich and chewed."

"You ever study for anything, Bob?" I asked.

"Not really. Frank is the smart one in our family." He took another big bite. The kid was hungry.

"My teachers in Pasadena compared me to my brother. I was never as good as him." He shook his head.

"That's crap. My sister's a brain. She went to this school and all her teachers wondered if I would be like her. I studied. I got good marks. They forgot all about my sister. Sandy and I work together every lunch period and we do well. Just try. You'll see."

"You want to have lunch with us on these steps? You'll have to study with us, otherwise spend your lunch hour someplace else." Sandy laid it on the line. Bobby looked at me, looked at Sandy and made up his mind. "Okay, I'll do my best."

"It's a plan then. We start today after lunch."

"Right," I said. "I've got two pieces of apple pie we can share."

27

Sunday morning. I got out of bed early, pulled on a pair of short pants, an old shirt and went to do my chores. I put water in the rabbit hutches, filled the pellet bowls, put fresh seed and water in the pigeon's cage, raked the chicken coop, scraped out all the droppings under the roosts in the chicken house and collected nine eggs. I sprinkled some corn on the ground, put mash in the chicken feeders and filled their water bowls. I left them scratching away at the corn, the big red rooster strutting around the coop. My sister made Sunday breakfast. We woke mom when the ham was ready to serve. I set the table. I put a large iced tea at each of our places. My Mom sat down in her bathrobe, very happy to be served. Gen's ham and eggs were terrific. I made the toast under the broiler. I gave mom the best pieces, Gen's were okay, I like burned toast. And so a peaceful Sunday began. I was dreaming about playing softball when mom informed me that we were going to visit my dad today. Gen had gone with mom yesterday while I mowed the front lawn. They came home and reported dad was not doing well. She looked at mom; I saw she wasn't very happy. "Mom, why not take Bruz next week, maybe dad will be feeling better."

My mom shook her head. "I think he better go today, Sweetheart, there's not much time left." Gen nodded. I didn't want to go at all. Let me remember him as he was. Why do I have to see him now, I thought. But I knew I would mind my mother.

"Thanks for a wonderful breakfast, Kids, it's nice for the working girl to sleep in. Bruz, wash up, put on nice clothes we'll go in about an hour." She went off to the bathroom. I helped Gen clean up the kitchen then went to my room to dress. I knew mom was in the bathtub so I washed under the faucet behind Jay's house, got dressed in clean pants and shirt and put black Keds on my feet. I sat on the front steps trying to think of anything but my father in the nursing home. My mom was very quiet. We got in the car and drove up the hill. We turned left on Airway. I could see a Ford Tri-Motor taxiing for take off. I wished I could jump out of the car and stand in the wind and never have to go to the nursing home at all.

We turned right off Sonora on to San Fernando Road. I could feel my stomach muscles tighten as the long brown stucco building came into view. It had a distinctive red Spanish tile roof. I knew my father had put on that roof. He was the best tile man in Glendale.

Mom parked in the corner of the big macadam parking lot. We walked to the glass front doors. She held my hand. I was scared, the ham and eggs rumbled in my tummy. She pulled the door open. Someone was screaming. I looked at my mother. She looked straight ahead, almost pulling me through the big ugly room. Empty chairs stood against the walls. We headed for a dark hall again. Someone screamed. I didn't want to cry, seven year olds don't cry, only babies cry. I felt tears run down my cheeks.

We walked by a nurse's station; three girls in green uniforms were drinking coffee. "Good morning, Mrs. Tyrrell, your husband was asleep last time I checked."

"Thanks Terry, we'll go in anyway." Why, I thought, let him sleep, we'll come back another time. Another scream. Very close to us. One of the nurses left as another said "Go shut Mrs. Meyers up or else she'll have to leave." At least it's not my dad, I thought.

The room was dark, almost too dark to see anything; a tiny old man lay in the bed.

"Bill? You awake?" No answer.

"That's not my dad. I don't know that person. We must be in the wrong room. Why did you bring me to the wrong room? I'm scared enough. Let's go home. I don't want to be here!" I was screaming as loud as Mrs. Myers.

"Calm down, son, your father has been very sick, he's lost a lot of weight. He loves you very much. I thought you ought to see him one more time."

"I don't care what you say, that's not my father, my father has big shoulders, my father has a round face with a shadow of his beard. My father is tall and strong. My father can fly!"

"Go wait in the car!" My mother's mad voice. I ran out of the room. I ran down the dark hall. Mrs. Meyer screamed. I ran across the red carpet in the empty waiting room, through the glass doors across the parking lot and into our empty car. I slid way down in the front seat and cried. My father was gone. He wasn't in the nursing home. They put some wizened up old man in my father's bed. He'd already left on his trip. I was still crying when my mother got into the car. She drove us home. She didn't say a word. We pulled into the driveway; I jumped out and ran into the garage. I would be happy among his tools. I could look at his crystal set and bring back good memories. His tools were gone. His crystal set was gone. The workbench was empty. I walked into the backyard. I looked at the pigeons he loved. I opened the gate. They didn't fly away. One or two jumped on my shoulder. The white one pecked softly on my neck like little kisses. I could feel myself relaxing. I sat on the tar barrel my dad kept by the cage. Almost at once I had birds all over me. Pigeons were sitting on my legs. Sitting on my arms, my shoulders. Pigeons, cooing happily. They had missed my dad in the hospital, in the nursing home and here I was a surrogate master ready to give them my love. I sat there for hours. The birds wandered over my body, they never left me. I finally stood up. The pigeons jumped into their cage. I didn't close the door, they were free to stay or go. I wandered to the front stoop and sat on the steps.

I could see the sick little man in my mind's eye. I couldn't get the picture out of my brain. I thought about the time my dad grabbed the porch roof and hoisted himself up and the sick little man flashed back in my mind. I couldn't shake the picture. I walked off into the walnut grove. I stood where Roy Rogers had stood when he sang on the radio. I enjoyed hearing the songs floating in my brain. I sat on the ground leaning on a tree as I had done thirteen times that first summer. It was quiet, my eyes felt heavy. I fell fast asleep.

Some one was shaking my shoulder. I opened my eyes. My mother smiled down at me. "Wake up, Bruzalah, suppers on the table." She pulled me up off the ground. "My, my, you're getting too big for me to haul you around." I laughed. I didn't think I'd ever laugh again. My mother was the greatest.

Every Sunday night at eight o'clock we listened to the radio. "One Man's Family." I got to stay up until nine because I couldn't miss what happened to Paul and Clifford in the house on the sea wall above San Francisco Bay. I lay down in my little bed. The breeze filtered through the screen. I closed my eyes. There was the tiny sick man in the bed. There were the screams in the hall. I couldn't take my eyes off the man they said was my father. He wasn't. He wasn't. I sat straight up in my bed. It was three o'clock in the morning. Everything was quiet. I walked out the back door and sat on the steps. I watched the moon flickering through the waving branches of the walnut tree. I looked at Jay's house and wondered where he was sleeping tonight. He hadn't been home for months. I went into the kitchen. I drank some milk out of the bottle. I sat in dad's place at the table and remembered him serving dinner. A tear rolled down my cheek. I slept till morning. School was a chore. I couldn't get my mind on anything but my dad. I made it through the day. Gen made something for dinner. We had some of mom's canned peaches; they made any dinner a feast. I was in bed by eight.

I was in a dark hall. Someone was screaming. I was pushed into the little room; the tiny sick man was in the bed. His face contorted in pain. He was groaning.

"Bruz. Wake up Bruz." I opened my eyes. A man stood at the end of my bed. A big man, wide shoulders, in need of a shave, his big hands holding the bar at the foot of my bed. My father was standing there. I was dreaming. He smiled. "I'm leaving on my trip. They let me stop by to say so long. You remember our agreement?"

"Yes Sir, I have to be the man of the house, do all my chores, keep up the lawn and the hedges, get Uncle Fred to fix whatever breaks, take care of Mom and Gen and get a small job, magazines or newspapers."

"Exactly. You have to stand in for me. Jay has Kitty. Mom and Gen only have you since I have to go. Remember me as you see me. I'm in my work clothes because I have a lot to do. Always remember your mother and dad loved you with all their heart. Grow up and be a strong honest man that can help your mother if she needs it. I have to go. I won't be back.

163

Now sleep well and be happy because I'll be happy where I'm going."

I opened my eyes. It was daytime. There was no one at the foot of my bed. My dad was gone. He'd said goodbye. I felt content, ready to live my life. They sent me home from school at lunchtime. Mom and Gen were sitting in the living room. Mom looked at me. "I have some news from the nursing home." My mom said.

"I know. Dad's gone on his trip. He came last night and told me I was to be the man of the house, take care of you and Gen, do my chores, get Uncle Fred to fix anything that breaks and find a little job to help with money. I can do all of that, Mom. Don't worry, I can help." Gen was crying. My mom looked at me and started to laugh. My dad had died. I never saw my mother cry. She never mourned. She worked, she stretched our money, she kept our home together. My dad went on a trip and mom became mother and father. We were still a family and mom was still in love.

28

Wednesday morning. I was eating sugar toast in the breakfast nook. I heard the iron wheels on the wagon the newsboy dragged along delivering his papers. I opened the front door. "Roosevelt and Garner elected in landslide…Roosevelt and Garner elected in landslide!" He called, hoping to sell some extra papers. He put a paper on the Baumer's porch. The cabinet business must be good, I thought. "What's the boy yelling, Sweetheart? Mom asked from the bathroom door.

"Roosevelt and Garner were elected in a landslide, whatever that is." I answered.

"Big majority." She answered. "Your father didn't get a chance to vote."

"Yeah but they won without him. I'm going to school."

"Wait a couple of minutes, I have to be at Grand Central at eleven but I need to see the principal. I'll walk with you."

I couldn't take the short cut through the walnut grove with my mother so we walked down Hazel, crossed over to Lake Street, my mother moving right along. I was nearly running to keep up with her. "I like my job," she said, "not a very high class position but they pay me seventy-five cents an hour. That's six dollars a day and it's close to home. I work eleven to seven this week, then nine to five next week. We change so no one gets stuck getting home late all the time. I have to quit the PTA; I'm going to tell the principal today. My vice president, Mrs. Hardy is married to a lawyer. They do quite well. She'll be happy with the challenge." We were there. She kissed me and flew away to the principal's office. My mother was full of pep for a brand new widow. I went to my class.

"Well, boys and girls, it's coming up to Thanksgiving and we need to see who will sit where for the next couple of months, so next Tuesday I'm giving you an examination. That long word means a difficult test. Should take at least two hours,

I'm trying to make it like a high school exam so you get some experience in taking long tests. I don't know how to tell you to study; you figure that out for yourselves. Tuesday. Test day, now get your history books."

"Okay, let's get to our notes," Sandy said, sitting down on the kindergarten steps. "We have today, tomorrow and Friday to study here. You guys come to my house on Saturday morning so we can work all day, then Monday we can go over anything we missed. Agreed?" Bobby sat on the bottom step, looking at Sandy and nodding his head, I guess he was agreeing.

"Sounds good to me," I said. "It's your plan, Sandy and you're always right." She laughed. Bobby was still nodding.

"And if I'm wrong we'll be sitting in the back row." We all laughed. The worst we could do is flunk. We didn't waste a second of our lunch hours, we got to Sandy's at nine-thirty and we finally decided we had had enough when Sandy's parents walked in and told us it was six o'clock and they wanted their dining room back. Monday we searched through our notes and the questions we had made up to see if we missed anything important. It was all a jumble of information. Our brains were in overload. We put away all the papers and silently finished our lunch.

Tuesday morning everyone sat forward in their desks waiting to see the test we had in store for us. Mrs. Hurley sat at her desk, a pile of papers on the front corner. She looked from student to student, nodding, smiling. Her eyes locked on mine. "Now I've got you, Louis!" They said. I looked at Sandy. She was clicking her nails in rhythm atop her desk, no sign of worry on her pretty face.

Mrs. Hurley stood up. She picked up the pile of papers and came down to the first row. She put a stapled pile of papers on Sandy's desk. Sandy looked at it. She didn't move. She dropped a pile on my desk. I read, "First Term Examination. Louis Tyrrell."

I peeked at the questions on the first page. Review questions from our classes, Sandy was right. We studied the right material. I relaxed. We had it made.

"Now, children I want you to begin at 9:45. You have two hours. You may run over till noon if you have to, I will deduct some score from those people not finished by 11:45. Put the exam papers on my desk and go straight to lunch. Class will resume at 1:15. Everyone had the exams; we sat watching the clock click forward. 9:45. I answered the first question, everything was easy. I was quickly at the top of the third page. I read the question. "Write the first one hundred words of an original story about your life. They will be scored for originality, aptness of thought, grammar, spelling and handwriting. I was stopped cold. We hadn't studied this. It was an unfair question. I said to myself, but if I don't do it I'll be sitting with the dumbbells. I looked out of the window; a couple of grey and white pigeons flew by. Pigeons, I thought. I'll write about my father's pigeons. I carefully wrote in my best cursive letters about my father in the hospital and his lonely pigeons accepting me in his place. I counted the words. 105. I went to the next question. I put my finished exam on Mrs. Hurley's desk at eleven forty. Sandy's exam was already there. Mine was second. I walked out the door and headed for the steps. "Wait up, Bruz!" Bobby Hessong yelled. Our slow partner had finished under the deadline. If we scored we could all celebrate.

Thanksgiving was strange without dad. We were going to have chicken for our dinner and someone had to kill the bird. My mother said she would chop its head off if I would pick out the chicken. I knew the bird I would like to eat for Thanksgiving dinner. A mean white leghorn hen that always pecked me when I was collecting eggs. She was the worst layer in the coop. Maybe she would be delicious roasted.

Mom waited, hatchet in hand, while I chased the chicken into a corner and grabbed its legs. She flapped her wings and squawked as I carried her to the executioner. My mom took hold of the hen's legs. "Dad always let go of the bird when he chopped off their heads. He said it was better for them to bleed on the grass than on his pants and shoes." Mom nodded her head. She laid the hen's shoulders on the block; the nervous bird kept moving her head. I petted her neck like my dad used to do and she relaxed on the block. I pulled my hand away.

"Now, Mom!" I said. "Whap!" The hatchet took off the hen's head, the body bounced into the back yard; it ran in circles, blood spouting from its neck where it's head used to be. Mom looked a bit queasy. She said nothing. Our Thanksgiving dinner finally fell over. I grabbed it, carried it over to the big washtub near the back porch. My sister came out the back door with a steaming teakettle and poured the boiling water into the tub. I put in cold water till the temperature was right. We doused the bird. The hot water loosened the large feathers and made plucking much easier. "Get all the feathers off and bring the bird into the kitchen, I'll singe it over the stove."

My mother and sister left me pulling out long white feathers from the wings, shorter feathers from the tail and many small, smaller and tiny feathers from the body. I wouldn't get pecked when I pick up eggs anymore. More important, I hoped she cooked up nice and tasty.

We sat around the table and ate a delicious Thanksgiving dinner. Chicken and stuffing, sweet potatoes, pickled beats, cranberry sauce and my mother's wonderful pumpkin pie. I didn't even know she'd baked them. I must have been fast asleep.

Monday morning, Thanksgiving was over. Today we learned how we did on Mrs. Hurley's test. My worst experience yet in my short school history. "Take it like a man," I could hear my dad's voice in my head. I laughed walking along Lake Street. How could this be a bad day? I had two chicken sandwiches and two pieces of pumpkin pie in my lunch bag, so what if I sat in the back row, my stomach would be full. The kids gave me funny looks as I laughed, walking into the classroom. I dropped into the second desk and waited for Monday to begin. Sandy smiled sitting in her first desk seat. All the kids sat quietly as Mrs. Hurley made her entrance loaded down with exam papers. She put them on the desk and turned to the class.

"Action! We've had some action! People will move up and people will move back. Changing seats will give us all the feeling of success or failure and that's one of the most difficult things to learn in grammar school.

Let's begin at the top, because that is where everyone wants to be. Miss Blaine will you stand up please." Sandy was shocked. She didn't know what to do. She had always been first in her class. She looked at Mrs. Hurley, a tiny tear in the corner of her eye.

"Don't be upset Sandra, you're still among our best, you take Bruzzy's second desk. My heart went up into my mouth. I aced that exam. How did I mis-figure my results. I was flabbergasted. Sandy sat in my desk. I stood and watched her. Third or fourth isn't too bad, I tried to sell myself.

"Now, Bruzzy, you had the top score in the exam. Please take your place at the head of the class." Sandy laughed out loud. Bobby clapped his hands from the rear. "No applause." Mrs. Hurley snapped. "I would like to add that Bruzzy's high marks were helped by his excellent essay. I never thought you had that talent, Bruz. We'll try to help you improve." She gave me my paper, "A+" in red on the cover page. She handed Sandy hers. She had a plain red "A," I was first because of a little plus. Sandy would be back in this chair after the next test.

"Megan Roberts, in the eleventh seat will move to number three." A cute little blonde girl came and sat next to Sandy. She had a red A on her paper too. Bobby Hessong in the fourteenth seat will move to number four." The class went wild. They clapped and hollered. Bobby, very shy, sat next to little Megan. He was so scared his hands were shaking. Somehow, though he thought he was dumb, he really was smart. Sitting in the fourth chair would give him the courage to believe it.

There was no Christmas party, no special presents. The big tree was decorated but Christmas wasn't Christmas anymore. Old man depression had snuffed out Santa Claus. Mrs. Hurley wished us happy holidays at lunchtime and we were on vacation. We walked Sandy to the corner; she kissed Bobby and me on the cheek and ran off for her Christmas. Bobby and I walked up the hill to E. J. Toll Junior High School. The Glee Club was singing holiday songs. Genevieve and Frank were singing solos. The show was scheduled for one o'clock.

We arrived about 12:30 and stood on the auditorium stairs listening to the rehearsal. I heard my sister sing Silent Night and a male quartet belt out God Rest Ye Merry Gentlemen.

A big voice said, "Okay, go relax. Half an hour till show time. We'll go onstage at one straight up, audience or no audience, I'm going home to San Francisco for Christmas this afternoon!"

They soon opened the doors, we got seats in the third row, I saved a seat for my mom who promised to get there somehow even though she was working. The house was full, standing room against the back wall; someone took the seat I was saving for mom. The glee club entered. They sang "Deck the Halls." It was a great arrangement, a swinging version that bounced along. The audience joined in on the second chorus. A standing ovation boomed out from the jammed auditorium.

As people sat back down I caught a glimpse of a blue and white uniform topped by a pile of red hair. My mother was standing in the back. I couldn't get out. I couldn't give her a seat. She was stuck back there with the janitors and maintenance men. My sister, dressed in her beautiful pink gown, walked to the podium. The crowd became still. The choral director blew his little pipe. "Silent Night, Holy Night," filled the auditorium. Nothing said Christmas like "Silent Night." My sister's voice was beautiful. You could hear her every word. They said she was the 'Kate Smith' of Toll. No one in this audience would argue with that. On the third chorus the conductor faced the audience and signaled for us to join. It was the only Christmas spirit we had that year. I saw my mom leave when the applause for Gen died away. She had to get back to her variety store. I waited on the front steps until Gen came out. I told her mom was there to hear her sing. She hadn't seen her. She was happy that mom could squeeze us in. "She's working too hard. We have to watch her, something always happens when she's in her working mood."

Christmas morning. A sad little tree decorated the radio. A bowl of nuts, hard candy and a few candy canes were under the tree. There were no presents. Mom came out of her room. "We'll kill a chicken today, Bruz. We'll have a nice Christmas dinner."

"I'll kill the chicken, Mom. Dad said I was the man in the house and that's what I'm going to be. I'll pick out the chicken, I'll kill the chicken, I'll pluck and clean the chicken. All you'll have to do is singe and roast the chicken. Agreed?"

Mom smiled. "Okay my little man, I always did what Bill told me."

Mom's fruitcake made it a merry Christmas. Where she found time to make it was an unsolved mystery. Mom worked, Gen made our dinners, I kept the animals fed, the lawn mowed, the hedge clipped. Our house was as happy as it would ever be. I was eight years old and going back to school on my birthday.

At the end of March a new president was sworn in. He told us, "all we had to fear was fear itself " But the depression didn't go away. Mom worked every day at the variety store. Her salary gave us lamb stew instead of ox tail, liver and onions instead of creamed salmon and every couple of weeks on her day off we'd celebrate with braised pork chops.

Every Tuesday and Thursday after school I would walk up the hill and visit mom on her job. The boss wasn't too happy to see me but he didn't tell me not to come. I would visit for ten minutes and walk down the hill to the flying school where my trusty broom waited for me to push it around.

I happily sat in the number one desk for a whole two months. Bobby, Sandy and I continued our studies on the kindergarten steps. We were ready when Mrs. Hurley laid the second tests on our desks. But there wasn't an essay question, it was a math test. Not my best subject. When all was said and done Sandy was back in her number one position and I was number two. This time the red A plus was hers. I was happy to see her eyes sparkling. Bobby, beamed holding on to his fourth place. I walked up the north side of Sonora, across the street from the airport, walking in the street past the long vacant lot. I crossed the train tracks into the parking lot behind the Grand Central and climbed the steps to the wide back porch. The variety store was empty. Nobody shopping, I didn't see my mother anywhere. I heard a voice behind me.

171

"Your Grandmother got sick. They took her away." I turned around. It was the young girl I'd seen my mother training. "She's my mother not my grandmother." I was upset.

"No matter," she said. "She's gone."

I opened my mouth to question her when my mom's boss stood next to me.

"Bruz." He said, "Your mom had a gall bladder attack after lunch. We called an ambulance. The young doctor on board said she should go to the hospital. She followed the ambulance in her car. I just got a call that she was operated on and she'll be able to come home in four days. She said you and your sister should take care of yourselves while she's away. They said she was feeling better this afternoon.

"Thank you very much, sir. I'll go home and tell my sister. I'll come back tomorrow and see if you have any more news."

"I'll be here," he said and patted my head. I gave the dumb girl a dirty look and went out the back door. I walked down the hill thinking about mom in the hospital. When dad went to the hospital he never came home. What would Gen and I do if mom never came home? I didn't like these thoughts. I shook my head to get rid of them. I nearly walked right past the Flying School. I went in. I was early but I got out my brooms, the dustpan and a couple of rags. I dusted all the furniture and the desktops in the reception room. No one was there. I picked up the pieces of paper that littered the floor. I threw them in the Teletype wastebasket.

Fred Fuchs came in the back door, pulling off his helmet. The young man behind him left his helmet on, his goggles high on his forehead. "Okay Tom? Tomorrow same time?" "Right you are, Freddie!" the man said strutting out the front door. We watched him jump into a fancy yellow convertible and speed away. Fred Fuchs shook his head. "Rich men's sons. God help us."

"You teaching him to fly?"

"His money is good. He signed all the papers. If I don't teach him somebody else will. I'll make a better flyer out of him than most guys if I don't punch him in the mouth first. How come you're here so early?"

"I went to the super market to see my mom, she got sick this afternoon. Gall bladder, the man said. She got operated on. My sister and me have to take care of ourselves for four days till she gets home. My dad went to the hospital and never came home. How do I know she'll come home? I'm kind of scared."

"Well, let's find out. Sounds like she's in Glendale Central. Let's give them a call." He sat at the desk picked up the phone, listened, said, "Glendale Central, please." I watched in awe. He was so controlled.

"Yes. You have a patient named Dorothy Tyrrell, gall bladder I think, could you give me a report on her condition?" Quiet.

"Yes?" Quiet. "Thank you." He hung up the phone. "She's fine, Bruz. Everything went well, she had a fine surgeon, she's all back together and will even have supper. You're right. She'll be released in four days. So tell your sister not to worry and act like she's away on vacation. You can feed yourself, right?"

"Oh sure, we can take care of ourselves, I was worried they weren't telling me the truth but you got the truth so I don't have to worry. Four days will go by in a jiffy."

"Okay, don't leave before you sweep up." I laughed.

My sister worried for a couple of minutes and then asked if mom would be home Monday. "That's four days." I said. "Ha. Ha." Gen said, "Very funny." We both laughed. Sunday I did away with another of our chickens and helped my sister make a big pot of chicken soup for Mom's return home banquet. We would have to start buying eggs in the store soon if I kept chopping the heads off our hens.

173

Mom was sitting in her chair listening to her programs when I walked in. It sounded like Myrt and Marge music but the sound was very low. "You kids kept the house up very well, Bruz. I'm proud of you." I kissed her. "How do you feel, Mom? When are you going back to work?"

"Tomorrow." She said as Gen walked in the front door.

"Tomorrow. What?" My sister asked.

"I'm going back to work." Mom answered.

"Don't you think you should rest a couple of days Mom, after all you did have an operation?"

"I've been talking to my boss. The girl who's working in my spot has some kind of market connection and they're trying to have her replace me because I'm old and sick. I don't want to lose this job cause there aren't any other jobs around so I'm going back tomorrow. And that's that." My mom had spoken.

"Well just relax, I'll put supper on the table at five thirty. The doorbell rang. I'd never heard it ring before. I opened the door. A big black sedan sat at the curb, a driver behind the wheel, a little round bald-headed man was at the door. He looked at me. "You must be Bruz?" He said. "Yes sir." I answered.

"I'm your Uncle Eddie, your mother's older brother. Is my sister home?" I opened the door. Mom jumped up and came across the room. "Eddie, how in God's name did you ever find me?" He stood in the doorway, surveying the small comfortable room.

"Your friend, Dan Pink, gave me your address. I wrote him when we decided to come out here." He didn't walk into the house he just stood inside the door. "Come in, come in. Sit." Mom said.

"In Jersey City. Niggers live better than this. Just what your father predicted when you got yourself involved with that roofer." He stood shaking his nearly bald head. My mom walked right up to him. He wasn't very tall because they stood eye to eye.

174

"You're still the same hateful bastard you've been all your life. You'd be living like a nigger too if you hadn't stole our inheritance. Dad said share, not steal. Turn yourself around and walk back out of my life, you bastard. I won't even introduce you to my kids." She grabbed him by the shoulders pushed him out the door, locked it and pulled down the shade. I didn't even know there was a shade.

I looked out the bay window. He backed down the steps walked backward to his car got in and it drove away. He never returned.

Mom smiled at me. "I think I'll lie down a bit before dinner." She disappeared into her bedroom leaving my sister and I full of questions. She never mentioned the visit again.

29

Roosevelt and his helper, Harry Hopkins, were doing everything they could think of to get people back to work. Constitutional, unconstitutional, it didn't make any difference to a country that was hungry. Where yesterday's bank president was selling apples in Grand Central's parking lot. The current hot idea was the CCC, The Civilian Conservation Corps. Men, who were 18 from families on relief went to work for the CCC to build parks, maintain federal lands, clean the beaches, do anything to earn 30 bucks a month with 25 dollars sent straight home to their families. FDR needed people to have a little money so they could buy a bottle of milk from the grocer, which he bought from his supplier who paid the farmer that ran the dairy. Money in circulation could breathe some life into the economy of the world.

It was a hot day in the last week of June. School was out. I was the star of the fourth grade. I was taking care of our last two pair of rabbits; they had to be pampered when the weather turned hot. They needed water, water, and more water. Shade from the direct sun and moving air. Otherwise you had a stiff body lying in the hutch. Your animal had gone away. Missing his date with the stew pot. "Hey, Son!" A soldier yelled across the back fence. "Your dad around?

"My dad's dead." I answered. Not being very friendly. But true. A couple of young men in green shirts and pants joined the officer. "Whose the man of the house?" The soldier wouldn't give up.

"I am. How can I help you?" They laughed. I didn't think it was funny. "I don't know what you're laughing at, my dad said I had to be the man of the house when he died. He died, so I'm the man of the house and if you're looking for some kind of help you're sure not impressing me with your knowledge. Right now I have some rabbits to keep alive so stop wasting my time." The officer walked over close to the fence and looked me over closely. Let him look I was too young for the army. Suddenly he spoke to me in a very business like voice. I listened.

"Well, son, we have been assigned to clean up these walnut groves. We can't seem to find an owner. You know who owns them?"

"Every once in a while some men show up and pick several sacks of nuts, they hang around a week or two and go away. A friend of my father owns this land. He rents it to us. If I was the army I wouldn't worry about some unknown guy I'd just do the job I've been assigned. If the owner doesn't like it you can bet he'll show up. My dad says the strongest guy always wins and nobody's stronger than the army so do what you like."

The soldier smiled. "How old are you son?"

"Nine, in January. I'll be in fifth grade next year."

He nodded. "What do they call you?"

"Bruz." I said, "Is there something you need me to help you with, I have a lot of chores waiting." They thought that was funny and laughed again. The soldier kept a straight face. "This operation is brand new, our office is all screwed up. We have to get a dormitory for sixty men built, over by that white house, right away and we're nowhere."

"My Uncle Fred could build it. He can build anything. He lives on Lake between School and Union."

"Could you take half an hour and show us. I'm sure your Uncle would like your help."

"If we go right now. I've got to get the eggs out no later than five." I went out the back gate. We got into a brown army car, I told the guy where to go. As we drove down Lake I caught sight of my Uncle in Sandy's garden. "You guys park in front of that little grey house. I'll get my Uncle. I ran across the street into Sandy's back yard. My Uncle saw me and looked scared. "What's the matter Bruz. Somebody hurt?"

"No uncle Fred, this army guy needs to build a dormitory for sixty guys behind our house, I told him you could do it and he's across the street waiting for us. I think they're in time trouble so don't be cheap." He laughed.

"You're Bill Tyrrell's son all right. Okay, Bruzzy, whatever you say."

We sat on Uncle Fred's front porch. The soldier had plans he laid out on the cement floor. Uncle Fred looked at the plans, played with some numbers and gave the man the price, plus or minus ten percent. They shook hands. Fred would get his men together and start tomorrow.

I told the story at supper in the dining nook. My mom and Gen got a big kick out of it. Next morning Fred pulled up in front of the house and yelled for me. I ran out to see him. He watched me come down the steps. "Put your shoes on, I need you to help me with this project. Hurry up. We'll wait."

I ran into the house, my mom watched me run past. I put on my shoes. I headed for the front door. "One minute, young man, where are you off to?"

"I'm working for Uncle Fred on the dormitory. I have to go. They're waiting." She kissed me on the head and patted my tush as I ran out. We drove Fred's truck around the corner. He had six men. Three used to work for my father, the other three were young guys. We parked in the white house driveway. The Soldier was waiting for us near a stake in the ground. "Good morning Captain Irving," Fred said, "This stake, is it the beginning of the land or the building?"

"Make it the right front corner of the building, Okay? If you don't need me I could use the time in the office."

"Right, Captain." Fred said and walked off to get his men started. The captain looked at me. "Thanks Bruz, you were a great help. Your old man would be proud of you if he was still with us. Make sure Uncle Fred takes care of you for selling this job." He chuckled.

178

I didn't know what he was talking about. The captain left. Fred got his men working. The long tape measures came out, lines were run, men began digging the foundation, stakes were driven into the ground, lumber arrived, cement and sand piles appeared. It was a mad-house. I was supposed to make sure no one was thirsty, keep the nail buckets full, pick up the short pieces of lumber and put them off to the side laid out in lengths. It was a lot of work. It didn't stop till we ate lunch and then went on till five. Day after day the dormitory took shape. No owner showed up. Nobody told us to stop. In two weeks, twelve days to be correct, Fred forgot the painting time. We stood looking at the first CCC dormitory in Glendale. The Captain was ecstatic. His men would arrive tomorrow; they would be at work in the groves the first of the week.

I was pooped. I relaxed on the back porch of the white house that had been empty since prohibition was ended. Captain Irving wandered over. "Bruz, you want to work with me this summer? I need a couple of runners to keep track of the guys out in the groves, a kind of messenger job. I could use you and one of your friends. I'll pay you guys a quarter an hour, seven hour days, six days a week, Okay?"

I was still pooped but sat up smiled and almost yelled "Great, Captain Irving, I'll get Larry Doyle. He's a couple years older than me but I'm smarter. He doesn't have a father. His mom could really use the money." The Captain was laughing at me again. Am I some kind of comic?

"Perfect Bruz, You and Larry come to my office in the dormitory Monday morning, 8:30, that's the day we start turning these old groves into a Walnut tree park."

I walked home every bone in my body aching. I heard my dad's voice in my head. "A good hot bath will relax all those muscles, you'll feel a lot better." "Thanks dad." I said aloud. I lounged in the hot water, the work pains melting into the bath. I dried myself feeling ready for a couple months hard labor in the walnut grove.

Mom was home by seven fifteen. She got out of her blue and white uniform and joined us for dinner in her mother clothes. Gen made creamed salmon, it tasted just as good as mom's.

We were a working family. I gave mom the twenty-one dollars I had earned from Uncle Fred. She smiled and put the money in the Mason jar. She sat down, "Uncle Fred gave me the money you earned as commission for selling that job. I put the hundred and fifty dollar check in the bank, we'll use it for clothes and things, is that all right with you?" I nodded. I didn't know about hundreds of dollars. I could handle quarters.

My big sister said, "You're a regular business man, Bruz. Your dad is smiling somewhere tonight."

"Yeah and I'm going to work all summer for the CCC. I'll give it all to you Mom."

"Eat your supper, Sweetheart. Enough money talk. There's peach cobbler for desert."

Larry and I reported for work at Captain Irving's tiny office in the dormitory. The front wall was a large map of the groves from Sonora all the way to the airport and behind the East West runways to where the trees ended at the river.

The 60 men were broken into groups of ten, five groups would work in the groves, the sixth would service those groups with a hot lunch. A morning break and an afternoon break. It was a very military-like operation. Larry and I were busy all the time, running here and there, back to the office, back into the groves, carry this, and lift that. I was almost happy that school would soon be starting.

The groves were sparkling clean, the trees trimmed, all the dead leaves, old nut cases, dead animals and garbage had been picked up and discarded. They removed the big limb off the tree in our backyard. No more nuts fell on my bedroom roof. The Glendale CCC was doing a yeomen's job keeping young men busy, improving the town and helping snuff out the great depression.

They replaced Larry and I with two young CCC men. And my mom put $94.50 into the Mason jar. It was almost time for fifth grade.

My two pair of rabbits lived through the summer. They had grown too big to eat. Big rabbits get very tough and lose their sweet taste. I was taking care of two sets of losers. The ladies weren't getting pregnant like they did when dad was alive and the males were eating, growing and wiggling their noses.

I went into the garage and looked through one of dad's notebooks. Sam, Thousand Oaks, hand printed across the top of a page. Chickens, Turkeys Pigeons, Rabbits, Chicks, Ducklings printed down one side. There was a phone number. It said "Long Distance." I never did long distance on the telephone. But I was alone in the house so I would give it a try. I went into the kitchen and picked up the phone, "Number Please?" the lady said. "I'm calling Thousand Oaks, Long Distance, can I do that?"

"Number?" I read her the number and the phone began to ring. I was about to hang up when a voice said "Thousand Oaks Farm." I answered, "Is Mister Sam there?"

"Who's this?"

"It's Bruzzy, Bill Tyrrell's son."

"You that little blonde kid came out for the turkeys?"

"Yes sir. I'd like to ask you about our rabbits."

"Ask your dad, he knows more about rabbits than I do."

"He's dead."

"Oh shucks, son, I'm so sorry."

"Don't be sorry, he was happy to go. He's on a long trip. He's not coming back."

"Your mother tell you that?"

181

"No, he did, the night he died."

"Okay… talk to me about your rabbits."

"I have two pair, male and female, they're too old to eat and they don't seem to want more babies, I can't afford to feed rabbits that don't multiply or go in the stew pot. What should I do?"

"You still have those pigeons I gave your old man a couple of years ago?"

"Yeah, they're my pigeons now, they won a homers contest before dad died, he really loved those birds."

"The birds wear tags?"

"Yes sir. Dad and I tagged them just before the race. They were tied for first but won because they all got home. Dad had a certificate I don't know where it is now."

"I'll give you a dozen hens and two male rabbits, ready for the table, if you'll let me take your birds."

"You'll take our old rabbits, too?"

"Sure. Bruz, I'll come in and get them unless you're driving the truck now." We both laughed.

"Plymouth Rocks or Rhode Island Reds, I don't like leghorns."

He laughed. "As you say. You still on Hazel Street in Glendale?"

"Uh huh."

"See you Saturday before noon."

I watched dad's pigeons land Friday night. One or two of them hopped on me. They were tired, must have taken a long trip. I got my two birds into the cage and closed the door for the first time since dad left on his trip.

I didn't sleep too good knowing my pigeons were leaving but I was getting 12 good dinners in place of them I wouldn't have to feed those lazy old rabbits anymore. I was raking the chicken coop when Mr. Sam came up the driveway calling my name.

"I'll be right there, Mr. Sam!"

I met him by Jays house. He didn't know me I was practically a baby when he last saw me. Now I was almost nine and grew six inches over my busy summer.

"Christ, Bruz. You're a man!" He laughed.

"Not yet, but growing. Want to see the bunnies?"

"Sure." We walked back to the hutches. He looked at the fat lazy inhabitants of the last two hutches.

"You tried mating them?"

"I don't know what you mean. Dad did all the rabbit stuff, I only put water and pellets in the bowls and gave them lettuce every once in while and tried not to get bit." He laughed.

"Domesticated rabbits need a little assistance if you want baby bunnies." He laughed. They'll do very well in Thousand Oaks. You want to keep those hutches? They look custom-built. Did Bill build those?"

"Yes Sir."

"Beautiful. I'll give you two bucks apiece and a buck for those three tables. Thirty-five dollars for you and all that yard space back. You could grow a lot of tomatoes."

"Got room on your truck?"

"Let me see those pigeons." I walked him to the cage. The birds cooed. He reached in and grabbed a bird. It sat in his hand. He dipped his hand getting a feel for how much the bird weighed. "These the birds I gave your dad?" He couldn't believe the change in the birds he had brought and the birds that had been raised by Bill Tyrrell. He looked at the tag. "WT17" He read. "Can I keep the WT registration?"

"WT is gone, you can be the new WT. You going to race the birds?"

"I was going to eat the birds. But anyone who would eat these birds would be a cannibal. Yeah, I think I'll race them."

"Dad would love that. I'm glad you've decided to race them. They loved it. I'm sorry you're so far away. I could help you a lot if you were closer."

"You're a good kid, Bruz. Maybe some summer come out and stay with me, work my farm with me. I'll pay you a little, feed you a lot and we can race your old man's pigeons together."

"Sounds terrific." I said.

"I'll give you thirty five dollars for the cage. I see it all comes apart. He built enclosures for six birds. I could screen them and take them home in their own cage, they'll only know they moved the first time they fly. You got some tin shears?

"In the garage. Thirty-five dollars is more than fair. Lets get the chickens into the run and I'll help you get those hutches apart."

He had a big old truck. He found a roll of door screen, I gave him dad's tin shears. He measured one of the pigeon cages and cut six pieces of screen. He used my father's masking tape to keep the pigeons in their nest and stored them against the back of the trucks cabin. Within an hour everything was on his truck.

184

We had one small problem. We had two young male rabbits that needed someplace to live before they were dinner. We looked at each other, the chickens were happily scratching in the chicken run. The pigeons cooed in their own nests. But two unhappy rabbits pushed and pulled in a wooden box with no home to go to.

Sam looked at me. "You're just going to eat these guys. right?"

"Right." I said

"Who's going to kill and clean them?"

"I might be able to get my brother Jay to do it."

"Let me do it now and we'll both save a lot of time. You toss them in the refrigerator and your mom will cook them in no time and we'll be all done with it. Okay?"

Mister Sam drove his truck back to Thousand Oaks with his new racing pigeons riding happily in their own homes. His two pair of rabbits had fourteen hutches to fill with new babies and he had a smile on his face contemplating the fun he'd have when the pigeons learned where they lived. I watched him drive away. Two cleaned rabbits were in the fridge, a dozen new hens in the yard and seventy real dollars clutched in my fist. Mom was going to enjoy a happy dinner tonight.

30

Fall. Time to go back to school. My new teacher was so tall he had to duck his head coming through the door. His long black hair was turning grey at its ends. He stood looking at the class that had been seated by his teaching assistant. He picked up an erasure and tossed it from his left hand to his right hand. Back and forth. Back and forth.

"There are forty students in this class. That's a large class. We won't have any time for fooling around. If you're not here to study you can leave right now. Miss Harris has a fifth grade class right down the hall she is a pussy cat next to me." He tossed his erasure back and forth waiting for someone to leave. "I see none of you have the nerve to walk out. Well, you may be sorry because I have a reputation of being a tough teacher. And, I must say, I enjoy that reputation. If you study, get decent marks on my tests, we'll get along famously and you'll enjoy fifth grade. If you can't meet my measure you'll probably have the fun of repeating this class next year. So, make that decision. Cooperate, study, raise your hand when I ask a question, be part of the class. Those of you who sit on your hands may not get through. My name is Mister Walters. I'm the assistant principal and the fifth grade teacher everyone tries to dodge. Well, you guys are here, so you're in my power. You are in your assigned seat. Miss Mayo will now hand out the textbooks we will use. You will go to the library and select three books you will read for book reports that will be due every three months. Every Monday morning I'll give a test on what we studied the week before. Ten questions, each worth ten points, miss three questions and you fail. Welcome to the fifth grade."

I was sitting on our friendly steps in what once was a friendly school. Mr. Walters had been on our backs right up until he pointed at the door and said "Lunch!" loudly over the ringing bell. "Wow. This guy is a pain, Sandy, were in for a tough time." I complained.

"I'll bet he'll be a pussycat when he finds out who his good students are; we'll study like always and ace his first test then I bet he takes it easy on us." Sandy smiled.

"Easy for you guys," Bobby sighed, "I got through with Mrs. Hurley but she was a doll."

"Don't worry, Bobby, study, we'll help you, we'll be just fine."

I walked up the back steps of the Grand Central Market at about three in the afternoon. My mom worked the day shift, she went home at five. I walked in and searched the store for the lady with the red hair. I saw it bobbing up and down in the pattern department. That sale would involve her for a while. The store was filled with customers counting their pennies. I waved to my mother's friend the butcher and went out on the back porch. A thin man in a light brown suit was leaning against the wall. I sat down on the top step watching one of the flying school Jennys taxiing to the head of the runway.

"You interested in flying?" Brown suit said.

"I work for the Flying school, just trying to figure who was driving the plane."

"What do you do there?" He inquired.

"I've been keeping the place clean since I was five years old. Someday I'm going to learn to fly one of those old kites." I turned to look at him.

"How old are you now?" I looked at the man. He really was interested in me. What did he want?

"Eight," I said, "I'm in fifth grade."

"Fifth grade? You must have skipped. Pretty smart," he said. "You want a job that could make you a little bit of money? You're supposed to be nine for me to offer you a job, but eight in the fifth grade will fill the bill."

"I go to school everyday, sweep up the flying school at five on Tuesday, Thursday and Saturday and take care of 20 chickens. Can I fit your job into that schedule?" I asked with a grin.

"You can sell magazines anytime and anyplace. You could sit right where you are and ask someone walking up the stairs to buy the Saturday Evening Post, just five cents. If they take it you get a penny. Ten people climb the stairs you could make a dime. It's not quite that easy but I'd bet you could sell twenty or thirty a week right on this porch."

"A lot of people don't have a nickel to waste on a magazine. How do you get them interested?" I was interested. My dad said selling magazines was a good job. I was going to give it a try. He threw a copy of the post over to me. It was a neat magazine. It had a picture of Benjamin Franklin on the front, right next to a big 5 cents. I opened the book it was full of stories, ads and pictures. People would like it, looked like a lot for a nickel.

"You need to fill out this form and get your mother to sign it, then I'll put your magazines on your front porch early Thursday mornings. Want to try thirty posts?'

"What happens if I can't sell them all?"

"You'll leave your unsold copies on the porch Wednesday night. We give you a bottle to use for the money, I take what the company gets and leave you your share. Still interested?"

"Sure. Let's fill out the form, my mom works in the market, I'll go get her to sign and I can start Thursday, right?"

"I have to offer you a couple of more products to sell, you can refuse and just sell the post. We also publish 'The Ladies' Home Journal,' every month very popular with housewives. Costs ten cents. You get two cents, the company eight. And finally another monthly magazine for men called 'The Country Gentleman.' Full of men's fashions, men's stories but mostly clothes styles. A lot of men buy it.

I could put you down for 15 Journals and 10 Gentlemen. You have a whole month to sell them. You keep three cents. That would make you sixty cents. So if you sold out each month you'd earn a dollar eighty cents. Not a bad way to waste your spare time."

"Let's try. What do you say?" We sat there and filled out the form, we went to find my mom. She was standing by the cash register looking around the store. We walked over.

"Hi mom, I met this man on the back porch. He gets boys to sell magazines, like dad said. I'm going to try but you have to sign the permission slip, like for school."

"Hi Mrs. Tyrrell, I'm Brad Appley, I run this territory for Curtis Publishing. I have 37 boys selling our products in the 25 square miles I represent. Your son would have this territory to himself, no competition, he's bright, he could do well."

"Thank you, Mr. Appley, my husband thought Bruz could be good at selling magazines. So let's find out if he was right."

I walked down the hill to sweep out the Flying School with a new job. I was the new Saturday Evening Post boy. I walked into the reception room. No one was there. I looked out the door to the field. All the planes were gone. This was a new experience. I'd never seen the tarmac empty in front of the school. Something strange was going on.

A yellow piece of Teletype paper lay on the floor. I leaned over to pick it up. It stuck to the floor. I yanked it off the floor revealing a glob of pink bubble gum. Our Japanese clientele didn't chew bubble gum. Here was a clue to our new business and a rotten job to start my evening. I found some alcohol and an old knife. I sat on the floor and scrapped off the gooey mess leaving a bright spot on the seldom, if ever, washed tile. I was going to earn my five cents today. I searched the big closet. I had taken my brooms and dust pans out for nearly five years never paying any attention to mops and buckets.

189

This surely wasn't covered in my contract but I couldn't let that clean spot prove we ran a dirty shop. Nope, time for the mop. Perhaps I could get away with the space in front of the weather machine. I got some warm water from the rest room, the bucket barely getting under the hot faucet. I filled the bucket a quarter full. I could still lift it out of the sink.

The mop was actually stiff like a dead rabbit. I stuck it in the sink and let hot water run through it. Finally it was soft enough to go in the bucket. I don't think I had ever mopped anything before in my life. This was a first. I was experiencing something new. I didn't think floor mopping would add a lot to my resume but it would make Fred happy.

I got all the tools into the reception room. I put a little alcohol in the bucket and squeezed the mop into the water. I pulled it out dripping water in the bucket. I wrung it out until it was fairly damp. I put it on the bright spot on the floor. I pushed it back and forth. The spot was gone. Now I had a bright box. It was apparent even to this smart eight year old that the only thing I could do was mop the floor, the whole floor, not half, not most, but the whole floor. I mopped around the desk. I mopped under the desk. I moved the chairs and mopped where they had sat. I mopped everything, everywhere. The floor was blinding clean. Brown and tan tiles shone. I always thought the floor was black and brown. At least I wouldn't have to sweep the reception room. It was sparkling. I wiped off the desk and the chairs with the damp cloths. The room looked brand new. I swept out the schoolrooms, emptied the trash and was putting my tools away when I heard our planes taxiing toward the school. It was after six I was late getting home but I watched each Jenny kill its engines. The pilots I knew climbed down and two strange instructors and five students I'd never seen were walking toward my sparkling clean floor. I ran to the door. Fred Fuchs was the leader.

"Wipe your feet, no oil on your shoes I just broke my butt washing the floor. Don't ruin the job." Fred started to laugh. He held up his hand to the guys behind him. "Gentlemen!" He spoke loudly, "Our chief of maintenance here, Mr. Tyrrell, asks that you clean your boots carefully since he has just finished washing our floor. A job I know has not been done since before he was born.

Let's cooperate since I can't afford to lose him."

They all looked at me and smiled. They cleaned their shoes and didn't mark our shining floor; one of them even carried his shoes, walking in his stocking feet.

"I have never seen the real color of this floor. It might even be called pretty. What in god's name provoked you to wash this floor? Now we'll have to keep it clean."

"One of your guests left some bubble gum on the floor. Someone stepped on it and covered it with Teletype paper, when I scrapped off the gum and cleaned it up, there was a bright round spot on the floor. I got the mop and made a big bright square. I had to clean the whole thing. It was a big pain in the ass." All the men collapsed laughing. I didn't think it was funny at all.

"Bruz, this is Major McDowell, United States Air Corps, he and Lt. Seivers, over there, are going to train some army pilots on our Jennys for some special project. We'll be pretty busy for the next while so this clean floor is welcome. Mop it every third week and I'll pay you an extra quarter."

"Nice meeting you, Major. I'm glad you're paying attention to these beautiful planes. They may be old but they look great up in the air."

"Pleasure meeting you, Bruz, I'm sure we'll see a lot of you over the next six months. I need to talk to you Fred, alone."

"Run along Bruz. Come in my office, Major." I went home wondering if I was going to find out why the army was flying our Jennys. I didn't get a chance to sell any magazines.

Thursday morning I woke with first light. Big Red was crowing his head off. I couldn't understand why he was so proud. Maybe because most of our chickens were Rhode Island reds and he really felt in charge. I jumped up, pulled on some short pants and headed for the chicken coop.

Big Red was strutting around the run pecking at this hen, bumping another. Big Cock of the walk on the make. I put twelve eggs in my basket, gave the roost a quick scrape. I knew I'd catch hell for if dad were alive, filled the water, the mash trays and threw out several handfuls of corn. I wanted to see my new magazines that waited for me on the front porch. I ran through the house, opened the door and looked down at an empty Post canvas bag, a small bottle with Benjamin Franklin painted on it and a blue piece of paper. I grabbed the paper.

"Sorry, Bruz, had to send your application to the office. Just routine. They approve you get magazines next Thursday. Left you your cash bottle and your magazine bag. Good luck next week. Appley."

The steam spilled out my ears. No magazines to sell this week, just Mr. Walters and school. I washed up, got some breakfast and walked slowly to school. I sat on the steps of the kindergarten watching all the kids arrive; finally I got up and went to face the lion in his den without the benefit of a chair or a whip.

Miss Morley sat at his desk. Half the class was seated. Some already reading their history books. He always started with history. I smiled at Sandy and sat in my seat two rows behind the pretty blonde head. Bobby wasn't here yet. Still five minutes to the bell. I looked around class. I had been in school with most of these kids since kindergarten. They were all older than me but they all seemed to have forgotten that. I was just one of the regular guys. Bobby came in; he leaned over as he passed my desk, "Come home with me, Mrs. Sapporro needs to talk with you." He sat down as the bell rang. "School's in"

The front door swung open, he ducked his head through, looked at us and smiled. "History this morning." He walked to the center of the room, "And who would like to read first?" I put my hand up, Sandy's hand flew up, Bobby followed suit. Half the hands in the class were in the air. He stood, full height, looking for his reader. "Mr. Tyrrell," he said, "Please start at the top of page seventy-eight."

My book was open to seventy-eight; I was waiting to be chosen reading was my specialty. "As a result of the Intolerable Acts, which had been passed by the British Parliament, Colonists in the Americas become increasingly convinced that they needed to take more aggressive steps in order to protect themselves and their liberty."

"So, we had history and English this morning that means math this afternoon. You read good, Bruz and you did too Bobby, you're going to be the teachers pet." We munched and studied, asked each other questions on the first Continental Congress and what we learned about adverbs and the use of commas in sentence structure, Sandy was a natural teacher. Bobby and I knew exactly how lucky we were to be sitting in the sun filling our brains with Mr. Walter's wishes.

Mrs. Sapporro was on her knees in the carrot patch. Turning earth over with a small trowel. She stood up when she saw Bobby and me come around the water tower. "Oh Bruzzy," she called "I need to talk with you. Thanks Bobby for bringing him home." I walked over to the garden where she worked and shook her hand. I was actually a couple of inchers taller than her. Made me feel like a big man.

"I met your mother at the Grand Central Market yesterday. Bobby told me she worked there. I needed a new zipper and she found one for me. I heard someone call her Mrs. Tyrrell so I asked if she was your mom. We had a nice talk. I found out she's good friends with Mr. Ianelli who owns the produce department there. He's not crazy about Japanese. Gets his lettuce and tomatoes from out in the country. My son thinks he can get him to buy ours if he can talk to him. Bill thinks you could get him to talk to us. Could you try to work it out? We could use the business and Bobby's folks would be helped out too." She looked at me, her Asian eyes very wide.

"I'll talk to mom. We'll figure something out. Give me a couple of days."

My mom was dead tired but her lamb stew was delicious even a couple of days old. She was sipping ice tea and looking off into the distance, her mind miles away. "Mom?" I said. Her eyes refocused on me. "Would you introduce me to Mr. Ianelli. He doesn't buy from Japanese and I want to tell him about the Saporros who run Bobby's step father's farm."

"Just go see him. He's the little guy with the big gut, tell him I'm your mom. He'll talk to you. I don't want to be involved. They're your friends you work it out." Mom had spoken. I went home with Bobby. I talked with Mrs. Sapporro's son. He told me his plan. Saturday morning we walked up the steps of the market. I saw Mr. Ianelli sprinkling water on some carrots, I left Billie Sapporro waiting and walked up to the little man with the big gut.

"Mr. Ianelli?" I said. He gave me a funny look. "I'm Dottie Tyrrell's son, Bruz. She said if I came in early this morning you'd talk to me."

"What can I do for you, Bruz?" Still had that funny look.

"I know you don't like to buy from Japanese but my friend owns a farm on Western Avenue and the farmers are Japanese. They run a wonderful farm and my friend Bill Sapporro thinks he can give you a fresher product and make you more money selling it."

"Well, if he's a friend of Dot's tell him to be here same time next Saturday." I waved my hand signaling Bill. He walked over.

"Bill came with me this morning can you see him now? This is Bill Sapporro, Mr. Ianelli." I smiled and walked away. I went out to the back porch and sat on the top step watching the Saturday morning action at the airport across Sonora. It wasn't very long until Billie sat down beside me. "He made a three month trial deal. If it works out the way I say we'll make it long term. Thanks Bruz. Now, what can I do for you?"

"We got rid of our rabbits and our pigeons and I've got space for a garden. I want to raise some tomatoes and carrots and I don't know how to start."

"Forget it. I'll be your gardener. Just rake the place, pull up all the weeds and I'll come over and make you a garden. I have to be here 3 times a week; I'll just stop by your place keep your garden growing and go home." And so the Tyrrells became the only people on county welfare to have their very own Japanese gardener.

Saturday was supposed to be an off day but I promised to be at Sandy's at 10:30. We were going to make sure we were ready for Mr. Walters' Monday morning surprise. Page by page we perused every note we had made. If we weren't the tops in the class it wouldn't be for lack of effort. I walked up Sonora toward the flying school, satisfied we were ready for anything. I turned the corner onto Airway. The tarmac stood empty.

All the planes were gone. It looked like everyone was working except Fred who sat on the trunk of his car waiting for me. Fred stood up and waved. I guess I wasn't in any trouble if he waved.

"Come on over here, Bruz, let's sit on the sewer." I sat down next to him on the high curb. "The Major and I were talking and we decided you had to know what was going on so you wouldn't say something dumb over dinner or to the kids in school. You ever hear of Adolf Hitler?"

"No, sir." I answered.

"Well, this guy Hitler and his gang of Nazis have taken over Germany. They quit the League of Nations and refuse to honor the treaty they signed after the last war. They're breaking every international law, rebuilding their army and rumor has it they're building a new air force. The British want some concrete evidence so they put together a fake advertising company in France. Signs towed by planes can get near these suspect factories and see if they really are building the aircraft. The tow planes are Curtis Jennys, like ours. Modified so they can do the surveillance. Our Air Corps is training the pilots in our Jennys while the Brits modify theirs. It is a secret. It's a war secret.

195

You can't tell anyone. Not your family, not your friends, not anyone. Whatever you see or hear around the school is secret. Got it? Remember, keep your mouth shut." He looked at me. I nodded.

"Sure. I never talk about the school to anyone anyhow and I don't know anything about that war, I think we learn that in Junior High. Anyway it's nice being treated like a grown up. I'm just sorry I mopped the floor." He patted my shoulder and laughed.

"Okay, go sweep up."

War? Nazis? Spies? What happened to our nice quiet depression?

31

There were flat green wide-leaved weeds, little green stalks with white hairy flowers, big flat leaves all along the fence, little bunches of leaves like four leaf clovers, weeds, weeds and more weeds growing in the empty ground where the pigeon cage and the rabbit hutches had lived. I pulled, I chopped, I filled a gunnysack. I got dad's gloves and pulled some more. Hour after hour I piled up weeds that I didn't even knew existed just yesterday. Finally, while the sun beat down from high in the sky all the weeds were gone. Two fat gunnysacks for the garbage man, two sore hands for the gardener. I got the rake. I started where the chicken coop met the back fence and raked till I reached the gate to the chicken run, turned around and raked back to the fence. The rake broke up the topsoil giving the hard ground a kind of brown rubbery look. Finally, I stood where Jay's house met the side yard fence. Admiring my handiwork.

"Don't you think you should break for lunch, Son? You can't keep working and not feed the machine. What are you doing anyway?" My mother was home. I forgot it was Sunday morning. Somebody else was watching the variety store.

"Billy Sapporro is going to plant carrots and tomatoes. He's going to be our gardener because we set him up with Ianelli. That's pretty good, right?"

"Come Sweetheart, let me get you some lunch. Wash up out here, you're done working for the day." She went back into our little house. I pulled off my shirt and washed in the cold water from the faucet. I grabbed a towel in Jay's room, rubbed myself dry and ran into the kitchen. I smelled sugar toast sizzling under the broiler and saw a tall glass of milk at my place in the breakfast nook. Heaven.

I sat in my place and tasted the cold milk. Mom put a plate of four pieces of sugar toast in front of me. "Twice as much as usual for the hard working man." She said, sitting in my fathers place. "Tell me about this garden."

"When Mr. Sam took the pigeons and the rabbit hutches I saw what a nice piece of land we had and decided to plant tomatoes and carrots. I didn't have any idea how to start so I was going to ask Mrs. Sapporro at Bobby's. Then she asked me to get Ianelli to talk to Billy and when they made a deal yesterday Billy said he would make our garden. I should pull the weeds and rake. He would do the rest. That's the whole story." I took a bite of sugar toast and drank some milk.

"You are your father's son, before you think about it it's done. Let's rest this afternoon. Maybe we'll get some ice cream tonight." She walked to the fridge took a big peach cobbler out, cut a big square, put it on a plate and set it in front of me. "Here, Bruzzilah, work like a man you can eat like a man. I'm going to lie down for an hour." She kissed my head and slipped out of the kitchen. She didn't seem to be her happy old self. I worried but kept eating the treats before me.

"Good morning Boys and Girls. Mr. Walters asked that I give out these tests and stay with you until you are finished. When you feel you've done your best you may go to lunch. Mr. Walters will begin today's class after lunch break. Good luck." She didn't say another word. She put a test paper on each desk, made a note if the student was absent and sat at Mr. Walter's desk. "There are three students absent. They will get a different test later. You may all begin now."

I looked at the pile of paper on my desk. The Cover page had my name the date 9/17/34 and a title, "Advancement Examination #1," very disconcerting. Page one was question one with ten parts, a serious test. I knew the question so I didn't worry, the rest of the pages were the same. One hundred chances to fail. I looked up. Sandy was smiling at me. I smiled back. I spent the next hour and a half using my best handwriting, being as neat as I could completing every question with what I knew were the right answers. When I was absolutely sure everything was as perfect as I could make it I carried the paper to Mr. Walter's desk. I was second. Sandy's paper was already on the desk. "Win some, lose some," I thought. I headed for the kindergarten steps.

Sandy had three milks at her feet on the sun filled steps. "I was done so early, I went downstairs and got us some milk. That was a cinch, this is going to be an easy year."

"Don't count on that, Mr. Walters is pretty deep, if he thinks we've got it too easy he'll change something. Don't get cocky, stay loose, we'll quietly get through the year."

She laughed, "I love it when you start making smart noises. I wish I was as young as you." She laughed again. I looked at her and decided it was funny so I laughed right along. "Ah, Bruz, Bruz, you're so smart since they cut your hair."

"I hate it when you talk over my head, if you shut up I'll share my mom's peach cobbler with you."

"I knew you'd try to buy me off." We both laughed. Bobby limped up. "Boy that was a bitch. I don't think I got half them right." He slumped on the steps, Sandy handed him a bottle of milk.

"You wouldn't know if you got them right or wrong, you just see TEST and you freeze. I'll bet you got 100 just like Bruz and I did. So shut up and wait till Wednesday, don't spoil our good times." He took a swig of milk shaking his head.

"You're right. I'll wait."

It was Wednesday afternoon. The classroom was hot. A warm breeze flowed in the open windows. Mr. Walters stood tall next to his desk in his shirtsleeves, his jacket hanging on the back of the desk chair. "Four people got a hundred. That's four out of forty! Ten per cent! That's not good enough for this class. One quarter. Twenty-five per cent should get a hundred. So we're not going to discus grades on this test. We're going to take three more tests then discus the marks when I have four sets. Each of you know how you scored, so work, this class is a work class. The next three weeks will be hell, my friends, until I feel I have the majority of this group headed in the right direction. The minority can stay and do it over.

Bobby Hessong, take your math book and do problem nine-A on page fifty-six on the blackboard. The class will discuss it when you've finished. Pay attention, watch how Bobby proceeds with this problem, I'm going to be asking some questions."

The next three weeks passed without too much effort. We had our study method and I was sure we were in that top ten per cent. Walters stood in front of the class pressing some students, commending others, pushing for us to work, threatening another year in the fifth grade. The second Monday we did "Advancement Examination #2" I spent an extra half hour on it fixing anything that might upset our leader. Sandy was always smiling, Bobby worried and I grinned. Finally we had finished four tests.

Wednesday, October 17, 1934 Mr. Walters stood in front of his class. Spic and span. Jacket and tie. The epitome of the fifth grade teacher. "Students," he said, looking around the room, stopping here and there. "Fourteen people. Thirty-five per cent got one hundred on test number four. You see what can be accomplished when you make up your minds to work. Make up your minds to improve yourselves. Of course we still have two or three people who should be in Miss Harris' class. But they too will improve. Right now, after four tests I can practically guarantee that not one of you will repeat this grade. Right now my associate teacher will hand out the scores. He sat. He stuck his long legs out either side of his desk. He looked like a giant stork in a grey suit.

Miss Morley passed out the score recaps to each student. I looked at mine. Four one hundreds. I wasn't even surprised. I knew I had a hundred each time. I was surprised to see written at the bottom in very scratchy handwriting, "Nice Job, Bruz, happy to have you in my class. RW." I'm happy to be here, Mr. Walters, I said to myself.

After school, walking Sandy to the corner with Bobby, we compared our score recaps. Sandy's had the same inscription as mine; Bobby's was the same except RW wasn't happy to have him in his class. I kidded, "Mr. W. must have run out of ink when he corrected your test Bobby. Want me to write I'm happy to have you in my class?" We laughed.

"It's perfectly okay, my mom will only see mine. She'll love it."

Away from school I was in the magazine business. From that Thursday morning when I picked up my first thirty Saturday Evening Posts I spent time finding customers. Hazel Street was long, stretching from Lake to Airway. There were fourteen houses on one side, fifteen on the other. I hardly knew anybody who lived on the block except families who had kids. But I knocked on every door, pitched my product as best I could and when I was through had ten regular Saturday Evening Post buyers, two ladies who like the Ladies Home Journal and a bachelor who lived in the last house before Airway. He flew for TWA and bought the Country Gentleman. My business was in motion. Every afternoon I stood on the Grand Central back porch saying "Saturday Evening Post, Ladies Home Journal and Country Gentleman." Every time someone came up the steps. Every so often I would sell a copy. Mr. Ianelli bought the Ladies Home Journal for his wife. He liked me because I introduced him to Billy Sapporro. Go figure. Even Fred Fuchs chipped in. He bought the Post every week. I saw it atop the schools choice of reading matter but he also bought the Country Gentleman. I kept watching to see if his dressing style changed. After a couple of months I wasn't returning any copies with my money. All my regulars stayed with me I settled down to delivering my regular customers and four afternoons hawking on the Grand Central back porch. A second Mason jar was filling with coins on the back of my mother's stove.

There were two weeks left in school, Sandy and I were lunching on our favorite front steps. "This has been a wonderful year, Bruz," Sandy said, "Old Walters turned out to be such a pussycat. I think he's my favorite teacher."

"You only go for tall guys," I kidded. "Maybe we'll get a short guy in sixth grade." I laughed.

"I don't know if I'll be here for sixth grade. It's according to what happens with my dad. He's going to work for the War Department.

Something called The Office of Strategic Services. He has a friend who is running it and wants my dad in on the ground floor. I don't know what it's all about but my dad may wind up a colonel in the army.

If he stays in Washington DC, we're going to move there with him. This summer or during next school year. I'll call you if I have to go this summer."

I couldn't find my voice to answer. Sandy gone. My Sandy gone. What would I do, who would I study with, Sandy just can't go away, I need her. Finally I found my voice. "Sandy, you can't go away, you're my brains; you make me smart. What could I possibly do without you? You're my teacher. You're my girl! I'd starve to death with no one to eat with. Who'd get the milk?" She laughed. We went back to class.

After school, we were standing in front of her house. I hadn't headed home. I crossed the street with her. I went the wrong way just to stay near her. I was in a lot of trouble. I couldn't lose Sandy.

"Listen, dummy, nothing is decided. My dad has a new job. There are a million things that can change. Right now we live on Lake Street, I'm coming back to Franklin in the sixth grade and you're my best friend, let's just live and see what happens. The War Department is worried about this Hitler guy and my dad is going to work in an office that takes care of problems like Mr. Hitler."

She leaned forward and kissed me on my mouth. I was star struck. Now I couldn't talk. She laughed and messed my hair! She ran up her front steps waved and disappeared into her house. I stood there with my mouth hanging open.

32

I stood on the grass and watched as the kids climbed the steps for the last day of school. They would send us home at 12:30. They would lock up the school; lock up the playground until the day after Labor Day. Teachers were highly respected in the depression era. They made good livings, drove decent automobiles; some had summer cottages in San Diego or Santa Barbara. Some ran summer camps at Toll or Hoover where upscale kids spent their summer doing arts and crafts, playing softball or acting in shows to entertain their fellow campers. Being a teacher was a good way of life. I wondered if I could get into college and learn enough to make my living teaching kids. I kind of liked that idea. The morning bell rang. I hurried up the walk.

"Wait for me, Bruz. I'll walk with you." Sandy came up the walk her face wreathed in smiles. She grabbed my hand and with arms swinging we went to Mr. Walters' farewell performance.

He was very casual. Summer slacks a white short sleeve shirt open at the collar red socks and sandals on his feet. He was already on vacation, came by to wish us bon voyage.

"I just wanted to say to each and everyone of you that you have been my best fifth grade class in the eight years I have toiled at Benjamin Franklin. My dire predictions of failure never came true. You'll all be in the sixth grade in September. I want to tell you how proud you've made me feel and how much confidence you've given me in the future of your generation. You've had a difficult start in life in these very tough economic times and the problems in Europe don't hold out much hope of a normal life for your age group. Nevertheless, you're very smart and I'm certain you'll bring honor to your school and your country. That's all I have to say. Talk among yourselves or sneak off home. As far as I'm concerned school is over." He ducked through the door and it swung closed. We sat looking at each other when Miss Morley came in.

"I'm to hand out the report cards and supervise the class until twelve thirty when the school will officially close. Anyone may leave after they have their report cards." She went around the room handing out the cards. Some kids looked, some put them in their pockets, some in their school bags. Mine slid comfortably into my back pocket and I went over to Sandy.

"You going home?"

"No sense hanging around here." She smiled. She took my hand we went out the door and down the hall. We walked holding hands in the hall, a big no-no. Last day, no one cared. But I cared, Sandy was being too friendly, she had something on her mind. We went out the main doors walked down Lake Street crossed School Street and stopped in front of her house. "Have a wonderful summer, Bruz. I'll see you in September." She kissed my cheek, smiled and ran into her house. I stood looking at the spot where she disappeared and a little voice in my head said "Goodbye, Sandy, have a good life." I turned and walked past the school up Lake Street across Sonora along No-Name Street on to Hazel Street. It was summer. Time to take off my shoes and have some fun.

Twelve-thirty when school "officially" closed I was pedaling my Posts on the Grand Central back porch. I had eleven left, a couple of journals and three gentlemen. A group of people made their way out of the parking lot and came up the stairs. "Saturday Evening Post, just a nickel." I said. "That this weeks, kid?" A man called. "Came out yesterday." I answered.

"Give me one." He said. "For a nickel." I kidded.

He flipped me a coin. I rolled up the magazine and handed it to him. He went into the store. "You have a Journal?" A lady asked. "Yes m'am," I said. "Only two left till next month. She gave me a dime and took her magazine inside. I only had one Journal left. I wondered if Mr. Ianelli wanted one. I went to the produce department; he was stacking heads of lettuce on an angular table.

"Mr. Ianelli," I said, "You bought a Ladies Home Journal last month and I only have one left. Would you like it?" He looked at me not quite understanding.

"Oh Bruz. Yeah, yeah, the wife liked that magazine let me have that and save one for me every month." He gave me a dime.

"Happy to, Mr. Ianelli, that's nice lettuce. Looks wonderful."

"That's Sapporro lettuce, Bruz, and I have you to thank for it. I've more than doubled my lettuce business with Billy and I'm taking tomatoes and carrots from him now. He says some of the tomatoes come from his garden in your back yard. I told Dottie. She got a big kick of it." I laughed and went back to my magazine department on the back porch.

"Saturday Evening Post, Ladies Home Journal and Country Gentleman!" I repeated into the afternoon sunshine. Friday afternoon I was sold out. I would see how this went before increasing my order. I crossed Sonora at Airway and stood at the end of the main runway. I waited ten minutes as a Ford Tri-motor taxied out onto the runway. It came right at me, its three silver propellers flashing in the sun spinning on silver hubs. Fifty feet away it spun around facing into the wind. It ran up its engines, the wind blowing me around. I loved it. Then its engines whined under full power. It started rolling down the runway. I grabbed the fence to keep myself on the sidewalk and thrilled as the tin monster lifted off the ground. Headed for Chicago or Dallas or New Orleans. I walked home chuckling. My sister was sitting on the front step reading a book. I dropped down next to her. "I sold all my books. I sold all my books. One day and I sold all my books." I laughed.

"You're too much." My big sister said. The telephone rang in the kitchen. "I'll get it!" I ran into the kitchen and picked up the receiver. "Tyrrell household." I kidded.

"Bruz? Mister Sam, Thousand Oaks Farm."

"Hi Mr. Sam, got some chickens you want to give away?"

"You're joking right? Putting me on?"

"I sold out all my magazines in one day, I'm feeling very good."

"That's great, Bruz, you too busy to come here?"

"Come there? What do you mean?"

"My nephew, a couple of years older than you is coming to visit for five weeks, I thought if you had the time you and he could work for me for five weeks and get to know each other. Maybe we could race the pigeons. I'll give you five dollars a week and all the food you can eat, you'll take care of the chickens, help out in the meat market, keep the geese fed, big farm Bruz, lotsa work but lotsa fun too. You and Andy can bunk in the top of the barn, sleep under a million stars and go home with twenty-five bucks and a new friend. What do you say?" He made quite a pitch.

"I'll have to get my mom's permission, find someone to handle my magazine business and sweep out the Flying School, could I call you tomorrow? When do I have to be there?

"Nephews coming a week from Sunday. Maybe your mom could drive you out. We'll feed her and give some stuff from the farm, got a couple of rabbits begging to be rabbit stew. Ask her. Call me tomorrow, okay?"

I was ready. Ready to go be a farmer for five weeks. I was great with chickens. I'll get Larry Doyle to handle the magazines and the Flying School and Mom, Gen and I can have a nice ride to Thousand Oaks. Great! It'll be just great.

"Well, I don't know Bruz, Thousand Oaks is a big farm and you're only a little kid. Five weeks is a long time. If the job is hard you won't be able to get away from it, maybe next year." Mom was talking over dinner in the dining nook. Gen was quiet. I wanted to go.

"His nephew is coming this year, that's why he wants me to come so I can play with his nephew. I can take care of chickens with my eyes closed; geese are just funny-looking chickens. I don't know about the meat market what could it be? Stacking cans? Carrying bags out to cars? Sounds easy to me."

"If you go, you're stuck for the whole five weeks. I can't come out there and save you if you've made a mistake. If you think you can handle it go ahead. But don't come home crying if you were wrong. You want to be a man, okay. It's your decision. Gen and I will drive you out and then it's your problem." I laughed out loud.

"Boy oh boy it's going to be a great summer."

Larry agreed to take over the magazine business for five weeks. I showed him how to handle the money. I gave him a list of the steady customers. He would use our front porch. We wouldn't even tell Mr. Appley. He wasn't real happy about the flying school. He thought sweeping out was beneath him but I shamed him into doing it by convincing him I would do it for him. I packed several changes of clothes, took a second pair of Keds and was ready for five weeks of fun at the Thousand Oaks Farm.

207

33

Mom, Gen and I enjoyed a peaceful two and a half hour drive to the farm. Mom pulled off and parked behind the produce market that was built along the road. Mister Sam strolled over from his office in the barn. I could see the house halfway up a hill. It was three stories high, white with green trim surrounded by what looked like acres of green grass. The barn where Andy and I were to live was two hundred feet off the two-lane road that passed the farm. A small tractor was parked outside the barn. Mister Sam was in high spirits as he walked up to the car.

"Let me get in and let's drive up to the house, my wife has a nice lunch before you head back to Glendale." He climbed in back with me. Grabbed my knee and smiled. "Ready for five weeks of life on a farm, Bruz?" He laughed.

"Is Andy here yet?" I asked.

"About four thirty. My brother's driving from Bakersfield, the asshole of the earth. They'll be here for supper."

It was a huge house, very fancy furnishings for a farmer and his wife. The dining room table reminded me of our home on Lake Street. The farming business must be good, no depression showing here. Mrs. Ashton, Sam's wife, fluttered around the table making sure my mother and my sister were comfortable. We had delicious white meat chicken sandwiches with fresh lettuce and tomatoes and mayonnaise on slabs of fresh baked white bread. Tall glasses of ice tea slaked our thirst. Sam sat at the foot of the table watching his guests enjoy their lunch. Warm apple pie with vanilla ice cream topped off a magnificent feed. "I hope your lunch was worth the long trip from Glendale, Dottie, we should have done this when Bill was with us." My mom got up from her chair, "Thank you Sam for the wonderful lunch, I guess Bruz is going to come home pretty spoiled getting fed like this for a month." She smiled and shook Sam's hand. "Thank you Mrs. Ashton, I have the energy to head back to Glendale now."

"Thank you for bringing Bruz out, Mrs. Tyrrell, I know he and Andy will get along famously." She kissed my mom's cheek. We got back in the Studebaker and drove down the hill. Sam and I got out near the barn. "Take care of yourself, Bruz, remember you're here for five weeks, keep yourself clean, get enough sleep and don't work too hard." She looked at Sam. "Take good care of my little boy, Sam. He means an awful lot to me."

"Don't you worry, Dottie, this will be an adventure Bruz will remember all his life." He gave her his big farmer's smile. Mom and Gen waved and drove off down the two-lane road. Sam and I watched them disappear over the rise. "Well Bruz, why don't you wander around the place and get yourself acclimated. You and Andy will bunk up there. A big room, two big screened windows, great air and that big sky light. You can lie in your bed and count the stars in the sky. I'll be in the office just inside the door of the barn if you need me." He smiled and walked off to his office.

I stood looking at the big brown barn. It was a long two-story building. No cows, no pigs, no horses. Big square windows lined the building. Something went on in that barn. I would find out soon enough. I counted the chicken runs. I could see about a hundred yards up the hill. Seven big runs. That was a lot of chickens. I walked across the wide yard in front of the barn and discovered a long wide hill descending to a small stream that was probably the property line. On my right were six identical cottages. They were well kept; each painted a different color with black shutters a small front porch with steps to the door. A few little kids were playing on a swing set and see saw a little way down the hill. A fat Mexican lady was hanging white sheets out to dry on a clothesline. If I were a painter I'd have an award winning landscape portrait on my easel.

Just below the clothesline began the gardens, square after square being attended by Mexican men. Men were working garden after garden, running all the way down the hill to the little stream. This is some operation I thought, ten times the size of Mrs. Sapporro's. I was totally impressed.

I climbed the hill to take a look at the chickens. Seven big runs I counted forty leghorns in the first enclosure, two hundred and eighty chickens! More than two hundred eggs every day! I hope Andy has taken care of chickens. I could smell a problem. Perhaps my mother was right. I'm here now, I'm stuck, might just as well shut up and enjoy it. I walked further up the hill and heard a sound I hadn't heard since Pacific Avenue. The peep, peep, peep of baby chicks rang in my ears. I pushed the door open. Two Mexican men were feeding a litter of tiny yellow fluffs running round and round on gunnysacks laid on the dirt floor. I could see three incubator stations. Mr. Sam had a serious chicken-raising operation going here. I heard Sam say, "Take care of the chickens" in my head. I worked a couple of hours a day taking care of twenty chickens! What was I going to do with nearly three hundred? I could see my five weeks of fun dissolving into five weeks at hard labor. My dad's voice filled my brain. "You promise to do a job, you do the job, no matter what." The Mexican said something in Spanish. I smiled and backed out of the coop. I walked around to the top of the hill and looked back down at the neat row of chicken runs. I shook my head. Sam called it a working farm. I didn't realize it would be me doing all the working!

I sat against the trunk of a little peach tree that grew near the gardener's cottages. The sky was cloudless, a ceiling of blue over the rural beauty of Mr. Sam's farm. I day dreamed of studying with Sandy, laughing at her jokes, sharing my deserts. I looked forward to our days on the kindergarten steps.

A new blue Pontiac pulled up in front of the barn. A skinny version of Mr. Sam climbed out of the driver's door and shook the cricks out of his muscles. A little kid, not much bigger than me took his father's hand. They walked into the barn. I laughed, if that was my helper I was in more trouble than I'd bargained for. I strolled across the yard and leaned on the barn door. I heard my dad's voice in my head. "I know. I know." I said aloud. "A promise is a promise. I'll do the job, Dad. I just need to complain a little."

"Talking to yourself, Bruz?" Sam laughed, "I thought only farmers talked to themselves."

"Yeah," I answered, "You didn't have a roofer for a father." He looked at me like I was crazy.

"Yeah, well, come in to the office meet my brother and my nephew Andy." He walked away. I followed.

It was a nice plain office, a desk, a desk chair, two side chairs and a water cooler. Nothing expensive needed for Farmer Sam. His brother and his nephew sat in the side chairs. "This is Bruz Tyrrell, the son of a good friend of mine, may he rest in peace." He looked at me. "Bullshit." I thought smiling. "Bruz, this is my younger brother, Steve and his son Andy." I stuck my hand out to Steve, "Nice to meet you, Mr. Ashton," I said. I waved at his kid, "Hi, Andy." He smiled.

Sam pulled open the big drawer in his desk; he put out a pile of books, pushed the drawer closed and gave the books to his brother. "You might just as well go up to the house and get settled for the night, Steve. Maybe get started on the books so you can get out early tomorrow. I want to get the kids settled."

Steve got to his feet, "Right, Sam. See you at the house. Have a good night, kids, I'll see you tomorrow." He walked out. The Ashtons weren't a close family. We followed Sam out into the barn. It was really a BARN. Huge. Dirt floor. Hammers, hatchets, saws files, screw drivers hung against the wall. Wooden chicken feeder trays piled on a shelf. I grabbed my bag I'd left before lunch. Andy carried a small suitcase. We walked over to a hand over hand ladder. "See that green door in the brown wall. There're six stall showers, six sinks and mirrors and six johns in there. You'll probably be the only ones using them but the single Mexican guys sometimes shower in there so don't be scared if a naked brown guy shows up one day." He laughed. Andy looked at me. I shrugged. I wasn't afraid of a naked Mexican. "See the yellow door there? That's the dining room, that's where you'll eat. Remember, Blue door, Pee, Yellow door, Peanuts." He really laughed then. "Oh my." I thought.

Sam huffed and puffed up the ladder. Andy and I got our bags up to a wide balcony. We followed Sam into a door in the corner. We were in a fabulous room at least twenty-five foot square. Large screened windows in each wall, a nice breeze floating through.

A twin bed with a bed stand, lamp and dresser turned the space into the nicest bedroom I'd ever seen. The bed was twice as wide as mine on the back porch at home. And best of all, the floor was carpeted with thick wall-to-wall brown carpet. We might have to work hard but we would sure sleep well.

I took the bed on the far side of the room. I threw my suitcase on the bed and snapped it open. "Okay," Sam said, "Get your stuff stowed away and meet me in the dining room. That's the BLUE door." He walked out laughing. Andy sat on his bed looking at his suitcase.

"Come on Andy. Throw your stuff in the dresser and lets find out how hard we have to work."

He sat starring at his case. Finally he looked at me. "My dad said this was a vacation, he didn't say anything about work. I don't want to work. This is vacation time. I don't know one end of a chicken from the other, only thing I know about chickens is I like a drumstick. I want to go back to Bakersfield with my friends."

"Come on, Andy, let's go talk to the boss." I walked out the door climbed down the ladder walked into the yellow door and sat across a picnic table from Mr. Sam. Andy didn't show.

"No one told your nephew this was a job, Sam. He doesn't want to work. He doesn't know a thing about chickens. And there are nearly three hundred birds out there that need feeding and cleaning and watering and twenty odd dozen eggs that need gathering and you've got one nine year old kid who's taken care of twenty chickens to do all that. I think you're in a bit of trouble Mr. Farmer."

"Respect. Respect your elders, Bruz. You're right, that chicken shit brother of mine didn't have the balls to tell his kid he wanted to make a man out of him. God damned accountant. I give my regular college kids time off to celebrate their graduation. Now I'm stuck with no help. And I haven't the slightest idea where to find it. I knew you could do it and you'd teach that lily-livered nephew of mine to pull his weight, cause you're Bill Tyrrell's kid, you have to have big balls like your old man.

Don't sit there looking at me for Christ's sake. Gimme a hand. You got any ideas?"

"We have to get Andy to work. He could be picking up eggs and feeding chickens in a couple of days. When we see what we can expect from him we'll see who else is around. Those Mexicans have any kids?"

"Mexicans? What good's a Mexican kid, can't even speak the lingo."

"If he goes to school he speaks English. Let's talk to Andy. You're his uncle, he must love you, talk him into helping you out. I'll find him." I went to the yellow door and pulled it open. Andy was leaning against the wall his cheeks streaked with tears. "Come on Andy, we have to help your uncle out. Wipe your face. Maybe you'll like working around animals, it's better than stareing at your suitcase." He rubbed his face with both his hands and followed me to the picnic table. We sat opposite Mr. Sam.

"Andy," Sam cleared his throat, "I'm sorry we got you down here on false pretenses, I know you'd rather be sitting on your butt reading in Bakersfield. Your dad and I thought it would be good for you to do some work. Have a meaningful job. Christ, you're nearly thirteen, when I was thirteen I practically cleared that whole mountain where our gardens are and my old man didn't even say thank you." Andy started to cry.

"Don't cry Andy," I said, "Mr. Sam is from a different generation than we are, and their values were different. We have to help Mr. Sam because he gave his regular help time off. He thought we could do their jobs for five weeks. Your father was supposed to tell you so you'd be prepared. Well he screwed up; we can't let the chickens suffer because your father forgot to tell you about working here. We have to figure out how we get this job done. Now will you work with me and who ever else we can find to keep your uncles farm operating? Will you?"

He gave me a very wet look and nodded his head. Mr. Sam smiled. I shook my head. "Talk. Talk out loud. Say yes, Bruz,

I'll help keep the farm running."

He looked at me a tear trickling down his face, I felt sorry for the kid. "Yes, Bruz, I'll help to keep Uncle Sam's farm working. You have to teach me but I'll help."

"Okay, a promise is a contract. We now have a contract with Mr. Sam. Mr. Sam, can you tell us exactly what we have to do to run this farm?" Sam looked at me like I had saved his life. He pulled two sheets of paper from his pocket, handed one to me and one to his nephew. I looked at the list in my hand. My heart went up into my mouth. Work. Work. And more work. I could see we would be up with the rooster's crow, feed and clean chickens, pick up eggs, candle eggs, fertilized eggs to incubator room, unfertilized into cartons delivered to produce store. Get receipt from manager. Get list of chicken orders from meat market, select, kill, pluck, clean chickens, place order tags on foot and return to market. Pick up afternoon eggs. Candle, fertilized eggs to incubator, pack unfertilized and deliver to produce store.

"This is quite a day, Mr. Sam, twelve, thirteen hours at least. Did those college kids get this much work done? Certainly not for five bucks a week. We'll see how much we can get done and I think you better think about how much you're going to pay us. We can't buy a thing with those million stars you promise." I folded the paper and slid it into my pocket. Andy, three years my senior, looked at me like I was his father. Sam sat nodding his head.

Andy followed me up the hill to the chicken runs. I leaned against the fence. He looked at the chickens. "In a couple of minutes we're going into the chicken run. These chickens are leghorns. They're mean little bastards. They like to take a nip out of you when you're not paying attention. That big guy over there is the rooster. He's king of the run. If you act like you're afraid of him he'll be biting your ass everyday. If he comes at you lift your foot like you're going to kick him. He'll slam on the brakes and stay away from you. Sometimes you may have to really kick a bird. Go very easy. A dead rooster can really screw up a run. Come on lets go meet our leghorn friends."

I showed him how to fill a mash tray, how many handfuls of corn to toss around, where the water pans were placed. Then we went into the coop. Sunday. Nobody had cleaned the roost. The place stunk. There were morning eggs and afternoon eggs everywhere, forty chickens seemed three times as many as twenty. I grabbed a bucket and collected 31 eggs. Sam had a fine group of hens.

I carried the eggs to the incubator room, Andy right on my heels. I opened the door, two men were busily checking the incubators. "Hey, guys, either of you speak English?"

"What do you want?" The older guy asked. "Where's the candling equipment?" He pointed to a cabinet. "Good," I said, "How about egg boxes, where are they stored?"

"You know Blue Door and Yellow Door?" I nodded. "Black door in middle, cartons, boxes all packing."

"Thanks, One more thing, do you know a Mexican boy who speaks English?"

"My son. Fourteen."

"Would he like a job? Clean out the roosts everyday in the morning and the evening, seven of them, five bucks a day?"

"Start when?"

"They could use a cleaning right now, but they could wait until tomorrow." He walked to the door, pushed it open, "Jose! Jose!" He hollered. In two minutes a great big kid came in. "Yes, Dad?" He said.

"Get the hoe out of the barn and clean the roosts, it's a demonstration. Do good and you can clean them everyday for five dollars, Okay?" The kids face lit up like the sun coming up. "Right, Dad." I smiled; all I had to do now is get Mr. Sam to come up with five bucks a day.

We walked down the hill carrying the candling gear. We went to the black door and found a big room full of all kinds of boxes. I grabbed a box of cartons. We went in the yellow door. We picked a picnic table in the back row near an A/C outlet. I set up a candling station, showed Andy what to look for and went to gather the rest of today's eggs.

I got a receipt for 14 dozen eggs and gave my Mexican friends in the incubator room 22 future chickens. The roosts were clean, the chickens happy and it was after eight when Andy and I sat down for dinner. Burritos! Chicken burritos served for dinner. Mexican cooking. Neither Andy nor I had ever eaten Mexican cooking, but the burritos and Coca Cola tasted just fine. Bed time. Time to check those million stars.

Andy followed me through the blue door. I dropped all my clothes on the tile floor and went into a shower stall. I stood in the hot water letting it pound on my head, pound on my shoulders. I bent over and gave my back a chance. I could hear Andy singing in the next stall. We showered till the water turned cold. We grabbed towels from a tall stack in the corner and rubbed our bodies till they glowed.

"Bed time!" I said. Andy laughed. I grabbed my clothes and bare assed out into the barn, Andy followed still laughing out loud. We climbed the ladder. Went into our fabulous bedroom. I threw my clothes on the dresser and slid in between the cool sheets on the big wide bed. I looked up at the big sky light, no stars only dirt. I closed my eyes. The Rooster crowed. I opened my eyes, morning sunshine through the dirt in the skylight. "Andy!" I yelled. "It's chicken time!"

Jose stood by the gate of the first run waiting for me. "Do I get the job?" I forgot that his father had given us a demonstration, "Yeah, Jose. Watch out there might be a couple of eggs in that shit. Get started. Andy and I are going to put out the feed." He nodded and was gone. Andy looked at me. "There's a bag of mash and a bag of corn just inside the coop. Fill all the mash trays. I'll get the water, then throw about ten handfuls of corn around the run. I'll pick up the eggs and you take them to the yellow door and candle them.

I'll do the rest of the chicken coops and keep you supplied with eggs. We'll figure out what's next when the eggs are done."

Andy smiled and nodded. He smiled!

Jose was nearly half finished with the wide roosts. I picked up all the eggs; two would need a little cleaning, a couple of hens too lazy to find a nest. I carried the eggs through the blue door. Andy was busy candling and packing. He smiled at me but didn't stop working. Good sign. I took seven fertilized eggs up to the incubator room. I opened the door. My little yellow friends were in fine voice. "Seven future chickens from the first coop. Er, what should I call you? My name's Bruz."

"Big Jose. Little Jose is working for you. Is your guy candling these eggs correctly? You're getting too many positives. Mind if I check him out?"

"Not at all, I set up the candling but I have only a little experience. We raised some chicks and some ducks but I was much younger. I'll pick up the eggs in three and see you behind the blue door." He laughed. I'd never seen a Mexican smile, let alone laugh. I was stunned. The roosts in three were all clean and sparkling as I picked up the brown eggs from the Plymouth Rocks in run three, twenty-nine eggs, three Jose had rescued from his hoe. Andy was going to be an accomplished egg washer.

I headed down the hill to Andy. Big Jose came up the hill. "He's fine, nicest set-up we've ever had. Let's keep check on the number of fertilized eggs. We might have a mystery here." He laughed and went back to his chicken replacement work.

It was nine forty five in the morning. I carried ten dozen eggs to the produce stand. The manager gave me a funny look as he wrote my receipt. I walked up the two-lane road about fifty yards to the meat market. A guy with a white apron wrapped around his waist watched me come.

"Mr. Sam said I was supposed to do some work for you. What do you need?" He didn't say a word. Walked over to a high desk and handed me seven sheets of paper and seven yellow tags with names printed on them. "You're very early. The guys usually get here after lunch." My customers always bitch about late delivery."

"I think we'll be here this time every morning. We've taken care of the chickens. You're next on the list." He looked at me and laughed. "Well, I'll be God damned!" He said, still laughing.

"Strange farm." I thought walking back to the blue door. I sat with Andy. The big cook wandered over. "Huevos Rancheros?" He said. "Okay," I said, "Haven't any idea what you're selling but could I have a glass of milk and buttered toast with them?" He nodded and looked at Andy. "Me too." He said defensively. The cook wandered off.

"You ever see a chicken killed?" I asked Andy. He just shook his head. His eyes were big enough to pop out of their sockets. "Well, we have to kill, pluck and clean seven hens, so by lunchtime you'll know all about it. I'm going to chop their heads off. They'll flop around on the ground and bleed themselves dry. That's where you'll come in. We'll fill the sink with warm water, you'll dip a chicken in the water and count slowly to a hundred then all the long feathers will pull out real easy. Then you sit down and clean all the little feathers. Somewhere we'll find a set of tweezers to get the tiny ends out of the wings. Once you do one you can do a hundred, we should knock that job off in an hour, an hour and a half."

A big plate of sunny-side eggs swimming in tomato sauce was put in front of me. I tried very hard not to puke. I gave the cook a half-assed smile and took a bite of some delicious toast. I looked at Andy. He shrugged. The cook looked at us, his eyes saying, "What do gringo's know about good eating."

I was an egg dunker. I loved to dunk toast in sunny-side eggs so I dunked toast into sunny-side Mexican eggs. I put it in my mouth; it tasted pretty good, a lot better than it looked. It was hot, not hot hot, but hot spicy. I could handle it. I cleaned my plate and washed it down with cold milk. I felt ready to murder some chickens.

Andy and I went to the execution room in the barn. Everything we needed was within reach, far superior to the back yard behind Jay's house. In seven chops I had seven chickens bleeding out on the blood-soaked ground. Andy was plucking the first victim as I sent the seventh to chicken heaven.

I checked Andy's plucking job, he was a talented plucker but still had to use tweezers on the wing tips. I cleaned the birds, getting the liver, the heart and the gizzard out of the mess I threw in the garbage. The Andy/Bruz team knocked the job off in an hour. We were rolling.

Eleven fifteen I was back at the market, with seven chickens ready for our customers. Mr. "Apron" smiled at me as I entered his busy store. I handed him the chickens. "Beautiful!" he said, "You got a butcher hid in that barn?" He laughed. "Better than that, Mr. Apron," I smiled, "You've got a chicken killer trained by Bill Tyrrell, best chicken killer that ever lived."

He laughed. "Charley, call me Charley. Understand you're a friend of the boss?"

"Acquaintance, I think I'm an acquaintance, my dad was his friend." Charley kept on laughing. "Do me a favor? See that big guy over there? He runs the local diner. A very good customer. He needs two chickens right away. Some party came out of nowhere. Could you give me two chickens in less than an hour. I'll put in a good word for you with Mr. Sam."

"I don't need a good word. I like you. Let me go do a couple of chickens. We can do the paperwork later."

"Appreciate, Bruz. Bruz? That's your name right? The old man thinks the world of you." I smiled, who ever the old man was I thought the world of him too. I ran for the leghorn run, I loved executing leghorns. Thirty-five minutes later I handed two killed, cleaned, plucked leghorns to Charley.

He smiled and handed me a huge Hershey chocolate bar. The customer came over to Charley, "This is Bruz, he killed your chickens as a favor to me, I think he deserves a tip." The fat guy laughed, "He's already got a candy bar you'll wind up charging me for somehow, but okay, here's a buck Kid. You did me a really big favor." I thanked them and excused myself. I stopped at the produce market and got four quarters for the dollar bill. I walked through the blue door and joined Andy sitting at the candling station.

I threw fifty cents on the table. "The man who needed the chickens gave us a tip. Half a buck each. That's not too bad. Lets go sit under that peach tree across the way. We can eat this Hershey bar."

It was cool in the shade of the little tree. Andy and I were just chilling out. We didn't have a job till five, when eggs were due for picking. Somehow the job looked harder on paper than it was for real. Little Jose showed up and plopped down on the ground. I gave him a square of chocolate. Another kid walked up. He stood looking at us. Thirteen, I figured. He didn't say anything. "Sit," I said. "Have a piece of chocolate." Little Jose said, "Pino. He's Big Pino's son. Big Pino works with my dad.

"Can you talk, Pino?" I said.

"Sure I can talk." He replied. "What's to talk about?" I laughed. He looked at me. "I don't like gringos." He said.

"Shut up, Pino!" Little Jose snapped.

"It's okay, Jose, everybody gets an opinion." Andy looked scared.

"So, Pino, you go to school?"

"It's summer vacation. School's in the winter."

"When you go to school in the winter are there any gringos in your class?"

"All gringos. Me and another kid are the only Mexicans. The gringos hate us."

"You ever try to make friends?"

"I told you. They hate us."

"I go to school in Glendale. There're no Mexicans in our school. But I know a lot of Mexicans. I play ball with some good Mexican players. Some Mexicans helped build our ball field. I like Jose, I like his old man. I might even like you if you didn't have such a big chip on your shoulder."

"Yeah, you gave Jose a job. You didn't give me a job. Jose has to like you. Give me a job and I might like you too."

"That's not how it works. It was an emergency. Big Jose offered his son's services. His son earned the job. If your father spoke English he might have mentioned you. You might have gotten Jose's job and Jose would be in your position. My mother says honey gets a lot more than vinegar. If you're friendly you might get a job. I think they're more jobs for kids like us right here on this farm, right now. If that's true you'll get a chance. But you won't get a chance if the gringos think you hate them. Think that over. Here have a piece of chocolate."

I picked up the evening eggs. I found only sixty-two. Andy candled the eggs, eight were fertilized. I took them up to Big Jose and Big Pino. I walked into the incubator room. Big Pino looked up. "I speak English. I just don't talk as quick as Jose." I smiled, "Eight fertilized eggs for your incubators, Gentlemen. All I have to do is deliver the evening eggs and my day is done, dinner and bed. Thank God." We all laughed.

I delivered four and a half dozen eggs to the produce store. Customers grabbed them up as I waited for my receipt. "You feeding those hens something different? Fourteen dozen eggs yesterday, sixteen dozen today. What's going on?" I was very tired; I smiled and slowly made my way through the blue door to see what was tonight's surprise.

Tamales. Cornmeal and meat rolled up in cornhusks. Fresh tamales, delicious. I showered. I let the water pour over me. I climbed the ladder. I fell into bed. I slept.

It was Sunday morning. Our third Sunday of fun at Thousand Oaks Farm. We had finished and delivered our morning egg project and were waiting for Mr. Sam to pick us up for breakfast in the big house. No huevos rancheros this morning. Mr. Sam came in. "Come on kids, the missus is ready to feed you." Sam drove us up the hill in his pick up truck. No one talked. Andy looked out the window.

We went into the nice dining room. Andy and I sat across from each other. Sam sat at the head of the table, his wife at the foot. We enjoyed fried eggs, fried potatoes and fried bacon. No fattening Mexican food for us gringos.

"So what do you think about this egg deal, Bruz? How come the chickens are laying so much more?

"Come on, Sam. You know chickens don't lay more. Somebody is stealing eggs. And I'll bet the thieves are your favorite college kids. They probably change every semester or so. The ones leaving teach the ones coming and they all steal a little bit of your money. I'll bet it adds up to a bunch over the years, you ought to ask Andy's dad if he can figure out when it started so you'll know how much money you lost.

"I don't care what happened. I just want it to stop."

"Don't hire outsiders. Everybody who works for you should live on the farm. Jose and Pino can take care of the chickens, The eggs could be candled and packed by Big Jose and Big Pino in the incubator room. Make a six man dormitory out of Andy's and my room for the single guys and hire a family man to pick, kill, pluck and clean the chickens. He could move into the house the six single guys were sharing. You could expand your chicken business and serve the restaurants in the area.

Charley has contacts there and you'd never have to hire an outside guy again. Andy could have a real vacation at his Uncle Sam's house and like in a soap opera on the radio everybody lives happily ever after."

With fifty dollars in my pocket I waved goodbye to Sam and Andy as Mom drove the Studebaker on to the two-lane road that lead us home to Hazel Street. I had worked my butt off for five weeks at Thousand Oaks but I would never complain to my mother. I made a friend for life out of Mr. Sam and knew I would miss killing his chickens. Once you chop off a head it gets to be a habit.

34

Home. Didn't somebody say there was no place like it? I lay in my skinny bed. I was very comfortable, safe in its narrow confines. Home. I closed my eyes and floated away.

A rooster crowed, automatically I was out of bed about to wake Andy when I realized I was home. No Andy to wake, no 300 chickens waiting up the hill. I could jump back into bed if I wanted. But I pulled on a pair of short pants and went to take care of my chickens. I pulled the gate open. Big Red, the rooster strutted around the run, the hens were sleeping in. The run looked as if I had never gone away, freshly raked, mash in the feeders, some water in the bowls. Someone had cleaned the place on Sunday. When Billy Sapporro said he'd take care of the chickens he took care of the chickens. I spent ten minutes topping off the mash, tossing some corn around and filling the water bowls. I picked up three eggs. I counted only seven hens on the roost. They ate chicken every Sunday I was away. At this rate I'd be an ex chicken caretaker before school started.

I checked Billy's garden. Perfect. I saw the hedge needed trimming and knew the lawn was long. I grabbed the clippers and caught up with my chores. Ten o'clock I put the lawn mower in the garage and sat on the front step to rest. My mom came out the door in her blue and white uniform. "I have breakfast on the table, come let's eat, I have to leave in 45 minutes." I got up and kissed my little mother on the cheek. She squeezed my arm. We sat in the breakfast nook.

"Are you guys trying to put me out of the chicken business?" I laughed.

Mom smiled, "Sorry, Bruz, I had some company and I needed to show off my cooking. I'm thinking of leaving the Variety store. I might go into business with a friend. I don't want to talk about it until I'm further along with the money people."

"Wow, that sounds exciting. I can't wait to hear what happens next."

"What happens next is we eat our breakfast. You know Sam gave you an extra twenty five dollars?"

"Yeah, I kind of helped him out of a problem. Just stick it in the Mason Jar." She laughed.

I watched her drive up Hazel on her way to Grand Central. She was one terrific person. Maybe this new venture would make her happy again. I sure hoped so. I sat on the front step and my big sister sat down next to me. She had a soup bowl in her lap. A big red pomegranate, cut in pieces, filled the bowl. "Mom loves these things," she said, "want to share?"

"All they do is make my fingers red, I must spit out the good part 'cause I don't enjoy them at all. I know mom loves them, but you enjoy, spit the pits on the lawn."

"Mom has a doctor friend," she said, "He was over for Sunday dinner three times. Nice enough guy. Old. Invented some kind of medicine called Royal Hygiene. I think he's rich." She spit some seeds on the lawn.

"She was talking about going into business. You know what she's talking about?"

"The doc wants her to open a restaurant. Thinks they can make a fortune. I think mom is just stringing the guy along. Restaurants are hard work, I don't think mom wants to work that hard."

"Well, she doesn't seem to be in any hurry. Let's just wait and see what happens."

"I guess you're right. Want any of this? I'm going to throw it in the garbage."

"Nope," I held up my hand, "See, red fingers." We laughed.

Wednesday I got my magazine route back from Larry Doyle. He'd sold everything but one Country Gentleman. I left it on my front porch for Mr. Appleby to pick up. I left the bottle with all of Larry's money and a note. "Mr. Appleby, I was away for five weeks and Larry Doyle took care of the magazine route. He did well but didn't sell one Gentleman that you'll find on the porch. If he can sell out my route each week then I'm not taking enough product, so please leave me ten more Posts and five more Journals and Gentlemen. See you around the market one of these days. Thanks. Bruz."

"There," I said to myself, "If I sell out I make another sixty-five cents a month." I smiled and went to bed.

I spent a couple of extra hours on the Grand Central back porch and sold out my magazines every week. On the fourth week since my Thousand Oaks adventure I went to the front porch for my magazines. Under the Benjamin Franklin bottle was a fancy silver envelope. I thought they were raising their prices and my business would go right in the can so I tore the fancy envelope open. I sat on the top step to read it.

"Dear Bruz,

As one of one hundred top salesmen in Los Angeles County you are invited to a special Barbeque in Fremont Park this Labor Day. The party will begin at eleven in the morning and be over at four in the afternoon. Come. There will be hamburgers, franks, ice cream and cake with special contests, prizes and awards. Please RSVP. Appelby, Curtis Publishing." I would be there with bells on.

Monday afternoon. I had six Posts left. Everything else was gone. I knew all I had to do was stand here and the customers would come. I saw my brother get out of his Chrysler in the parking lot. What was he doing here on a Monday afternoon? And he wasn't wearing a tie. He came up the stairs.

"Hey, Jay, what's wrong?" I asked.

"Newberry's laid me off. Some big cash flow problem. They laid off three quarters of the office staff. I wanted to ask mom if I could move back into my room. Where does she hang out?"

"Come on, I'll take you." We walked across the store. Mom was near the cash registers. She saw Jay and me.

"What's the matter, Jay, you all right?" She looked worried.

"Newberry's laid me off. Can I move back into my room for a while?"

"You know you can. You don't even have to ask. You have any money?"

"I'm okay for now. I got a line on a temporary job. Fred works for this new government thing, WPA, Works Progress something. He's talking to his foreman. They're a guy shy fixing roads in Griffith Park. He's going to call me tonight. Twenty-five bucks a week but it's better than a kick in the ass. Sorry, Bruz." I laughed.

I rode home with my big brother. I helped him straighten out his room. I got him a couple of towels from the linen closet. "Why don't you go take a shower now, while everyone has something else to do. One bathroom doesn't go too far." He patted my head, grabbed one of his towels and went in the house. Gen called him from the kitchen, "You staying for supper, Jay? I'll throw some more lamb in the stew."

"I'm home for a while. Got canned. I'll grab a shower and tell you about it at dinner." Gen put some more lamb, carrots and potatoes into her bubbling stew. She knew her big brother's appetite.

Seven fifteen we sat in our dining nook. Jay sat in dad's place. Mom was in civilian clothes, her blue and white uniform finished for the day. Gen had served a big glass of fresh orange juice to start. Mom looked at her oldest child. "So, Son, what happened to your job?"

"Well, my boss called me in Santa Monica. The guy who runs that store is a real jerk. Anyway he says New York had screwed up the cash flow and we weren't going to get payroll for a while so he had to lay off nearly all the guys who keep the place running. I know it won't be long but it sure is inconvenient. Katie and I were thinking about getting married. Now she's the only one working. I don't think I'll be out of work a month. They'll probably have to close Santa Monica if I'm not there watching the operation." He drank his juice down. "That's really good. Haven't had OJ for a long time." The phone rang. Mom picked it up. "Fred Fultz for you, Jay."

"Fred?" He said. We watched him nod. Nod again.

"You son of a bitch!" He laughed.

"Yeah. Seven-thirty. I owe you one, Buddy." He hung up. Sat back in Dad's seat and laughed. "Well, I'm a government employee. I work for the WPA and start tomorrow morning at seven thirty. I'm meeting the truck on Lake at Sonora, then to Griffith Park and road work."

"You better take Dad's work gloves. Your soft hands will be hamburger before lunch." I said.

"How'd you get so smart so young, Bruz? You just knock me out." He messed my hair. It didn't mess anymore but I loved it. I loved my big brother.

I was standing in the driveway in front of the garage when he came out of his room. I held dad's work gloves. I wasn't going to let him forget them. He hadn't had a shovel in his hands for years. Without gloves he would be through by lunch. I knew he needed this job.

"Follow me, we'll go out the back way." He smiled. I opened the back gate and we walked though the trees past the CCC barracks and out onto Sonora. We crossed with the light at Lake Street then stood on the corner waiting for Jay's truck.

"You miss the old man?" Jay said. I was surprised, I'd never thought about it.

228

"I don't know. I think about him a lot. I know you guys had problems but he was great with me. I loved him a lot, but he told me he had to go on a long trip and I wouldn't see him again and since you were marrying Katie that I was the man of the house. I was responsible for Mom and Gen. So that's what I try to do."

"He tell you that in the hospital?"

"No, he came the night he died. He was in his work clothes, told me he had a lot to do where he was going. Told me not to mourn him because he was just on a trip but he wouldn't be coming back."

"You had a dream, Bruz."

"No I didn't. I was asleep but he woke me up. He shook my bed. He was standing at the foot of the bed shaking the bar. I opened my eyes and he was there. He talked to me and went away. That's how it happened. I haven't told anyone but you. Maybe you'll like dad more now you know how he worried about me."

"Here comes the truck Kid. I loved my father more than I like to think. I just worried about how much he loved me. You were the apple of his eye, Do No Wrong Bruzzy. Let's just remember we both loved him. Each in our own way. Now let me get on this truck before they fire me on my first day." Fred reached down and pulled Jay up into the truck. All the men smiled at me and waved as they turned on Sonora and headed for Griffith Park.

35

Mom dropped me at Fremont Park by the main ball field. It was ten minutes to eleven. "I'll pick you up right here at four o'clock. Got that? Right here at four." She waved and drove away.

I saw a sign with an arrow pointing across the park. "Curtis Publishing," it said. They had a large area roped off at the back of the park. Two posts with a crosspiece were wrapped in red, white and blue. A banner across the top welcomed The Curtis Top One Hundred. I walked through. Three men sat at a table a long list in front of them. A couple of older boys were ahead of me. I waited. The guy said, "Name, please?"

"Bruzzy Tyrrell." I said. He looked down his list. "I have a Louis Tyrrell." He looked at me. "That's what's on my birth certificate but my name's Bruzzy." He laughed. "Well, Bruz, if you want to come to the party today pretend your name is Louis, even if Bruz is better. Go get in line for the Bean puzzle." He pointed to a bunch of kids standing by a big round bowl nearly full of jellybeans. I wandered over. "Guess the number of beans in the bowl and win a wonderful prize!" A big sign said. Someone handed me an entry form and a pencil that had Saturday Evening Post printed down its side. I gagged, printing Louis Tyrrell on the form. I guessed there were 7,822 beans in the bowl. I folded the paper and put it in the envelope. A man took it and slid it through a slot in a big box. I walked on into the party.

"Hey Bruz!" It was Mr. Appelby, "Over here!" I walked over. He stuck out his hand. I shook it. This table is ours, I have ten of the top guys working for me, that's pretty good, don't you think?"

"That's great, Mr. Appelby, you're the best."

"Nope, I'm lucky. I have a great territory. Let's grab a hot dog and a coke and sit down. The rest of the guys should show up pretty soon."

I got a well done hot dog, smeared it with mustard and pickle relish and dug deep into a barrel of cokes for a cold one. I sat at the Appleby table. Three kids all a couple of years older than me came up. "This Tony Appelby's table?" The tallest kid asked. "Yeah." I answered. "He's over there getting a hot dog. Actually he's talking to some guy. Sit down. I'm Bruz Tyrrell." They sat across from me. "Where do you work?" One of the guys said. "Glendale. Mostly at the Grand Central Market." He shook his head. "I'm from West L.A., I do most of my business in the Ralph's parking lot about six blocks from home."

The oldest guy, probably fifteen, looked at me. "I work downtown Glendale. Don't you think you might do better at the airport? Lots of people pass through there."

"Nope," I answered, "The airport doesn't appreciate kids. They sell magazines inside the terminal. We're just competition. If you go near there the airport cops throw you out. The market likes me. I use their back porch. I get a stream of customers all day."

Mr. Appelby sat down. There were two franks on his paper plate and a root beer in his hand.

"Hi Tony," the kid from downtown Glendale said.

"Okay, first names for my best sales guys. This is Bruz Tyrrell; he's the best and youngest guy in my territory. Bruz, the big guy is Billy, the guy from downtown is John and the quiet guy is Terry. Now if you can remember you can call each other by name.

It was a great party. We ran in the three-legged race, Terry and I were last. There was a forty-yard dash. I would have won if some little kids hadn't run out on the course. They had some acrobats and a magician doing card tricks. I got a certificate as best salesman in Glendale. I got a Saturday Evening Post Tee Shirt and a Ladies Home Journal apron for my mom. Finally at three-thirty they were going to announce the jellybean winner. I was stuffed from eating everything in sight, pooped from the races and tired of shoptalk.

The Big Man from the front office was going to present the prize to the one who guessed how many beans were in the bowl. 7,822, I said to myself.

"Gentlemen." Mr. Big Shot publisher said. "Now it's time to find out who is the champion mathematician out of our 100 best salesmen in L.A. County. The entries have all been checked, the beans counted and the winner is Louis Tyrrell, seven thousand eight hundred and twenty two beans. Come down here, Mr. Tyrrell, and get this brand new speedometer for your bicycle. Let's hear it for Louis Tyrrell." I jumped up and walked to the table. I shook the man's hand.

"Here, Louis."

"My name is Bruzzy, Louis is my Grandfather." Everybody laughed.

Mr. Big Shot didn't know what to do. "Well, okay, whatever your name is you win. Go home and mount this beauty on your bike and you'll know how fast you're travelling and how far you're going."

"I don't have a bike." I said. The whole place roared with laughter. Mr. Big threw up his hands, "Here. You won this take it and I hope you get a bike soon so you can use it. Congratulations."

"Thank you very much, Mr. Curtis. Thank you for letting me sell your magazines." I couldn't understand why everyone was laughing. Anyway I had to go. I could see my Mom parked at the ball field across the park. "Thank you, Tony. Swell party. I've got to go." All my friends waved as I ran off to catch my mom and show her my new speedometer. I figured Santa Claus might take care of my bike problem.

It was the first day of school, Jay and I stood on the corner waiting for Jay's truck.

"I think my WPA career is nearly over. Katie heard a rumor yesterday that I was to be called back."

"That would be keen, Jay. You could wear a suit and tie again, look like a boss."

He smiled. "Here's the truck. Have a good first day of school." He grabbed the edge of the truck and vaulted aboard. They all waved and yelled "So Long, Bruz" as they headed up into the hills. I walked to school. I sat on the steps waiting for Sandy. Bobby Hessong showed up. He sat. "Good summer?" He asked. "Swell." I answered, both of us watching the gate for that familiar blonde head. The bell rang. We looked at each other. The sixth grade was in Room 115. We dragged ourselves into the room; the teacher shouting "Sit in alphabetical order!"

I made for the back row. I sat. I looked around. No Sandy. I was devastated.

"Good morning. This is the sixth grade. My name is Mrs. Gross; it's a pleasure to have you here. Mr. Walters has informed me of his feelings about all of you. I can't wait to see if you're as good as he thinks you are. Now, I like to have competition among my students. The way I make sure we compete is by testing you every four weeks then seating you based on your position in the class." She walked to her desk. She picked up a notebook, "Sandra Blaine, please take the first desk." She looked up from her notes. "Sandra Blaine present?" The class shook its head back and forth. Mrs. Gross turned a page in her book. "Louis Tyrrell, sit in the first seat." I didn't say a word. I walked to the desk, watched the person in the seat get up and dropped quietly into the seat.

In one voice the class called out. "Bruzzy Tyrrell. Louis is his grandfather!" They all laughed. Mrs. Gross' face went red. "Order. We'll have order in this class!" Bobby Hessong waved his hand in the air. "Yes, young man?"

"I'm Bruz Tyrrell's friend. Every teacher in every class we've been in has called him Bruzzy or Bruz. This is our last year in Franklin. The class would appreciate it if you carried on the custom, please." The class applauded. Mrs. Gross looked at me. She looked at the class. She shook her head. "Did Mr. Walters call you by your nickname?"

"Yes m'am." I said.

"Well, since you're number one in the class we'll carry on the tradition." The class applauded. "Enough!" Mrs. Gross stamped her foot. "Megan Roberts take the next desk." I watched Megan sit down. "Bobby Hessong, next." And so it went until everyone was seated in the proper order. The morning was a blur. I couldn't get Sandy out of my head. The lunch bell rang. I walked out of school, out the side gate, across School Street and stood in front of Sandy's house on Lake Street. It was empty. A blue and green "For Sale" sign hung on the front door. I was lost. Someone walked up to me and stood by my side.

"Bruz, she asked me to give this to you when I saw you."

I looked. It was Uncle Fred. He held out a blue envelope. I saw Sandy's writing, I grabbed. "Thanks, Uncle Fred, when did she go?"

"Couple of weeks ago. They wouldn't let her call you. She was very upset. She ran across the street and handed me this the day they drove away. Go read it, maybe you'll feel better." He patted my head and smiled. He was a good friend. I sat down on her front step and looked at the blue envelope. I tore it open.

Bruz:

My dad has been assigned to the London Office he is a full colonel. My mother and I are joining him. I'm going to a fancy American Girls school in London. I'm going to miss our studies on the steps. I'm going to miss Glendale. I'm going to miss your mom's peach cobbler, most of all I'm going to miss you. My dad talks about this Hitler guy, he's sure there's going to be a war. I just wanted to be in sixth grade with you, study with you, eat lunch with you but that's not possible. Maybe someday we will meet again in happier times. I love you.

Sandy.

So, there it was. Sandy was gone. Gone forever. Gone halfway around the world. I'll just think of her happily living in England with her father and mother and face sixth grade alone. I stood up, brushed off my pants and walked back to school. Bobby sat on the steps. I sat down. "Sandy's in England, she's going to a girls school she says goodbye and we'll always be friends. So, you and I will study together, so we can stay tops in the class." Bobby shook his head. The bell rang. We went back to class.

I sat in the first desk in the first row. I was number one in the class. Mrs. Gross sat at her desk. Megan handed me a piece of paper. I unfolded it. "I'm as smart as Sandy. Let me study with you and Bobby, together we can stay sitting right where we are. Please! Megan."

I looked at her. She starred back at me. She had dark curly hair; her eyes were green like my mom's. I shook my head yes. She smiled. The three of us would rule the class. I had a new partner.

I watched Jay climb down off his truck. We walked home through the trees. Billy Sapporro was working on the garden. He bowed when I introduced my brother. Jay went to take a shower. I watched Billy snipping here, shoveling there, picking tomatoes, and pulling up carrots. I put some tomatoes and carrots in the fridge and found Gen on the front porch. "Jay's taking a shower. Billy is taking some vegetables to market and I have a new study partner at school." She smiled. "Mom will be home a little after seven, we'll eat at seven-thirty. I'm making pot roast and baked potatoes."

"I'm due at the Flying School, be home for supper." And up the hill I walked.

Genevieve started dinner with a bowl of cut up cantaloupe. A present from L.A. County. The bags had arrived today. Mom was sitting in Gens seat because Gen was serving the supper. I sat between Mom and Jay. The breakfast nook was the best room in the house.

Gen sat down, we were enjoying our appetizer. Jay spoke up. "I talked to Kitty this afternoon. Sounds like I have two more weeks to work for the government. She hears they're going to give me the Burbank store. Somehow the guy who runs it has screwed up, supposed to get the official word tomorrow. I'm going to run over to Burbank after dinner and see what I can see." He looked at a plump piece of cantaloupe and popped in his mouth.

Gen cleared the dishes. She went to the sink to serve the pot roast.

"I have something to tell the family," my mom said with a big grin. "All of the financing has been arranged for our restaurant. I'm going to work at the Variety Store for another month, and then we'll put the restaurant together. We should open for Christmas."

Gen put plates of food at everyone's place. She sat in mom's seat, "Don't you think that might be too much work for you, Mom? You're not getting any younger." My sister looked right at her mother. I thought I might hide under the table

"I'll be 45 in April, young lady, I think I have a few good years of work still in me. I won't kill myself and I could make a lot of money."

"Get good help, Mom." Jay chimed in. "No rules you have to do all the work."

"I'll have an extra cook, two kitchen boys, a manager, two waiters and a counterman. I think I can palm off some of my duties on them. The cook will do breakfast and lunch; I'll do the dinner. Doesn't sound like I'll kill myself."

"Maybe I can help." I offered.

"Yes darling, you can come and eat. You can tell me how good it tastes. You can be our best advertisement." The table got quiet as we polished off Gen's pot roast. If they served food that tasted as good as this Dottie's Deli would be a great success.

Megan, Bobby and I copied our fourth grade study plan. We were sure to ace all the tests and stay at the top of the class. I stood on the corner of Lake and Sonora waiting for Jay. This was his last day digging roads for the WPA. He was going back to his suit and tie, back to running his own store, back to living his real life.

Saturday morning. I took care of my seven chickens, put three eggs in the fridge and put the hoe away in the garage. Jay came out of his room. Nice tan slacks, opened collar tan short sleeve shirt, all signs of the WPA were missing. He was the young executive again. "You want to check out Burbank with me?"

"Sure," I said, "You expecting any trouble?"

"Sure," He laughed, "That's why I'm bringing you along."

He parked across San Fernando Road from his new store. It was open. People were working, helping customers. He held my hand as we ran across the busy road.

We walked into the store. The floor was littered with little pieces of paper, candy wrappers, a paper bag. Jay walked up to a pretty lady. "The manager in?" He asked. She shook her head. Who is the floor lady?" She pointed to a tall skinny woman standing in the raised office in the back corner. "Thank you." Jay said and nodded to me to follow him. We walked to the office. "Miss?" He called.

"Can't you see I'm busy?" The girl snapped.

"I'm sorry. My name's Tyrrell, I'm the new manager, supposed to start Monday, but I gather you have some kind of problem."

"Oh! Thank God, Mr. Tyrrell. Phil didn't come in and the cash bag isn't here. I only have the money that was left in the registers and it's Saturday. What can we do?"

"First, we won't get excited. Do you have this Phil's number?" She nodded. "Call him. I don't think he'll answer but call him, then I'll call L.A." She asked for a number, we waited, she shook her head. "No answer." she said.

"What's your name?" Jay asked.

"Millie, Millie Washington."

"Well, Millie. Go back on the floor, tell the girls the new manager is here, check all the registers for money and put all the money at the candy counter, okay?"

"Yes, Mr. Tyrrell, I'm so glad you came in." Jay nodded. She walked away. "Well, Bruz, looks like we're working today." I went to find a broom. The one thing I did well was sweep. It was a very nice store. I swept it clean, picked up the mess and put it in a garbage can, carried the can downstairs to the basement which was crowded with piles of boxes, small packages and paint cans. I did a quick inventory and checked where I could put everything.

I went back to the floor and saw Jay speaking with a man in a suit. I joined them. Jay put his hand on my shoulder. "Mr. Donohue, this is my little brother, Bruz. He came to protect me and wound up sweeping the place out." Donohue laughed and shook my hand.

"You've got a terrific big brother, Bruz. I hope you appreciate it."

"Best big brother in the world. Nobody's better."

"You should have enough money to get you through today. Stay open till six. We'll check out the books and see what Phil relieved us of. Nice having you back, Jay. This should be a good store for you. Maybe we should transfer Katie?"

"Leave her in L.A. till I figure this place out, I don't think we ought to work the same store. I'm going to marry her."

"Terrific, you'll make a great couple. I'll see you Monday." He walked out. "Miss Washington!" Jay called. She rushed right over.

"Yes, Mr. Tyrrell?"

"Here's a bunch of cash. Set the registers up as usual and put what's left over in the safe. Okay?"

"Yes Sir. Thank you, sir. It's nice having a real manager around." She quickly walked away.

"I guess we're stuck here till six, Bruz. Anything you want to do?"

"Yeah, I think the basement could use a cleaning. Lots of stuff sitting around that should be on shelves. Let me see what I can do."

"You're a good kid Bruz. I'll make it worth your while somehow."

I laughed. "I like to keep busy. That way you keep out of trouble, that's what my dad always said."

"I wish I had a dad who said things like that!" Jay teased. We laughed. I headed downstairs. There were boxes of candy. Gum Drops, chocolates, tootsie rolls and something that sounded delicious. "Carmallows," caramel covered marshmallows. Too bad the box was closed so tightly. I couldn't steal a sample.

I found a brown door in the hall with a hand printed "candy" sign. I opened the door to what soon would be my favorite room in the whole store, a room twenty-foot square filled with every kind of candy imaginable. I was in candy heaven. I could work down here and eat candy all day. That was better than sweeping out the flying school. I might even work for nothing.

I found all the candy boxes in the basement and put them on shelves in the candy room. Finally all I had was trash. I pushed open an angled steel door that looked as if it went outdoors. It was a small patio with ten or twelve garbage cans lined against the walls. I got rid of all the garbage. I washed my hands and face and went back upstairs. I was shocked. The clock read five forty-five. Only fifteen minutes left in the workday. Jay was sitting in his office. I walked over. "We'll be leaving soon, Bruz. Do me a favor, go lock up. We don't need anymore customers."

239

The big round white clock read six, Jay held the door open for Millie, "Thanks Millie for all your help. I'll see you Monday, enjoy you're day off."

"Thank you, Mr. Tyrrell, it's wonderful having you here. See you Monday. So long, Bruz have a nice weekend." A car pulled up. She got in with some good looking guy, they drove away. I liked the dime store business.

Jay went behind the candy counter, straightened a sales sign atop the counter. We walked out he pulled the door closed and locked it. He tried the doors. When he was satisfied they were locked we climbed in his Chrysler and headed for Glendale. He reached in his pocket and handed me a large square object in brown waxed paper. "That's a 'Carmallow,' Bruz, my favorite candy in the whole world."

"I saw a box of them in the candy room. I really wanted one but the box was closed tight and now I get one, this is a perfect day." Jay laughed.

"Could you drop me at the flying school? I have to sweep it up before supper. Tell mom I'll be home by seven" I had busted my butt all day in Jay's store but I wasn't a bit tired. I liked the variety of work in a dime store, and I could sweep out the flying school in my sleep. I went to get my brooms.

36

Monday. I did the chickens, made my lunch, washed, dressed and headed out for school. Jay came out of his room. "Seven-thirty?" I said.

"First day, I want to check money and stock orders before all the people are around. Tell mom I'll be late, I'm going to look at an apartment I saw in yesterday's paper. Thanks again for Saturday, Bruz, you saved my ass." He headed for his car; I went out the back gate hoping he didn't take the apartment. I liked him living in the back yard.

I sat on the steps and studied with Megan and Bobby dreaming about Sandy. I needed to forget her. My mind flitted between Sandy, the Burbank store and Dottie's Deli. Suddenly my life was full of problems. I got home, grabbed my magazine bag and hiked up the hill to Grand Central. At five o'clock when mom offered to drive me home my magazine bag was empty. Another sold out week for one of the top salesmen in L.A. County.

I sat in the Studebaker as Mom drove down Sonora. "Jay's going to look at an apartment in Burbank. He'll be home late." My mom looked at me. "Should we wait dinner for him?

"He didn't say."

"I have a lot of papers to go over. We'll eat at seven-thirty if Jay is home or not."

I was sitting in the dining nook, watching Mom stir the creamed salmon when Jay came in the front door. No hello. He went into the bathroom and in no time at all he slid into dad's seat at the table.

"Sorry, I'm late, mom, that store will take me a year to straighten out and I rented a little place in Burbank so I'll be out of your hair. Nice place. Cheap. It's two blocks from work. I can leave my car in the garage. That stuff smells good."

241

"Wonderful, Jay. You can work late and still be home early." My sister had spoken. Mom put the creamed salmon on toast and handed our plates around.

"We've leased a two window store just off Brand Boulevard in the middle of Glendale. I was looking at some suggested plans and those windows just don't seem right. Has my bright family any suggestions?"

"Yeah, forget about it, stay at the variety Store, mom, you don't need all that responsibility. This stuff is good, any chance for seconds?" Jay, the store exec was speaking.

"Too late to turn back now, we signed a three year lease on the store, my doctor friend has laid out some important cash and I have to assume some responsibility."

"Dad said a promise is better than a contract." I said and got a dirty look from my mother and a chuckle from my big brother. My sister just shook her head. We watched Jay wolf down his seconds. "I made an apple pie last night, anybody for pie and vanilla ice cream." We all raised our hands. Mom laughed out loud. I got a wonderful feeling in the pit of my stomach.

We watched Dottie cut the pie, put it on a plate and pile ice cream on the top. When we were all served she sat down. "Enjoy!" She said. Jay spoke up.

"Bruz. I'm in trouble at my new store. You could help me out if it's okay with Mom. You handled the basement very well on Saturday. I need a stock clerk but there isn't any budget for a stock clerk. The girls can never do the job. I might be able to pay you 20 or 25 cents an hour. You'd have to quit your magazines but you would save your big brothers butt. What do you think?"

"I loved working in your store. I could get there by three or three fifteen and work till six thirty.

Then I could be home by seven, I could still sweep out the Flying School. I could work all day Saturday. I'll sell my magazine route to Larry Doyle. Would that work out for you?" I looked across the table.

"Is that okay with you Mom?" Jay asked.

"It's Bruz's decision, he's a big boy." They all looked at me. "I guess I'm the new stock clerk at JJ Newberry's in Burbank."

I was sitting on the top step resting my head against the warm brick wall listening to Megan pontificate on American history. I thought about working in Jay's store. Megan finished her speech. I opened my eyes. "Very good, Megan, you've got that subject beat." She blinked her eyes and smiled sheepishly. Bobby patted her shoulder.

"I'll walk you home this afternoon, Bobby, I'm going to Burbank and work in my brother's store."

"Shall we check some math problems now?" Megan pushed; Bobby had christened her 'the slave driver.'

I crossed the railroad tracks and turned left into no-mans land. Neither Glendale nor Burbank. Burbank started the block before the Cosmo movie house and Jay's store was in the next block. I walked in the right door. The place was full of customers. Everyone was working. Three or four people were trying to buy something at every counter. Was the depression over? Millie was working house wares and several women were waving pots in her face. "Bruz!" She called. "Come bag for me before you go downstairs." I stood next to her. She took the money. I put the pots and the strainers and the sink plugs into bags and handed them to the smiling ladies. In twenty minutes our rush was over. Millie went off to give another girl a hand and I went downstairs to my basement. Everything was as I left it Saturday except someone was pounding on the steel door. I pushed it open. Two Mexican kids stood there looking at me. I smiled waiting to see if we spoke the same language. "Mr. Phil let's us take the garbage cans down the alley where they pick them up on Tuesdays and Thursdays. He gives us a dime a can, Miss Millie says we should ask you."

"Mr. Phil is gone. My brother is boss now. I don't know if he has a dime a can, let me go up and ask. Sit on the steps I'll be right back." I ran upstairs. Jay was talking to some guy near the front door. I walked over. They were in deep conversation I wasn't close enough to hear what they were saying. The man took a pad from his pocket and stopped talking. I nearly yelled "Jay" then I thought better of it, I walked up to him. He looked at me like I was a stranger. "Mr. Tyrrell," I said, "Today is trash day, two young Mexicans tell me they were hired to take the trash down the alley to be picked up. They say they get a dime a can. I said I needed to speak with you. How do you want me to handle that?" He handed me two quarters.

"Tell them we pay a quarter for three cans, six cans a half a buck, Okay?" The man with the pad started talking. I walked away. I ran downstairs. "The new boss says three for a quarter, take it or leave it." They smiled and rolled the cans down the alley. I gave them the two quarters. "See you tomorrow," one of them said as I closed the steel doors. I went around the basement and found all the light switches. I turned on all the lights, it got a little brighter, they must put ten-watt bulbs in those fixtures I thought. I wandered down each aisle looking at what was on the shelves. Some stuff was brand new some had been around for a while.

There was a desk and file cabinet in the far back corner. A couple of yellow pads on the desk and a basic map of the basement showing the shelves and what was supposed to be on each shelf. I took the map and started comparing what I found to what the map said. Nothing matched. The map was a good idea but no one seemed to follow it. I found some carbon paper in the main drawer and some eight and a half by eleven paper. I copied the map. I walked around the basement, changed light bulbs and notated where everything was stored on the shelves. I was ready to start putting away the material laying on the floor. Jay's voice came down the stairs. "Hey Bruz, It's six o'clock I'm locking up. I've got fifteen or twenty minutes of paperwork then we're out of here. Okay?"

"Right! I'll be ready to go."

Twenty minutes later I watched him lock the right doors, check the left doors then stand back and survey his store. "Busy day. Haven't got any idea why, but it was the best day they've had since Christmas two years ago. Go figure."

"It's because it's your store, Jaywah, people love buying from a Tyrrell." He laughed.

"My car is across the street. I'm going into LA to see Katie. I'll drop you at Sonora, Okay?"

"Great!" I got to the flying school at six thirty-five. I was home at seven. I showered, ate dinner, checked the chickens and was fast asleep before eight o'clock. I was one pooped out stock clerk.

I woke up, picked up three eggs in the chicken coop and put them in the fridge. My mom was sitting at the table looking at her restaurant plans. I grabbed the Wheaties, a bottle of milk and a banana.

Mom looked at me. "I have lunch with my doctor friend and I still haven't got an answer for these windows."

I sliced my banana on the cereal, poured some milk and took a spoonful. "Remember that restaurant on Temple Street where dad liked the flank steak? We used to eat in the window. The table was up on a kind of deck, it was round six people could eat there. Dad thought it was very special. We went there just because he liked that table."

"I never thought about that until this minute, Sweetheart. That's perfect for us. Why didn't I think of it? Thank you my darling, you've really saved my day." I happily ate my Breakfast of Champions. I'd just done something good for the mother I loved.

We aced Mrs. Gross' first test and kept our seats. Megan was almost as good as Sandy but she didn't have her sense of humor. Bobby liked Megan a whole lot. It wasn't long before I became the third wheel in our study group.

Everyday I walked home with Bobby, checked out the expanding gardens behind his house, crossed the railroad to no-mans land and on down San Fernando Road to Jay's store. I was a fixture. Everyone expected me by three-fifteen. Millie kept a list of things to do for Bruz. I had the basement in great shape; I had become good friends with Jose and Manuel who took care of the garbage. They helped me tear up boxes and scrub the candy room floor. Never asking for more than their regular fifty cents. I worked the floor during busy periods. I restocked the counters; I filled the candy cases, made sure all the light bulbs were in stock. I found old stock hidden on the basement shelves. Jay held sales to get rid of the out-of-date merchandise. I cleaned the glassware, polished the pots and pans and hung strainers along the edge of the house-ware counter where customers would see them and remember they needed a strainer. JJ Newberry, school, five hens and a rooster were my main responsibility with the flying school squeezed in on Tuesday, Thursday and Saturday.

Christmas was coming. Boxes of Christmas products arrived every day. The Candy room was my favorite. I loved putting the candy stock away. Sampling every new chocolate cherry, every new candy bar, and every chocolate covered cookie. My problem was passing the brown candy room door without slipping in for a sample. Some days I was successful some days I failed, I still loved carmallows the best.

"Hang the green string to all the light fixtures front to back and the red one side to side, throw a lot of tinsel over both ropes then decorate the little tree and put it in the toy department." My manager was giving me my Saturday assignments; it was three weeks till Christmas. For the last two years Christmas just passed by in our house. Christmas couldn't be passed in a dime store. I heard someone say the store made a third of its income over the Christmas holidays. I was on a stepladder tying a red ball to a light fixture.

"Hey Bruz, come on, I'll buy you lunch." Jay called from his office. I met him by the door. "Let's get a burger across the street at Bob's, okay?"

"Great." I said. "Better than hanging red rope." We laughed. Bob's hamburgers are the best. I licked the catsup off my fingers as Jay paid the check. "Come next door, I want your opinion on something." My brother was being mysterious. We walked into the Burbank Second Hand Store. It was filled with Christmas. It made our store look like the Fourth of July. Jay nodded to a man, "Is it still back there?" "Yep." The guy said. "It won't be there tomorrow." Jay nodded. We walked to the back of the store. I saw a beautiful 'Roadmaster' Blue and Silver Bike, white walled balloon tires, Texas longhorn handlebars. I fell in love. I could see the price tag. Seven ninety-eight, my heart dropped, no way Jay could afford that. "What do you think, Bruz? Nice bike?"

"Great, I love it. Maybe someday when we get rich." He laughed. I saw him nod at the guy he'd talked to. The guy walked over and rolled the bike into the back. "I guess they have to fix something, come on we better get back to work. It's Christmas you know."

I worked hard. I got all the decorations done, the store looked great. I couldn't get that bike out of my head. I saw myself putting my speedometer on it. Saw myself riding home from the store. If I had that bike I'd be free as a bird. "Hey Bruz," Jay called. "Think you could put together some Christmas stockings? Little ones, middle size ones and big ones. Three prices. Make me one of each now and we'll see if they're salable. I went downstairs. The bike in my mind had been replaced with Christmas stockings.

For the next hour and a half I played the best Christmas game ever invented. I called it "Santa's Helper" while I filled red net stockings with cookies, nuts, chocolate cherries, foil covered St. Nicks, everything a kid wished for in his dream stocking. I weighed the cookies, counted the pieces of candy, put all the costs of what was in each stocking on paper so Jay could see if they were worth selling. I put the three stockings on his desk and laid the cost page on top. He looked at me like I was some kind of a genius.

"They look like a million dollars, Bruz, you're a regular designer." Millie looked over the top of the office wall. "Oh, can I see what Bruz did?" She came up into the office. "Wow, those are terrific, probably too expensive for our customers."

"I don't think so, Millie. The small one could sell for a buck twenty-nine, the mid-size a buck ninety-nine and the giant, say, two fifty-nine and we'd make out much better than selling the pieces. That doesn't count Bruz' labor, but he works so cheap we don't have to think about it." They laughed. I didn't know if that was a put down or a compliment.

"Bruz? Could you make nine more in each size and we'll see if they sell." I nodded and ran downstairs. I put the boxes of cookies and candy I used on the big table in the candy room. I got the stockings and filled each exactly as I had made the samples. I finished 27 stockings in an hour and a half, a little over three minutes a stocking. I found three Christmas boxes and filled them with our new product. Millie put them near the register at the end of the toy counter. She put three red and green price cards at the back of the box and stood back to check her artistic effort. A lady came to the register with several little toys. She looked at the stockings.

"Oh! Aren't these wonderful, I've never seen anything like them and so cheap." She took three large stockings. One third of my inventory sold before I had even walked away. This would be a Bruzzy stocking Christmas. I made batches of stockings every morning before doing my regular stock clerk work. The store was busy. It looked like it was going to be a good Christmas. Jay, Kitty, Genevieve and I were invited to Dottie's Deli for Christmas dinner. Mom's deli opened to the public Christmas Eve.

I locked the left hand doors at 9:10 Christmas Eve. We had to chase the last customers out of the store. I looked around, the place was a mess. Everyone was leaning against a wall, sitting on the floor, leaning on the candy counter. Jay yelled from his office. "I have to thank you all. We just had the best Christmas in the history of JJ Newberry in Burbank. Each and every one of you deserves a standing ovation. I think Bruz' stocking brought us luck. I've never seen a fake product sell like those stockings. Bruz, you made 312 stockings and we sold every one. You're going to be a Newberry's hero. Now, let's just leave this place in a mess. We'll clean up after Christmas. Thank you ladies, it's a pleasure working with you."

All the girls clapped. Jay laughed. I turned out the lights until only the last row over the candy counter remained. The girls got their coats. Jay grabbed a box of chocolate Santas from the candy counter. He stood at the door and kissed the cheek of each girl as they left. He gave them their very own Chocolate Santa. "This is in lieu of a bonus, but maybe next year. Merry Christmas." They laughed and walked out into the warm California evening. They would work for Jay Tyrrell forever.

I pushed open our front door at almost ten o'clock. Two hours past my bedtime. The front room was dark but I could see lights on in the kitchen. Mom and Gen were sitting in the breakfast nook. A tall iced tea in front of them. They were just looking at each other. I made my announcement. "Jay's store had its best Christmas ever and my stockings were the best seller."

"That's wonderful, darling. Get yourself some iced tea and join us for a Merry Christmas drink." She looked happy but tired. I sat down sipping the cold tea.

"Mom's restaurant opened today, remember Bruz? You'll be happy to know they did a knock out business too, even without your stockings." We looked at each other, we all laughed. "So, tell me Mom, did a lot of people show up?"

"We opened at eight thirty, breakfast was a disaster. I think we had three customers all morning, we all stood around looking at each other. I made Chicken in the pot for lunch on our opening day. People started coming in at eleven thirty. It was mayhem after that. I thought I would bring home chicken but they ate every morsel. I had to start selling our dinner menu when we ran out of lunch. Tomorrow is turkey dinners, from one till nine. Remember you guys are coming with Jay and Kitty at three. I'll sit with you if I can get out of the kitchen." She drank some tea. I looked at Gen. She smiled.

I looked at mom. She nodded her head. I sipped my tea. "If nobody minds I'd like to stand in a hot shower and get in my bed. I have never worked as hard as I did today."

"Jay used to say, 'Christmas comes but once a year. Thank God.'"
Mom laughed out loud, I giggled. "Shower, my baby, and get some sleep. Maybe we could have breakfast at ten. I have to be to work at eleven." I leaned over and kissed my sister, walked over and kissed mom went to the kitchen door and faced my family, "And a Merry Christmas to all and to all a goodnight." I gave a little bow and left.

37

I opened my eyes. Dad's old clock read 9:47. I sat on the side of my skinny bed. I was stiff all over. Dad's hot shower remedy had failed me. I guess it worked for roofers but not for stock boys. I found my bathrobe in one of Mr. Baumer's cabinets. I headed for the bathroom in the hall. The little Christmas tree sparkled on top of the radio, candy canes and cookies under the tree. Christmas had returned to Hazel Street. I washed my face, brushed my teeth and joined my mom in the kitchen.

She was at the stove making ham and eggs. I could smell the toast in the oven. Four plates were on the table. I couldn't believe it. She was cooking for the world every day and here she was making Christmas breakfast for her kids. I missed my dad.

Gen walked in, tying her bathrobe. "Good morning, Merry Christmas."

"Merry Christmas Darling, hope you slept well."

"Want me to do that? You'll be cooking all day?"

"Sit, Honey, this is Mother's work." She hummed a little bit of Jingle Bells. I stood there mesmerized by Christmas morning at the Tyrrell's. I heard some noise. My big brother came in, all decked out in his go out for Christmas dinner clothes.

"Good Morning." He said in a hoarse voice. "I was with Katie pretty late, she's going to take the Red Line in and meet us. I figured mom might feel sorry for us and make breakfast."

"Well, if my two boys will get to the table the ham and eggs are ready." It was a wonderful family Christmas breakfast. I think I was the only one who missed the big guy with the dark beard but that was because I was still only a kid. The eggs were gone, the ham was gone. The teas needed refilling when mom put slices of her Christmas fruit cake in front of us.

"When?" Genevieve asked, words failing her. My mom laughed. "I baked it yesterday morning during our breakfast failure. Not aged as well as I like but the sentiment is there." This was a Christmas breakfast never to be forgotten. I wiped my mouth and walked into the living room right into a blue and silver Roadmaster with white walled balloon tires and Texas longhorn handlebars.

"Jay you bought it! Jay you bought it!" I screamed at the top of my lungs. Mom, Gen and my big brother came laughing into the room. Tears were pouring down my cheeks. My brother had spent Seven ninety-eight, a small fortune so I could have a bicycle. What could I do to show him how much I loved him. I just stood there with tears running down my face. My mom hugged me, "sometimes tears are better than laughter, Bruzzalah. You have a wonderful big brother." I hugged him. He was totally embarrassed. Gen kissed him. "Oh, for Christ sake it's a second hand bike, not a Rolls Royce. Bruzzy broke his ass for me, never asked for a thing, this isn't half of what he deserves."

"I thank you Big Brother, now I'm going to test my new bike on the Hazel Street Hill and remember Christmas 1935 as the best Christmas of my life."

Katie was waiting for us when we arrived at Mom's restaurant. Jay kissed her and I realized that he really loved her. I would have to try to be nicer to her. I kissed her on the cheek, "Merry Christmas, Katie." I said quietly. She gave me a strange look. I tried to act nonchalant. Whatever that means.

We sat at a table for six in the window. Every table in the store was taken. Waiters scurried about. This was a successful restaurant. We had Mom's turkey dinner. It tasted like moms dinner. We just weren't sitting in the breakfast nook. We had sweet apple cider to drink. We never had that at home.

We had pumpkin pie, my mom's pumpkin pie, not restaurant pumpkin pie or bakery pumpkin pie but mom's pumpkin pie. Everyone in the restaurant knew this food was special.

They told their neighbors, they told their friends. Dottie's Deli became the talk of Glendale. Months later someone from the LA Times had a Glendale business lunch at Dottie's. He was knocked out. The Times review said if you wanted your mother's cooking get yourself to Dottie's Deli in downtown Glendale. It's worth the trip. The restaurant was jammed. My mom worked harder than she had ever worked in her life. Success was all around us.

Jay and Kitty got married and took up housekeeping in his little Burbank apartment. Genevieve was graduating with honors in June and my years at Benjamin Franklin Elementary School were numbered. Working in Burbank had been a cinch since I got Nellie, the name I hung on the seat of my bike. I rode to school, I rode to Burbank, I rode to the flying school, I was totally mobile. Nothing was too far away. Go to lunch at Mom's restaurant? Hop on Nellie and I was there. Then in the middle of May I lost my job. Just like that. Job today. No job tomorrow. Some executive in Newberry's New York office decided that two members of the same family could not work in the same store together. Either transfer one or fire one. No exceptions. Since there were no stock clerk jobs for eleven year olds in all of L.A. County I was retired. Jay tried everything but just got himself in the middle of executive nonsense. I was gone. Out of the dime store business. My responsibilities were now taking care of our last three chickens, mowing the lawn, trimming the hedge and sweeping out Fred Fuchs Flying School.

We had aced Mrs. Gross' last test, I was going to graduate first in the sixth grade class, the last time in my life I would be first in any class, top ten per cent, third in Physics, no more firsts for Bruzzy. In fact, not too long until Bruzzy would turn into Lou. My tired mom sat in the first row as the sixth grade paraded across the stage and got our diplomas. Mrs. Gross decided to pass on cap and gowns; sixth graders could save that for high school and college. Okay with me. It saved my mom four dollars, even though four dollars didn't mean much to her anymore.

Two days later Genevieve graduated from Hoover. My sister, the honor student, a trained secretary and bookkeeper already had a job waiting for her in LA.

Other kids waited to graduate to go job hunting. Gen found a job. Then she graduated. My mom was all decked out in her finest and we sat in the front row of the Hoover auditorium. My sister, looking very beautiful in her pink gown sang "God Bless America," to open the ceremonies. Her principal had introduced her as Hoover Highs' Kate Smith and all the kids cheered. We watched student after student accept their diploma, after all her name was Tyrrell and T was in the back of the class. Finally Genevieve Tyrrell was called. She walked straight and tall across the stage. The presenter spoke. "Genevieve Tyrrell is a member of the National Honor Society; She is one of only two students to have never been graded less than A in their time at Hoover. I know she will bring honor to her school in what ever she does in the future." I laughed. I knew she was going to work for a private detective.

We had dinner in Mom's restaurant. My mother was off that day so the second cook was in the kitchen. I ordered chicken in the pot. It was lousy. I told my mom. She shrugged her shoulders. Gen was happy. The food didn't bother her. She was starting her new job in L.A. on Monday. She looked forward to her new life. Mom drove us home in the Studebaker. She pulled into the driveway, turned off the ignition, pulled up the emergency brake and sat there looking out the windshield.

"We going to stay in the car or are we going in the house?" I said like a wise guy.

"I hate the restaurant business." My mom said to the windshield. Gen sat up in the back. I looked at my mom.

"I hate my life. I need a man. I have to quit this job. I have to go home and find me a husband. I can't go on living alone. Living from day to day. You kids are growing up. I don't want to be old all by myself. As soon as I can work it out, six months the most, I'm leaving that restaurant. It won't last too long when I'm gone. I'm going home to New Jersey. I'm going to find me a husband. Then we'll sit down and figure out what we'll do with the rest of our lives." She honked the horn. 'Shave and a hair cut two bits.' She laughed, climbed out of the car and walked into the house. I looked at Gen.

"I knew this was coming. She's been killing herself in that Dottie's Deli of hers. You know she never learned when to quit. I'm sure she will be off to New York just as soon as she can work it out and she'll probably leave you and me right here."

"Okay, with me. We can take care of ourselves. You're all grown up, you're out of school, you're a real person now. I can cook, clean house, make the beds, and mow the lawn. We can live here very comfortably till she finds her guy and we see what's going to happen. Let's not give her a hard time. Let her go. She misses dad and the hole he left when he went away. Let's give her some time."

"Okay, little brother, I'll put up with it as long as you will. You and me against the world." She reached across the seat and messed my hair.

38

I was alone. The chickens were taken care of, the hedges were clipped and the lawn was almost too short for the hot weather. I was out of work. I had nothing to do. Newberrys had dumped me. Mom was slaving in her restaurant, Gen was busily running a law office that featured its own private investigator and I was sitting on the front steps without a thing to do. My bike leaned on its kickstand in the driveway. I didn't even feel like taking a ride.

Maybe I'd walk up to the airport and get blown around by the planes. That was a good idea. I walked up the hill. Fred's parking lot was jammed with cars. Was he teaching flying for free these days? I could see a big old Ford taxiing away from the terminal. If I hurried I could play in its wind storm.

"Where you off to, Bruz?" I saw Fred Fuchs leaning on the fence. "I was going to play windstorm with that Tri-motor." I pointed across the airport.

"Annie got married. She'll be gone all summer. I was leaning here trying to figure out who could run this place and you walk by. Want a full time job? You can sweep up on your own time." He walked over and shoved me into the reception room. He pointed at Annie's chair behind the reception desk. "Sit there, I want to fill you in on our business problems." I sat in her chair. Comfortable, rolled around on wheels. This could be fun.

Fred sat on the corner of the desk. "I signed a contract with the Air Corps to train 10 man classes of fliers, using our Jennys until the PT-17 Stearmen are available. We're supposed to get two September or October. I have 2 Air Corps classes and a Japanese class starting tomorrow. Someone has to be at the desk directing traffic. You think you can figure it out?" Fred didn't say so but he was thinking. Hm, eleven years old.

"Things must be written down, I mean who is in what class in what room and who is in flight training with which teacher," the eleven year old asked.

He nodded his head. "Yeah there's a notebook that keeps track of each student in a class. You could have a set, then you'd know as much as anybody about what's going on. You'll have to be here from eight in the morning till six every day but Sunday. I'll pay you fifty cents an hour. You sweep out on your own time, okay?"

"You're going to pay me five dollars a day for seeing that your students are in the right place at the right time? And you're giving me a book that says where they're supposed to be? That's like stealing money. I'll take the job."

Fred laughed. "Nothing like getting down to the basics. You have to understand that this is government work. I'll only keep it till they get their training sites up and operating. There's lots of changes coming, Bruz. And you're going to be right in the middle of them." I smiled, not knowing what he was talking about but sure I could find good use for thirty dollars a week. That was a lot of Saturday Evening Posts.

I had twenty Army students for six weeks and ten Japanese for eight weeks. I made card files in three boxes atop my desk. I could find a name and where he was supposed to be in a second and I got better with every question. I was soon calling the army guys by their first names and the Japanese guys were becoming more familiar everyday. I was enjoying the job. I wondered at the discussions among the students. They talked of war, argued about planes, always agreeing that American fliers were the best.

I got home at six thirty. Gen got home at seven, we would find something to eat, I'd make scrambled eggs, or maybe there was something left over. Mom was late almost every night; work in the restaurant was never ending. In mid July mom came home around seven-fifteen, Gen and I were eating French toast, one of my new specialties. She sat in her seat and watched us dipping French toast in maple syrup.

"I quit today. I'm not working anymore. I'm taking a bath and sleeping all day tomorrow. Then I'm getting myself together and I'm going to Brooklyn and stay with my sister Bea.

I'll let you know what's happening. I'll pay six months rent on the house and leave you some money to live on. Jay and Kitty are around if you have any trouble. The doctor is buying the Studebaker. I'm planning on taking a bus to New York on the third of August. I hope that's all right with you guys. I appreciate you giving me a chance to straighten out my life."

We looked at her, taken completely by surprise. Finally Gen said, "We'll be just fine, Mom. You go home and find yourself a happy life. Right now Bruz is making money, and I'm making money. So go. Forget about us, we'll be just fine.

Seven-thirty in the morning on August third Mom and Gen pulled away from Hazel Street in the Studebaker. The doc would take the car, Gen would get the trolley to L.A. and Mom would board the bus for New York. Only Gen would be home for dinner. Right now, I had a date with a bunch of would-be fliers at the Fred Fuchs Flying School.

Eight o'clock, on the button, I sat at my desk in the flying school. I was making new notebooks, 20 new names of 20 new soldiers the air corps wanted turned into fliers. We were still using our five Curtis Jennys; Boeing was miles behind with the PT-17 and every plane that did come off the line went to army teaching centers. Fred wasn't upset; the Air Corps still paid their bills.

It was solo time. Our twenty fliers had three days to complete their solos. Then they were off to Randolph Field. We were doing four solos every hour and a half.

Old number five was getting a new engine, not exactly new, different was a better word. There were no new engines for planes that flew in the World War, just engines that worked versus engines that didn't.

Four instructors brought four fliers to my desk. They took the notebooks and signed each student off for his first solo. Everyone laughed and grabbed cold cokes, it was an all day party. Fred sat on the edge of my desk. "How old are you, Bruz?" He asked, a strange look in his eye.

"Eleven and a half." I answered.

"How old when you began sweeping out?"

"Five and a half." What did he want? Why the funny questions?

"You've worked here for six years? You're the most senior employee we've got." He slapped his knee and laughed. I smiled. Just to be friendly. "You want to go for a ride? I have to check out five. Want to come along?" I looked at him. I was tongue-tied. Do I want to come along? Why had I been sweeping up for six years?

"Yes! I'd love to come along."

"We should get your mom's permission." He said.

"She left for New York this morning."

"How about your sister?"

"She works in L.A., gets home after six."

"Well, I guess we'll have to wing it. If we crash someone will tell them." I looked at him. He winked and laughed. He pulled open the bottom drawer. All the way in the back a little compartment contained a helmet and goggles. He handed them to me. "Come on." He said. I was in seventh heaven.

We walked out on the tarmac in front of his yellow school building. Directly across the field stood the fancy arrivals building where all the commercial action was. There was old number five parked at the end of the tarmac, a mechanic buttoning up the engine cover. I pulled on the helmet as I followed Fred, the goggles swinging around my neck. I walked as tall as my eleven and a half year old body would allow. I was going to fly in a Curtis Jenny with the best pilot in the world. Fred bent over, made a stirrup of his hands, I put my foot in and he tossed me into the back cockpit. I wiggled around and got my butt in the soft canvas seat.

The joystick stuck up out of the floor right in front of me. I kept my hands in my lap. I found the seat belt. It was wide canvas and very long. I shortened everything that would shorten but I was still too small. Pulled as tight as it would go it still hung loosely around my body. But, what the hell, this flight was free and I was in the hands of Fred Fuchs himself, owner/operator of the Fred Fuchs Flying School. What could go wrong?

Carl, one of the mechanics who had just installed the engine stood in front of the plane as Fred climbed into the front seat. He pulled the propeller through a couple of times and yelled "Contact!" I don't remember much more until I felt the engine throbbing, the plane vibrating and Fred slapping the side of the plane. "Seat belt?" he yelled. I nodded. He taxied out on the runway. There wasn't another plane in sight. He turned onto the main runway, braked to a stop, gunned the engine twice and we were rolling faster and faster down the concrete and up into the air banking right over Riverside Drive. Magic.

I could see our house through the walnut trees and then the market where I sold my magazines. I saw the big HHH sparkling white on the hillside, advertising Herbert Hoover High where my sister just graduated. I was in heaven. He flew over the hills, down around the stores on Brand Boulevard. There was Dottie's Deli, doomed by my mother's desertion. He flew out over Pasadena, the new engine humming along. As I settled down to enjoy the flight he was lining up the runway to take us home. I didn't touch the stick, kept my hands away from the throttle, my feet didn't reach the rudder controls, I just stared over the edge of the cockpit feeling the wind in my face. I want to do this, I thought. How do I get to do this?

The plane touched down softly back on the runway. Taxied to the school and parked in the space we had vacated not fifteen minutes ago. But what a fifteen minutes! The best fifteen minutes of my life. I would have my own plane. "Nellie Two" I would call it.

Fred climbed out, went over to Carl, put his hand on the engine wall. I undid the loose seat belt, got my leg over the edge of the cockpit, found the stirrup and got on the ground in one piece.

I followed Fred back toward the school. He turned and called out. "Well, how'd you like it, Bruz?"

"Loved it! I loved it!" I screamed.

"I'll have you flying that sucker before this summer is over." I stopped and starred after the tall blonde pilot as he walked through the door.

I was flying five feet off the earth going to Grand Central Market. I had to make a good dinner for my sister to soften her rotten day. It wasn't any fun seeing your mother leave for the east. I got a small chicken and bought some ice cream. I ran back down the hill and all the way home trying to get the excitement of flying out of my system.

I cut up the chicken, rinsed it off and dried it with the dishcloth. I pulled out my father's big black iron frying pan and put it over low heat. I peeled some potatoes and put them to boil. We would have fried chicken, mashed potatoes and pickled beets for dinner. We'd eat the last two pieces of mom's apple pie and ice cream for desert.

I poured a little milk in a soup plate. I dipped a piece of chicken in the milk rolled it around till it was covered with flour and put it in the sizzling hot margarine in dad's frying pan. I turned each piece of chicken over and over till it was nice and crusty, sprinkled a tiny bit of salt and poured the left over milk into the pan. I put on the heavy cover and turned the heat low to let the chicken simmer, I mashed the potatoes with butter and milk and put the pickled beets in side dishes on the table in the dinner nook. We could sit anywhere we wanted since we were the only people in the house. Like she said, "Gen and me against the world."

I set the table at our regular seats. I heard the front door open as I put the last utensil in place. "Bruz?" My sister called from the front door. I went to greet her. She looked very unhappy. "I made chicken and mashed potatoes for dinner." She dropped into mom's chair.

"Thank God, brother dear, I thought I would have to make dinner and I didn't have any idea of what there was to cook. I got all upset with being left alone and you make the dinner. Thank you." She looked beat.

"I said I'd make dinner, didn't you hear me?"

"I thought you were kidding. I thought it was my responsibility."

"Your responsibility is eating what I cook, and that's going to be tough cause I don't really know how my stuff is going to turn out. So, I'll cook, you'll eat and neither of us will comment on the quality of my food. Get comfortable and we'll eat supper." She laughed going to the bathroom.

The chicken was great, soft and crispy in delicious gravy that made the mashed potatoes twice as good. Mom's pickled beets always hit the spot. I washed the dishes and cleaned up the kitchen while Gen sat listening to the radio. I stood behind her. "I flew in a plane today. Fred gave me a ride in one of the Jennys. He says he's going to teach me to fly. Will you sign the papers?"

"What happens if you kill your self? Mom will be very mad."

"So what," I laughed, "I'll be dead."

She laughed.

"We'll never tell mom, it'll all be over before she finds her new love. What she doesn't know won't hurt her." I pitched.

"I'll do it when I see the papers, okay? That is if you keep making dinner." We laughed. I liked living with my big sister. She was fun.

I had never been so busy, even taking care of three hundred chickens. I had to check class 201 out and class 202 in. Twenty new soldiers destined to be fliers. The army wanted 2,000 new pilots this year and we were there to help them out.

Fred stuck me in a pre-flight course. I learned about things I never knew, ailerons, vertical stabilizers, lift, magnetos, props, strange words for strange objects. The more they talked about them, the more you studied a tail assembly, the simpler it got.

I sat in back, Fred's voice squeaking in my ear, "Just put your hands on the stick. Easy! Not tight! Just so you can feel what I'm doing." Then I was at Annie's desk again, checking in 16 new Japanese who were as excited as I was about learning to fly. The days flew away. Suddenly it was Labor Day. I was starting in a new school, Eleanor Joy Toll Junior High School. Fred happily told me I was ready to solo. I screamed. "I go back to school tomorrow!"

"You'll go. You'll find out your schedule and you'll come after school. We just had too much going on with our five old kites to get you through any quicker. Another week, two at the most." He gave his famous Fred Fuchs' smile and wandered away.

I locked Nellie in the bike rack and looked up at the huge school I was entering. You could put six Franklins piled on top of one another and not match the wide brick building atop the long flight of stairs. I walked in the middle pair of double doors, I saw three people at a table marked Seventh Grade. I must have been early. There wasn't any line. I approached the table. A lady smiled. "You a new seventh grader?" "Yes m'am." I stammered. A grey haired man snapped, "Name?" "Bruzzy Tyrrell." I answered, realizing, now there was a line of kids behind me.

"Louis Tyrrell? Homeroom is 315, third floor, up those stairs over there. Opens at eight-fifteen. Next."

The clock above the stairs read ten to eight, twenty-five minutes to kill. I would walk slowly. I was the first person in room 315. The desks were different, chairs with a wide armrest where you could write or lay a book. I sat in the back row, that's where the Tees belonged. Little by little kids arrived, all strangers. Then Megan Roberts walked in. She saw me and screamed. I stood up, smiling. "Oh Bruzzy! I'm so happy to see a familiar face. At least we'll have homeroom together."

"Maybe we'll get lucky and be in some other classes together. We can keep the old study group going." She laughed we sat down. I didn't recognize anyone else. No Bobby Hessong, nobody, they must be in another homeroom. This wasn't like Franklin at all.

"Ladies and Gentlemen, sit where you will, this will be your regular home room. Today I'll hand out your schedules, tomorrow you'll report here at eight a.m. sharp, this homeroom is only eight minutes long and we have many things to accomplish each morning. Attendance. Saluting the flag. Morning prayers. Then all the information the school feels you'll need to get through the day. Now, I'll call the roll and give you your schedule, Robert Abrams?"

"Here!"

Megan and I stood in the hall comparing schedules. We had fifth period lunch together and third period English. I was done after the seventh period; Megan had a study period and got out eighth Period. It was strange now, but in three days it would be routine. I was happy to be out at 2:15. I could be at the flying school by 2:30. I would be a real pilot before I knew it.

I flew down the hill heading for the flying school just making the light to cross San Fernando Road. I locked Nellie to the wire fence and walked into the flying school at twenty-five after two. Fred was going through notebooks with Annie who had a pained look on her face. Fred looked up. "Bruz?" He said. "Can you get here this time everyday?"

"Sure, unless they close Sonora or we have an earthquake or something." He didn't laugh. We were being serious. I put on my business face. "You need me, I'll be here."

"Just for a couple of months, Annie needs time in the inner office to keep the company on the straight and narrow, if you could get here before two-thirty she could work 3 hours a day while you run things out here. Okay?"

"Sure. Will it screw up my solos?" I gave him a "poor me" look."

"We'll do them this Saturday and Sunday. I'll work with you weekends on whatever bothers you. Meanwhile you'll take care of Uncle Sam's boys, right?"

"Right you are Mr. Fuchs. Go, Annie, I'll run your desk."

She grabbed a pile of books kissed me on the cheek and disappeared into the back office. I sat in her comfortable chair waiting for classes to break and questions to start. I unlocked Nellie at six thirty and flew up to the market. Bought some hamburger and a package of rolls. Everything else I needed was home. I was in the kitchen at a quarter to seven, hamburger patties sizzling in the pan, rolls warming in the oven. Sliced tomatoes and sliced raw onion and catsup on the table. I would throw some potato chips in a bowl, fill the ice tea glasses and dinner would be served.

Gen walked in the front door. I went out to welcome her. "I smell hamburgers, perfect, just what I wanted for dinner. I'll wash my hands and meet you in the dining room." She kissed me on the cheek and went into the bathroom.

School took third place behind keeping house and running the flying school. The army wanted exact answers as to how their fledgling pilots were proceeding. We had to fill out the forms the right way. Use the right words or hear complaints from the officers who dropped by now and then. Annie was discussing a form I had filled out, pointing to a specific answer I had written when a soldier standing by the desk put in his two cents. "The problem is there's your way to answer, the right way to answer and the Army way. They want the Army way, grab the next officer that shows up, sit him down and find out what he wants the form to say. Than make the form his way and you'll never have another problem. Simple." He patted my shoulder and walked away.

Saturday morning Fred watched me taxi old Number five to the main runway. I took off. My heart was in my mouth. I flew the assigned route doing each maneuver Fred had suggested. I was back at the school in just under forty minutes. No problem. I felt like I'd been flying all my life. I parked, shut everything down and jumped to the ground.

265

"Got back in one piece?" Fred called. "That's half the battle." We walked into the school. An Air Corps captain sat at my desk going through a pile of forms we had prepared. I walked over and watched him reading. He looked at me like I was a bug that needed stepping on. I smiled.

"Sir? One of your men told me that we had to learn how to fill out those forms the Army way. Would you mind showing me what he meant so you guys will be happy with our reports?" The captain gave me a strange look.

"You mean one of the soldiers told you to do it the army way?"

"That's right, he said I should ask an officer to show me the Army way and we wouldn't have to worry about our forms. Could you do that?" Fred began to laugh. The captain cleared his throat. I stood waiting for an answer.

"That's a joke. It's a very old joke. 'Do it your way, the right way or the army way.' It's a joke." My face fell.

"You mean we just go on doing our reports the way we've been doing them? Then find out that you guys think they're wrong. And you can't tell me the right way?"

"Forget it, Son, your reports are head and shoulders above the reports we get from our own schools. Soldiers have to bitch about something so they pick something easy to bitch about like reports. That's better than bitching about the planes or the instructors. Forget it. Just do what you've been doing. If something is really wrong you'll hear about it."

I shrugged. "Thank you Sir, You've been a great help."

Over the next two weeks I finished my solos and passed the tests Fred gave me. He brought me a pile of typewritten pages with places for about seven signatures. "Get your sister to sign these and have them notarized. Give them back to me and soon you'll be a licensed pilot, just like me, except you can't fly at night. That's some more school you'll have to take. You don't want to fly at night anyhow. You can't see a damn thing."

Gen signed the seven places and took the papers to her office where they were notarized. I gave them back to Fred on Wednesday. My training days were over.

I didn't like the forty-five minute classes at Toll. I didn't make any new friends but I had lunch and discussed things with Megan every day. She wondered what happened with Bobby. I worked at the flying school every afternoon so the next Saturday I rode my bike over to Western Avenue. The big white house was right where it always had been, Bobby's mom was in her usual rocker and Bobby was sitting on the top step. He saw me and ran over.

"Hey Bruz! Glad you came over; I'm going crazy sitting around. We're going back to Texas, Mom thought it would be dumb to start Toll and leave in a week so I'm waiting for my step-dad to take us. He's waiting for a new pick up truck due any day now. Most of our stuff is shipped already. Have you seen Megan?" He stopped to catch his breath

"She's in my homeroom. She's fine. I can't get used to changing classes all the time and different teachers in every class."

"Will you give her a note for me?" I nodded, he ran into the house. His mother looked at me and smiled. I sat on the steps. A fancy black Chevy pick-up pulled to the curb. Gar, Bobby's stepfather got out. He nodded coming up the stairs, kissed his wife's cheek on his way inside. I walked to the curb to inspect the fancy truck. The front door swung open, Gar held it while half a dozen young Japanese men carried boxes, suitcases, clothing bags and a couple of large frying pans to the truck. Gar jumped into the truck got everything loaded, covered and tied down. Bobby came out of the house wearing a light jacket. He handed me an envelope. "Megan" was printed on the front. He climbed up into the truck, sat against the pile and waved to me. Gar and his wife got in the front seat. The truck's motor started. They drove away, Bobby waving from the back.

"My farm now, Bruz." I turned around, Billy Sapporro and his mother watched the truck disappear over the railroad tracks. "My farm. Now we're real Americans!"

I gave Megan the note, I told her how Bobby had left for Texas. She never mentioned his name again.

39

My mom had been in New York for two months. Her letters were full of news about our Aunt Bea, Aunt Annie and Bea's husband's dress shop on Atlantic Avenue. Her letters sounded happy, carefree. She was dating some guy who was her boyfriend before she met my father. Mom knew what she wanted and we knew she was going to get it. Gen and I had worked out how we would survive being left on our own. We were actually having fun.

Friday afternoon, I locked my bike against the airport fence and made my way through a crowded reception hall. Classes had just ended so all the soldiers were discussing what they had been taught. A crowd of Japanese stood on the tarmac just outside, laughing together. It was like homeroom at Toll. Fred was talking to a guy I'd seen around the school a couple of times. I walked over and waited for a break in their conversation. Fred looked at me and held up his finger. They finished speaking.

"Bruz, Annie's going to stay on the desk. We have a problem and you are the answer. Charlie here is with the Express. They're doing a story about Rainbow Pier, he needs to take some pictures. I've been out with him on several flights. Very straightforward flying, easy stuff. Five is available but I'm all tied up with classes this afternoon so you're going to fly Charlie and do what he asks. Okay?" I didn't know whether to laugh or cry. I had no experience flying anyone around except myself. If I killed myself? So what. But Charlie? That was another question.

"I've never flown a passenger, Charlie, you might wind up in the drink."

"I'm not a passenger, Bruz, I'm a photographer. Fred says you're a natural. I'll put my life in your hands." He laughed. I shrugged. I'd love to fly out to Long Beach instead of handling a bunch of students.

"Get going Bruz, Charlie has a deadline to make. Oh, and good luck."

I tore the weather report off the Teletype. "Rain, heavy at times this evening. Thunder storms and rain tonight and tomorrow," the yellow paper predicted. My watch said 2:45 we'd be there and back before the storm. Fred handed Charlie his gear and walked us out to good old number Five. I watched Charlie and his big camera drop into the rear cockpit. I walked around the old Jenny to see if there were any obvious problems, got myself together and climbed into the front seat. Carl pulled the prop through, and the Curtis Jenny came to life. "Seat Belt, Charlie?' I used the intercom. He waved. I taxied to the main run way, the airfield was dead, ran up the engine a couple of times, Mags checked. I took off.

I leveled out at a thousand feet and pointed the nose toward Long Beach. Before we knew it we were looking down at the Rainbow Pier. Charlie slapped the plane and pointed down. He didn't talk. I took us down to two hundred feet. I could see the people walking around the pier. Pay attention I said to myself. This is where you can get your ass into trouble.

"Could you bank right, so I can get some clear shots?" The intercom crackled. I gulped, slid the stick over and flew in circles around the pier, keeping the altimeter at 200, watching people stare up at us. Twice around and Charlie was happy. I was even happier, straightening out the old ship, heading back to Glendale.

Over my shoulder I could see great clumps of black clouds. The six o'clock rain following us to Glendale. I banked to the right over the Sapporro farm and went straight in, taxied back to the school, parked in the spot we'd left. Shut down, closed my eyes, took a deep breath. My first passenger was back in one piece. I jumped down and helped Charlie get his camera out of the cockpit and down on the tarmac. He chattered along about the great pictures he'd taken and how steady I'd kept the plane. The one thing I knew. I'd never be an airline pilot. Carrying people made me too nervous. We walked into the school. Annie was alone in the room. We'd only been gone forty-five minutes, even though it felt like it was all day.

"Okay, flyboy, take over, I have some important numbers inside."

I smiled and sat at the quiet desk. Maybe I wasn't meant to fly. I looked around the room. I only had a couple of weeks before this job was done. My life was getting less interesting every day.

About five all hell broke loose. All the planes returned. The ground classes broke, there were people everywhere. I did my thing. Answered questions, showed the weekend schedule, found some stamps for a young soldier. Then order returned.

Fred Fuchs was standing next to the desk. "Charlie loved flying with you, says you're the steadiest flyer he's ever flew with. He wants you all the time. That was my client, kid, you stole my client." He laughed and handed me a twenty-dollar bill. "Charlie says you earned this. Better run home. Bruz, it's going to rain like hell. Go. Right now."

It started to rain as I ran across the lawn up the front steps into the house. It was dark night and it wasn't even six o'clock. I warmed yesterday's lamb stew, cut a couple of slices of rye bread made a lettuce and tomato salad and set the table. Gen came in.

"It's raining cats and dogs!" She screamed. "Stole this lousy umbrella from the office, I'm still soaking wet. They say this is going to last the whole weekend. I'm getting out of these wet things, make that stew nice and hot." I stood smiling like a dummy, the rain beating down on the roof.

We listened to the radio. The news said this was a bad storm, we should expect some local flooding. They forecast rain both Saturday and Sunday. Gen was listening to some drama that I didn't understand. I kissed her cheek and went to bed. The rain echoed off the roof. I'd never heard such a noise. The wind blew the rain right through the screened windows. My bed got soaked. I went into the living room. Gen was completely immersed in her story.

"The rain's blowing in the windows my bed's soaked."

She waved her hand. "Sleep in my bed. I'll sleep in Mom's room."

I crawled into her bed. Comfortable. On the wall, were the Ten Commandments and the Lord's Prayer that hung there when I shared the room a long time ago. Thou shalt not kill. Thou shalt not covet thy neighbor's wife. I fell fast asleep. I woke up. It was dark. The clock read eight, the rain pounded on the roof.

I went in the kitchen. It looked like nighttime out the windows of the breakfast nook. I turned on mom's kitchen radio. The man was talking about the worst storm to hit southern California in twenty years. The barometer was still falling and the rain was getting heavier. People should stay in their homes. Go out only in emergencies. Rain. Rain. Rain. I heard a strange new noise. It was a kind of muffled roar. It was the water in the river racing past the flood control panels. I began to think about local flooding. I opened the front door and looked out at the river running down Hazel Street, garbage can tops, milk bottles, empty cans cascaded down the street. I thought about the ball field at the bottom of the hill. This flood wasn't going to do it much good. Gen came out of mom's room in her bathrobe.

"This is pretty bad Bruz, I can't remember a storm like this in my whole life. Should we call Jay?"

"What's he going to do, he's up to his ass taking care of his store. It's Saturday, the busiest day of the week. We're okay; it's just a lot of noise. Want some breakfast?"

About two in the afternoon Gen's boyfriend pulled up in his little car. The only thing I liked about him was the little Henry J. he drove. It was like watching a clown car in the circus to see this big hunk unwind himself from the inside of the tiny car. He loped across the lawn, jumped up the three steps and pushed the front door open. He stepped inside. "Christ. I've never seen rain like this. The roads are all rivers, but my little baby just sails right through. You want to go to the movies? 'Petrified Forest' is at the Alex. You love Bette Davis. We could grab the three o'clock and go to Bob's for some burgers. You up for that?"

"The weather is so rotten, Joy. Poor Bruz would be stuck home all alone and we'd be out in that storm."

272

"Go ahead. You guys have fun. I don't mind hanging around here. This place isn't going to wash away." I said. Joy laughed. I watched that cute little Henry J. pull away about two thirty. I had the afternoon all to myself. I spent it reading Jane Austin. I was doing a book report on "Emma" for my English class. I got hungry about six-thirty. No sign of Gen and her friend. I made myself an avocado sandwich with lettuce and tomatoes on white, heavily smeared with Hellman's mayonnaise. I laughed hearing my father's voice in my head. "You could eat a shit sandwich with that much mayonnaise!"

I sat in the glass breakfast nook and watched the rain pour down, enjoying my sandwich. I took a quart of ice cream out of the freezer and ate as much as I wanted right out of the box. No mom, no sister. I could do exactly as I pleased.

The rain poured down, the roar from the river got louder, it was eight o'clock, no Joy, no Gen. I tried to read but I was beginning to worry. I saw car lights flicker in the wet street. It was the Henry J. Gen jumped out and ran for the porch as the little car drove off down the street. She ran into the house, only slightly damp. She laughed. "A lot of the streets are closed in Glendale we had to keep driving around. Joy left. He's worried about his mom. She's all alone." She fell into dad's chair and relaxed. I sat on the ottoman.

"How was the movie?"

"Great. Bette Davis was terrific. I can't wait to see it again. I had a great hamburger and some of that new soft ice cream. Joy and I had a nice talk."

"I don't like him. He doesn't talk to you nicely. Thinks he's a big shot."

There was a huge flash of lightning, the thunder crashed, the windows shook. Gen and I were scared out of our minds. This storm was the real thing.

I'm glad it didn't happen while I was over Rainbow Pier. My bed was soaking wet so we continued last night's sleeping arrangements. I was just relaxing in bed when Gen stuck her head in the door. "You hear that roar down the street? Sounds ominous to me."

"It's the river. It never has any water in it and suddenly its full, the water makes that sound going round the bends with the concrete walls, I don't think we have to worry. Let's go to sleep, maybe the rain will stop before morning."

It was worse in the morning. The roaring sound was louder still. I opened the front door. The water cascaded down the street splashing up over the curbs. I looked down the street. I couldn't understand what I saw. It was a lake, water all across the street coming up the hill! It was three houses away. I could see the water covering the lawns, the wind blowing small waves against the houses. This was a sign of big trouble, the one thing we didn't need was a flood. The rain poured down, the wind howled. The flood crept ever so slowly up the street. Gen looked at me questions flashing in her eyes. "It's moving so slow, you can't tell if it will get here or not. We've got hours. Maybe the rain will stop. We're a far piece from the river. I'm surprised the water has gotten this far."

"What shall we do?" My sister was scared.

"Well, the house won't float away, maybe we'll get our feet wet but I think we should just wait it out. It's going to stop raining sooner or later." I gave her my bravest smile and watched her relax. I found our Chinese checkers set and put the board on dad's ottoman, Gen sat in his chair and I sat on the floor, we played game after game. Every so often I'd peek out the door. The water would be closer. Finally, we stopped for supper. We ate out of the fridge, anything that was edible we got rid of. We could have tomatoes from the garden for breakfast. We turned on the radio.

"Cecil B. De Mille presents Lux Radio Theater." It was eight o'clock. I peeked out the front door. Our lawn was covered with water; it was three inches from the top step. I began to get scared. I was the man of the house. I had to protect my sister. I'd promised my father I'd protect my sister. Now how do I do that?

274

I saw a trickle of water come under the door, I ran to the linen closet grabbed some bath towels and pushed them against the front door. No water came through. Thunder crashed. Windows rattled. The Lux Radio Theater dissolved into static then the radio died.

Two huge lightning flashes, the thunder so loud it hurt our eardrums. And the rain stopped! Quiet. The river roared in the background but there was no more rain. I pushed my nose against the glass. I could see the water was backing away down the hill. Further and further it receded leaving everything covered in thick black mud. The inside of the house had escaped but god knows the damage done to the outside. Only daytime would tell.

I woke up. I sat up in my sister's bed. Quiet. No river roaring, no thunder clapping, no rain pounding. Quiet. I pulled on a pair of shorts, slipped into a tee shirt and crept for the back door. Monday morning, but nobody was going to work. I was certain the Red Line would be out of service.

My bed was a total loss it would never dry, the wood beams would rot with the dampness. A new bed needed for Bruzzy. That is if I was lucky. The back yard was mud. Everywhere mud. I took off my shoes and waded into the muddy mess. Sapporro's garden was gone, no tomatoes, no carrots. It was a mud farm. Three muddy lumps lay in the chicken yard. Why the chickens came out of the coop was a good question. But they would never answer it. The last white leghorn and two Plymouth Rocks had succumbed to the storm. My friend Biddy had gone to chicken heaven. They missed their chance to do the headless dance.

Except for its muddy bottom Jay's house had survived. Everything else in the back yard was choked by sticky black mud.

I grabbed a shovel out of the garage. I cleared a portion of the driveway. The concrete looked fine. Get rid of the mud and life could return to normal. It took me an hour and a half to shovel the driveway clean. I threw mud on top of mud on Hazel Street. It was mud from curbstone to curbstone. Some of the neighbors were standing on the street looking at the mess. Floyd Baumer came over,

"My dad says we have to start up at Airway and shovel down to the Ball Field. If we all work together we could clean the street."

Every male on the block had a shovel, we broke up into teams of five. We started at the top of the street. The first five shoveled mud down the hill till they could shovel no more, and then the second five took over shoveling.

They found three wheelbarrows and several of us went ahead and filled barrow after barrow of mud. They dumped it on the ball field. Some of the women brought water and iced tea to the muddy laborers. Some women relieved their husbands shoveling up the stinking black mess.

I would bet that Hazel Street was the first street cleared in the whole city. The airport cleared Airway and the city cleared Sonora. By suppertime we could get to Grand Central to resupply the house. Gen made a big pot of ox tail soup. We ate at nine o'clock. I stood in a hot shower again, fell in bed and was fast asleep by ten thirty. Next morning the sky was bright blue, the sun shining down on the mess left by the storm.

My sister called her office, they were happy to hear from her. She could come back tomorrow. She hung up. The phone rang. It was Jay. All the phones had been out of order until this morning. He and Kitty survived the storm. They lived on the second floor so they had no damage at all. The mud never reached San Fernando Road. It stopped ten feet in front of the flying school. For the first time since Friday planes were flying out of Grand Central, cars drove up and down Hazel Street. Our ballpark was gone, our garden was gone, our chickens were dead, my bed was ruined but Genevieve and I were in perfect shape. Then the mail arrived with a letter from Dorothy Tyrrell.

40

Dear Kids, I'm having a wonderful visit. Reminiscing with Bea and Annie, seeing our old home, going to places I went as a kid. But I worry about you guys. Living all alone there on Hazel Street. We hear about that terrible storm on the radio and I wonder how you got through it. I've spoken with Jay. He and Kitty are moving to a new apartment and I convinced him to rent a two bedroom and let his brother and sister live with him while I sort out my future. He would talk with Kitty and then discuss it with you and Bruz. I would feel much better if I knew you guys were safe and sound with your family. I'm seeing a man I dated when I was a kid; he's a very nice guy. His wife died four years ago. He lives with his daughter, Miriam, although his business is in a small town in New Jersey. Please discuss the move with Jay and for my peace of mind make the move. Love.

"I don't want to live with Katie. I don't even like Katie. I want to stay right here." Tears were rolling down my cheeks. I was mad at myself. Pilots don't cry!

"Let's talk with Jay and see what's up. I don't think they want us around, Jay knows you're not crazy about his wife. He's a good guy, let's wait and see." Genevieve was trying to keep me calm. I was going to be twelve in January. Twelve year olds don't have much control over their lives.

The next evening we were having dessert in the dinner nook when Jay came in the back door. "Wow, this place is in really shit shape. How're you going to rid of all that mud?

"I cleared the driveway. I'm going to try to save the front lawn but I'm going to leave the backyard alone. It's just too much work for no reason. I'll see what mom says when she gets home."

"You have any more ice cream? I'll have some while we talk about mom's latest bright idea." I made him a big bowl of ice cream. We sat around the table.

"Look," Jay said, "I know you guys would like to stay right here. I know Bruz isn't crazy about taking orders from my wife but when we come right down to it the problem is money."

"We have money. We don't need your money or mom's money. Gen earns money and I earn money. We can live just fine. Mom paid six months on this house, that's two more months till we have to give them more money; we'll worry about that then. We're doing just fine." I took a breath to go on.

"Hate to tell tales out of school, Bruz, but your mother only paid four months on this house, figuring she needed more money to support herself in New York. The place is only twenty-five dollars but I hear the man who owns it wants to clean up the mess, fix up the house for his daughter whose about to be married. So I think you're out whether you join Katie and me or stay on your own. We could use mom's furniture in our new place. We don't have any furniture and my forty-five bucks just gets us through the week, Katie has to give money to her family so it would make things much easier on me if we lived together."

"Okay, okay, if it's easier for you then I'll move into your place, I'll try to get along with your wife, I'll follow the rules. You've been a great big brother and I won't give you any trouble. But I need a new bed. My bed's ruined." Jay laughed. He looked at Gen. She shrugged her shoulders.

"Listen," Jay, said, "There's this new apartment house on Dryden Street, two blocks off Brand Boulevard. We took a one bedroom, but we can change to a two bedroom if you guys come. It's got a big back porch, just as good as your room here, Bruz. We can get you a good bed across the street from my store where we got your bike, okay? Gen would only have two blocks to walk to the Red Line. Katie goes to L.A. everyday so you guys might even ride together. Let's make a deal.

278

We could move in there in two weeks and get on with our lives." So the deal was done. Goodbye Hazel, hello Dryden.

Friday my job ended at the flying school. I told Fred I had to move away. He hugged me like he was losing a brother. He held my shoulders and looked into my face. "Listen to me. Soon as you enter Hoover join the Air Corps reserve. They'll be very happy to have a licensed pilot. There's going to be a war. You will be a lot better off flying than fighting in the mud. Promise me you'll do as I ask. I taught you to fly so you'd have this choice, do it, you owe me that." I was speechless, war, mud, what was he talking about, but it was my friend Fred. Next to Jay he was my best friend. I promised. He shook my hand, we said goodbye. I never saw Fred Fuchs again.

I pedaled Nellie slowly along Dryden Street. It was a long way from Hazel Street. I looked for the big pink house with the wide front yard. There it was at the end of the block, two blocks this side of Brand. Just like Jay said. I looked at the wide pink building. An avocado tree loaded with fruit filled a square of lawn in the front right corner. I loved avocados. These were round, the size of baseballs; they were getting ripe as I watched. Some lay on the ground pecked full of holes by gourmet sparrows out for breakfast. I stuck one in my pocket. I rode my bike around to the back. I saw the garage and the back steps with back porches at every level. Twice the size of my back porch maybe this would be a good move.

I told Gen about my adventure, about the avocado tree and the big back porch. She had no comment. I put the avocado in the salad I made for supper. She said it was good.

Jay said he had movers for Sunday. Asked me to come have a hamburger on Saturday to buy my new bed. I locked my bike in the patio behind his store and walked around the block to meet him in front. He waved as I came around the corner. "You're getting big, Bruz. We better buy you a long bed or your feet will hang over." We laughed. We got across San Fernando alive. I followed him into Burbank Second Hand Store. They had at least ten cots, anyone of them would do. I found a three quarter model, extra long that I thought would be great.

It was Seven dollars and ninety-eight cents. I didn't let Jay pay. I took out the twenty I had earned flying around Rainbow Pier and paid for my new bed. Jay let me pay with a smile on his face. He paid for lunch. I said hello to all the girls in the store and left before I let myself miss working there.

Sunday was moving day. All the furnishings of Hazel Street moved to Dryden Street. My mother's bedroom became Jay and Katie's bedroom, my sisters room went into the second bedroom and my new bed appeared on the back porch with a tall brown dresser pushed against the wall for my clothes. It was a large space, good air and I hoped comfortable. The lot was surrounded with tall Pine trees making the back yard very private. By eight o'clock Sunday night Dryden Street was very livable. I found a deli on Brand and bought a quart of Neapolitan ice cream. We had a party in our new living room. Katie reminding us not to spill our ice cream on my mothers carpet. Oh well.

The major problem with the new place was one bathroom. Every one who lived in the apartment had to be out early every morning so a bathroom schedule had to be made. I was first and had to finish by seven fifteen. It was an easy task for me. Gen and Kitty were next. They had to be on a train by eight thirty or they would be late for work. Jay was last in line for the bathroom. No one would fire him if he was late and he had a short trip down to San Fernando and out to Burbank. Ten minutes if he was quick. It got easier every day and soon wasn't a problem at all. I was a five-minute walk from Toll. I left my bike in my room and walked everyday. I was home at two fifteen with absolutely nothing to do. I would walk along Brand looking in the store windows. There were a lot of people buying things; money seemed to be more available, a lot of packages being carried to cars. I walked home, pulled a ripe avocado off the tree and went upstairs. White bread, mayo, smeared with half an avocado was a perfect snack. I put the left over half in the Frigidaire which used to sit in the Hazel Street kitchen.

Kitty always got home first, about a quarter to six. She worked 9 to 5 and her store was right on the red line. I was lying on the couch reading a history assignment. I heard her key.

The door opened, "Hi, Kitty!" I called. She came in, she was a very pretty lady, I could see why Jay liked her. "Take your feet off the couch, Bruz, you've got your shoes on." I had been putting my shoe covered feet on this couch since the day I first wore shoes. I couldn't understand why she would say that. I did what I was told. I didn't say another word. I sat up on the couch and kept reading although nothing was going into my brain. She went into the kitchen. I was reading about the battle of Waterloo but couldn't figure out who was beating whom. Kitty walked in. Half an avocado held in her hand.

"I see you've stolen another avocado, Bruz. I thought I asked you not to take avocados from a tree you don't own." I looked at her. She was a total pain in the ass.

"I picked it from the space I rent." I went back to my book.

"You don't rent that tree, that tree belongs to the management, those avocados belong to them not the tenants."

"Then why don't they pick them instead of letting them rot or be eaten by the birds. I like avocados. These are good avocados, nobody gives a damn that I'm eating an avocado every so often. Why does it bother you so much?"

"First, watch your language. There's no cursing in this house. I'm a grown up, you're a child. I tell you not to pick an avocado, you say yes and don't pick an avocado. I don't have to argue with you. You live in my house and you'll follow the rules."

"Listen, Lady, I've lived in several houses where I put my feet on this sofa or I got a bottle of milk and drank it, as far as I know my mother pays half the rent on this apartment so I can live here, we'll make believe I'm putting that avocado in my part of this apartment instead of in my refrigerator that happens to be in your house and I don't have to take any shit from you." I got up and walked into my room. Later Gen looked in. "You having dinner?"

"No." I said.

After dinner Jay walked in. Before he opened his mouth I said. "The trouble with having your room on the back porch is that anyone can walk in any time. There's no privacy. Dad put a door on my room in Hazel Street because he understood a person needed their privacy. But he had to die and put us in this position. I know I was disrespectful to your wife but she was disrespectful to me first. I try to follow your rules but it just doesn't work out if I can't have an avocado sandwich without a meeting of the Supreme Court. Now, how can I help you?" He shook his head and walked out. Maybe I could rent the room on top of the water tower from Billy Sapporo, I thought as I fell asleep in the new used bed I bought and paid for myself.

The next morning I dressed and was gone before anyone in the house was up and about. I went into the Toll cafeteria and had sunny side eggs, bacon and toast with a cup of hot chocolate, it cost me eighty-five cents. If I could find some place to sleep I wouldn't have to go to Dryden Street ever again. I went to homeroom. I walked past the pink building on Dryden Street at twenty after two. I kept on walking. I turned right on Brand and went to the Show Shop, ten cents anytime. I watched Hopalong Cassidy win the girl twice and wandered back out on the street. Five fifteen I walked up the back stairs and went into my back porch room without a door. I lay down on my bed and tried to understand how the English managed to win at Waterloo. I heard someone in the house, I figured it was Kitty; there was no one in the world I wanted to see less than Kitty. I kept fighting the Napoleonic war. My sister came into my door-less room.

"Bruz, you can't hide out in here for the rest of your life. You're going to have to make up with Kitty or we can't go on living here." She sat on the edge of my bed.

"Good. Where can we move? I've got more than three hundred bucks I earned at the flying school, we can move someplace for that." She smiled, a kind of tired smile. "I don't want to move. This place is okay with me. It's handy to the train. Cheap. I don't have to cook. You don't have to cook."

"Yeah, great, if you like tamales and burritos every day. I haven't had a good meal since I've been in this place, I know its only weeks but it feels like years." Jay walked in. He must have left Burbank early. Was he sick?

"Well, Bruz, I'm sorry you don't like it here, I find it very comfortable." Jay said.

"You're in love with the cook." I interrupted. He laughed. "You're right, she's my wife and when you're married you'll find out that your wife can do no wrong. So we have to straighten out this problem and this problem is you. Katie was raised differently than we were. She lives her life differently. It took me a while to understand her and fall in love with her but she isn't a Tyrrell, she can't even understand how a Tyrrell views his life. Your dad trained you to be a perfect Tyrrell, much more than your sister or me. You've had a free hand since the day you were born. The sun rose and set on you. Now your protector is gone. You have to lose some of that Tyrrell freedom or you can't live in this house."

"Where would you like me to go? Tell me and I'll take it under advisement. You live with everything that once was my home. How can I take my feet off the sofa I've put my feet on for ten years? You have an answer for that?"

"Yes. The answer is your mother. Go to your mother, you can't get along here? Go to your mother."

"That's pretty funny, she's off in New York trying to make a new life. She's only got enough money to keep herself together and you want to saddle her with me. You should have left us to fight out our lives in Hazel Street. I could handle that. What I can't handle are people who won't meet me half way. If my mother wants me, I'll go to New York. God knows I love California; I've had the greatest childhood of anyone until I moved to Dryden Street. You're my big brother, tell me what you want me to do." He sat down on the bed, my brother and sister looking at me like I was five years old.

"Your mother is marrying some guy named Kahn. They'll have a place for you to live the beginning of December. If you transfer out of Toll over Christmas vacation you won't screw up your schooling. Live with us for the next few weeks, go to New Jersey with your mother in December and everyone will be happy. How about that, Mr. Tyrrell?"

"Okay. I know when it's time to go home. I'll make up with your wife so we can live in peace till I go to my mother. You're my big brother, I've looked up to you for years, I love you, still, under the circumstances, I don't think we can ever be great friends, but I will never forget the bicycle you gave me. That was one of the happiest days of my life, just as I'll remember today as a day almost as bad as the day dad left on his trip. What's for supper?"

41

Eventually that fateful Friday morning in December came. The day I was going to use the 38-dollar bus ticket to Linden, New Jersey that my mother and new father had air mailed from the east. Gen kissed me goodbye on her way to work in L.A. Kitty said something under her breath as she left the apartment. I sat on my mother's couch with my mother's suitcase I'd filled with my clothes. My big brother was getting ready for his job. The bus left the station in Glendale at nine-sixteen. Jay would drop me off at eight forty-five so he would be in time to open his store in Burbank.

Everyone was happy to see me go. I was the fly in the ointment. I was the rule breaker. Without me they could live happily ever after. I was feeling pretty good. At least I was heading for a place where dinner didn't come from the deli and someone kissed you goodnight before you went to sleep. I was interested in meeting my new stepfather. I wondered what kind of man could replace the irreplaceable Bill Tyrrell. I would discover there are many personalities in fathers and John Kahn would turn out pretty good. I could hear my brother singing a little song as he shaved his heavy beard. I knew I took after my mom in the beard department.

"Well Bruz, you ready for your journey?" Jay said, putting on his jacket.

"I'm sure it'll be different. I'm looking forward to a lot of hot roast beef sandwiches and mashed potatoes." We laughed.

"Come on. Sorry I have to drop you off, but you know the store. I have to run the store."

"They fired me cause I was your brother so fuck them." It was the first time I'd ever said the F-word. I kind of liked it.

"Too bad, we were a great team. Never forget those Christmas stockings. Newberrys put out instructions on how to make them. They are standard Christmas specials today and you invented them.

Of course the New York guy didn't know that when he canned you. Come on let's go catch a bus."

I stood in front of the All-America Bus Depot, waving goodbye to my big brother till his car turned at the corner. I carried my suitcase into the tiny waiting room. A chalk-board announced the 9:16 to New York was leaving from lane four. I bought a Mounds and an Almond Joy from the newspaper store. Sometimes you feel like a nut, sometimes you don't.

I carried my mother's suitcase out to lane four. There was a red and white bus parked facing the curb. "New York" printed in big black letters, displayed in the windshield. It looked like a shrunken Greyhound Bus. I guess if you paid forty percent less for the ticket you got forty percent less bus. "You get what you pay for." My dad always said.

The heavy-set driver studied me through the closed glass door. Finally he figured out I wasn't there to steal his money and swung the door open. "You the kid going to Linden, New Jersey?

"Yes I am." I answered politely like a normal eleven and a half year old kid would do.

He shook his head, eased his big body out from behind the wheel, edged himself out the narrow door, opened a hatch in the side of the bus and stowed my suitcase away. "You look like a nice kid, but you're traveling alone and the driver is responsible for your safety. You sit up front next to me. We'll make sure you get to your destination."

I nodded. A couple of weeks ago I was ordering grown men around, flying photographers over the Pacific Ocean. Now I had to sit up front so some fat driver could make sure I got safely home. I laughed. He looked at me like I was crazy. I climbed up into the front seat that was surrounded by a chrome pipe fence. This would be my home for the next three days. I was ready to go. All we needed were the rest of the passengers.

A man and lady helped a very old woman up the high steps into the bus. She must be a hundred I thought. They helped her halfway down the aisle where she sat in the window seat. They put her handbag up in the rack. Kissed her and left her sitting alone. She should have been sitting next to the driver. She needed taking care of much more than I did. The man watched the driver put the lady's suitcase under the bus. He handed the driver some money. I heard him tell the driver she was going to St Louis. Make sure she got off. The driver smiled. "We'll take good care of her, Sir. Don't worry, she'll be fine."

Suddenly a gang of very happy, very noisy Mexicans filled the sidewalk. Men, women and children were standing around, yelling at each other in their native tongue. Sounded like gibberish to me. The driver patiently sorted them out, the drunks staying on the sidewalk while the sober ones boarded the bus. They took over the back and continued they're conversation. It never stopped till I got off in New Jersey. A young man, an older man and a middle aged lady filled out the roster of companions I would join as the All-America bus backed away from the platform and pointed its red nose east.

In what seemed like no time we were on a two-lane highway flying toward our first stop. I ate half of my Mounds bar and half of the Almond Joy. I put the other halves into my pocket for tomorrow. I watched the white dashes painted on the roadway flash past. Zip. Zip. Then they were double orange lines curving with the highway. A no passing zone where there was no one to pass if you wanted to. My eyes got heavy. The lines disappeared and I was fast asleep.

"Barstow! Barstow! Rest stop! Fifteen minutes!" brought me back to my All-America seat. The door was open. The driver helped the people who needed a rest out of the little bus. The old lady was sitting in her window seat, not moving. I walked back. She looked at me through rheumy eyes. No smile. "Could I bring you some water or some tea? Do you need the ladies room?" The driver was taking care of me. Nobody paid attention to the little old lady. I was sure she'd have to pee before we got to St. Louis.

So as usual I stuck my nose in where it didn't belong. I helped her up the aisle and down to the street. We were at a truck stop in Barstow, California, asshole of the earth. I held her arm as we inched our way toward the Ladies Rooms inside a ramshackle building that catered to busses and trucks and wasn't designed for little old ladies. Lucky for me the middle-aged lady came out of the building. She walked up to me and took the old ladie's other arm. "You're a good boy, son, to worry about your elders. Let me take over your job. I'm a little better equipped." She smiled. I happily gave up my responsibility and the old lady smiled at her new companion. I didn't have to worry anymore. My middle-aged friend saw to all the old ladie's needs till she met her family in St Louis.

A rest stop in Needles. A rest stop in Flagstaff. A bus trip seemed to break down to resting and sleeping. I was very good at both. We had rested a lot but for some unknown reason we hadn't eaten. I found out that lunch was in Barstow when I was busy taking care of my fellow man or woman as the case might be. I was looking forward to supper in Albuquerque, New Mexico.

"Albuquerque! Albuquerque! 45 minutes, rest stop and supper break. I'll be leaving you here. I hope the rest of your journey is enjoyable." I was surprised. I thought this guy would drive us to New York. "The new driver has his instructions about you, Tyrrell, don't worry he'll look after you."

"I'm not worried. Have him help the old lady, I can take care of myself." He nodded, not listening to what the kid had to say like most people put in charge of kids. After all what does an eleven year old know about the real world?

I got off the bus. It was cold. I had never felt cold. I climbed back into the bus and got the heavy jacket Kitty made me take in case it got cold. I was last off the bus. I walked toward the big well-lit building that was a bus stop, a truck stop, sleeping accommodations and a sprawling restaurant with a long counter. I stepped up the front stairs when the doors swung open and a huge black man came through. I had never seen a black man before in my life.

My stomach flipped over, I was scared stiff. The black paid me no notice whatever, joking with his white friend, heading back to their truck to continue their journey. I couldn't get his face out of my head. I saw a laughing devil in my brain. I was visibly shaking. I sat in the first booth and threw my coat on the opposite seat. I tried to calm myself down. So the man was black. So what? I'd seen pictures in National Geographic of black men. They were always little naked men, dancing around fires; they weren't huge muscular giants laughing on their way to their eighteen-wheeler. I pulled myself together. I had no problem with men, white, red, brown or black, I'd have to figure out why this one scared me out of my wits.

I managed to wrap myself around a hot roast beef sandwich, even ate the mashed potatoes. The fear was disappearing into my full stomach. I walked out of the building, climbed aboard my All-America transportation resting my head against the seat back.

"Tyrrell? I'm Charlie. I'm supposed to look after you from here to Tulsa. Don't give me a hard time, okay?"

"Forget about me Charlie, just drive your bus." I fell fast asleep.

I was sitting in the breakfast nook finishing my sugar toast when my dad came in from the back yard. "You doing anything important Bruz?" I laughed. I was five years old; it was the beginning of May in 1930. The depression had wrecked my father's bank account and his roofing business, but he kept up a happy face for his family. "Come out to the garage with me I want to show you something." I stuck the last crumbs of my sugar toast in my face grabbed his hand and walked with him out to his garage. My father was a tinkerer. He built little things for the fun of it. He was enchanted with this new thing called radio. He built his own crystal set and spent hours listening with his headsets on his head. "Bruz, when I was a young man I was a pretty good ball player. Used to play some semi pro with a New Jersey team. I was a good catcher and could hit with some power. I tried out to be a Yankee. That's the best ball team that has ever been. Frankie Crossetti was the shortstop and he and I became good friends. I didn't come close to making the team but Frankie and I saw a lot of each other.

289

Some off seasons he'd work for us if he couldn't find an easier job. Anyway, I've been a Yankee fan ever since. There's a clear channel station in Philadelphia that broadcasts coverage of the Athletics. Today the "A's" are playing the Yankees. You want to listen with me? He split his headset in two. He handed me my half putting his up to his ear. I put mine next to my ear and listened. All I heard was static. Dad fumbled around with the crystal on the pile of condensers, coils and wire that was his radio. Suddenly a voice was talking baseball words and you could hear the crowd yelling in the background. Lefty Gomez was pitching. Bill Dickey caught. We listened together for two hours. The Yankees won. "So what was the best part, Bruz?' My dad smiled down on me. "When Baby Ruth hit the homer, Dad. Can I be a Yankee fan like you?" "We'll be fans together, Son." My dad said messing my hair. "Oklahoma City! Breakfast! Rest stop! Oklahoma City!

The hours passed. The drivers changed. The highway rolled along under the red and white All-America bus. The drivers caps said All-America, their shirt pockets were emblazoned All-America their jeans said Levi. Go figure. We were in St. Louis. The old lady limped off the bus, helped by two handsome young people. They were probably her grandchildren. They looked happy to have her and she looked twenty years younger. Love had a way of doing that.

We had dinner in Terre Haute, Indiana. I had rabbit stew. It was very good. Not as good as my mom's but very tasty. I was stuffed but managed to force a piece of apple pie and ice cream into my full tummy. I burped getting comfortable in the big front seat. I saw a new driver behind the wheel. He hadn't said a word to me. I relaxed. The bus pulled out on the highway. It began to snow. I watched it float down. We were moving into eastern weather. That meant I'd need my jacket. A light flashed in my head. I didn't have the jacket. The jacket was on a seat in the first booth of the truck stop in Albuquerque. My rabbit stew came up into my throat. I guess I had eaten too much. "Hey driver, think you could pull over for a second, I think I'm going to throw up."

"Pain in the ass." He looked in his side mirrors and looked ahead we were all alone in the world. He pulled over.

I jumped out. It was freezing. I bent over and got rid of my dinner, wiped my mouth on my sleeve and climbed back aboard the All-America red and white beauty. I fell into my seat. The driver said, "Pain in the ass." And we were on the road again. I fell fast asleep, my stomach grumbling.

My brother Jay shook my shoulder. "Come on, Bruz, open your eyes. You wanted to come hunting, get your ass out of bed, Fred's waiting in the car." Oh my God, I thought, my big brother finally asked me to go hunting and I overslept. The clock on the nightstand said two in the morning; I was supposed to be ready. We were sleeping in the sand to get an early shot at the jack rabbits in the Mojave Desert. We climbed in the car. Fred and Jay up front, me in the back. Rabbit hunting with Jay and Fred. What could be better for an eight year old who missed his dead father? Jay turned around in his seat and handed me a long white package. "Here," he said, "a present from Fred and me." I couldn't believe my eyes, a long white package. I tore the paper and saw what I'd dreamed about since my brother got the shotgun that Christmas. I had a brand new Savage, twenty-two automatic. I'm hunting with my own rifle. I'd kill every cottontail in the Mojave today. I had the best rifle in the world. Fred and Jay laughed at my reaction.

We spread our blankets on the sand lit by a huge low-hanging moon. It was cold. I rolled myself up in the thin blanket. Fred was snoring. Jay looked at the moon. "You'll remember this day all your life, Bruz. Like I remember Dad giving me my first Savage. It's kind of like becoming a man. Remember. Never point the gun at anything unless you mean to pull the trigger. It's not a toy. You could kill somebody with it if you don't pay attention. Owning a gun means you are a reliable citizen, you own a tool that has a special use and you will only use it to do what it was designed to do. If you don't think you're old enough to meet the responsibilities of gun ownership, use it to hunt today and give it to Fred or me to hold for you until you're old enough."

"I'm old enough. I hear what you're saying. I'll only fire it when I'm hunting with you. All the other time it will hang on my bedroom wall. I'll look at it falling asleep and dream of hunting with you and Fred." We stopped talking.

The moon got lower and lower in the sky. I laid on my stomach and fell asleep. Fred snored. Jay's breath would catch in his throat. He'd cough but wouldn't wake up. Every time he coughed I opened my eyes. The sun was peeking above the desert floor. You could feel the temperature rising. Twenty yards away from me, sitting on his haunches, licking his front paws was the biggest jack rabbit I had ever seen. Eight, ten pounds. Might be very tough meat. Stupid things were running through my head. I grabbed my rifle. Of course it wasn't loaded. I reached into Jay's bag I pulled out a box of cartridges. .22 Long. Did my rifle take .22 long? I didn't know. I knew it was an eight shot automatic. I slid eight cartridges into the little hole in the stock. They Fit. I screwed the chamber closed. I turned on to my stomach. Mr. rabbit was still doing his nails. I sighted high at the rabbits head. I took a deep breath and squeezed the trigger. The gun bucked against my shoulder. The big rabbit fell over like a doll at the carnival. "I got it! I got it!" I shouted as Jay and Fred sat up, scared by the .22's report. "Got what?" Jay managed. "The biggest jack rabbit you ever saw. Look, laying right out there on the sand."

Between us we shot twelve rabbits that day. Not one half as big as my first hunting trophy. Mom cooked it in her big rabbit pot. It was the best dinner I ever ate. I remember her saying, "Pittsburgh! Pittsburgh! Breakfast at Pittsburgh."

I got out of the bus. I was cold, light snow floating down. There was a line of half a dozen stores next to the big restaurant that served our breakfast. I walked into an Army-Navy store. The man behind the counter looked at me. "We don't carry candy, Son." He smiled.

"I need a heavy sweater. I lost my jacket so could you show me a sweater?"

"How much you want to spend?" Treating me like a kid.

"As much as it costs. I haven't got all day, Mister. I'm on that bus and I have to have breakfast, so where's your sweaters?"

Suddenly he was all business. I bought a brown angora sweater. Expensive, but I was loaded with Flying School money so I gave him sixteen ninety-five, slipped into the sweater and, warm as toast, went to order breakfast. It was all downhill after Pittsburgh came Harrisburg. Then Philadelphia. It was getting dark, the snow falling heavier and heavier, filling up the cones of light made by the headlights on high beam. We were in New Jersey. A two-lane highway, the white dashes flying passed under the red and white bus, then turning orange on the curves, a no passing zone.

"About fifteen minutes to Linden, Tyrrell," The fourth driver of the trip told me. "Better get your things together I don't want to stop for too long, I'm late into New York and you can't trust that Holland Tunnel."

Now it was dark, the snow was icy. You could hear it hitting the windshield. I had all my stuff in a paper bag on my lap starring out into the darkness of New Jersey. There, two, three hundred yards ahead was a lighted bus stop. Two people huddled together out of the snow. My mom with my new stepfather. My stomach began to tighten up. The All-America's air brakes hissed as he pulled to a stop in front of my parents. My mom waved. Smiling. The man was taller than mom, fine looking with a grey mustache. Was I going to like this guy?

"Come on, Tyrrell, move your ass we haven't got all night."

"Thanks for the ride, Kind Sir, I'll recommend All-America to all my friends." The guy actually smiled.

"Okay, wise guy, you're here in one piece. I'll get your bag and be on my way."

He put my suitcase under the roof of the bus stop. "Here's your son in one piece, Mrs. Tyrrell, he was a fine traveler. Goodnight." He climbed aboard, the door hissed closed and the bus pulled away leaving a stink hanging over the bus stop.

I kissed my mother. I shook John Kahn's hand. "We're just a short walk to home Bruz, I'm so glad to see you, I've missed my family.

You can call your new father, 'Pop,' that's what his kids call him."

I grabbed his hand "Well Pop, you can call me Bruz, that's what everybody calls me. You look like a nice guy and any guy my mom could marry must be terrific. 'Cause she is only used to the best."

We all laughed. We walked out into the snow. Mom held one of my hands. Pop held the other. Three against the world.

"Oh Pop?" I said. "You ever considered moving to California?"

I had so much fun writing this story of when I was a little kid. Much of that fun came from checking with my sister Genevieve who at ninety-one was eager to tell me where I went wrong. Luckily I was born with a photographic memory so the tales I tell are as true today as they were 83 years ago. I say I had fun writing this book but the truth is every time I read a section tears fill my eyes and my throat closes up.

I want to thank my former son-in-law, Dan Charnas, for telling me to write the book after reading a story in my blog also a huge thank you to my brilliant son-in-law Richard Levine, a real writer, director, producer for reading the first three chapters and agreeing that the project was worth the doing.

Special thanks to my live-in editor, Leah Jay who is the best wife in the world, the best business partner, thoughtful critic, faithful cheer leader and a Phi Beta Kappa English major who makes sure I'm writing some kind of English. I'll love her forever.

Now, I'd like to say goodnight to Dottie and Bill Tyrrell, my loving parents, whose love kept our boat afloat in choppy waters. And to Dr. John Kahn, my stepfather, who never acted like a father but was a best friend. And finally to my big brother Jay, who taught me how to be a man.

A Kid in the Great Depression
Table of Contents

Made in the USA
Monee, IL
21 March 2025

14383867R00164